Prosciutto
Bread

VILLA DI ROMA
HOUSE MARINARA
NET WT. 24oz (680g)

CITY OF CLEVELAND
LANDMARKS

LITTLE
ITALY

Historic District

ALSO BY AMERICA'S TEST KITCHEN

FOR A FULL LISTING OF ALL OUR BOOKS

CooksIllustrated.com

AmericasTestKitchen.com

CONTENTS

WELCOME TO AMERICA'S TEST KITCHEN

This book has been tested, written, and edited by the folks at America's Test Kitchen. Located in Boston's Seaport District in the historic Innovation and Design Building, it features 15,000 square feet of kitchen space including multiple photography and video studios. It is the home of *Cook's Illustrated* magazine and *Cook's Country* magazine and is the workday destination for more than 60 test cooks, editors, and cookware specialists. Our mission is to test recipes over and over again until we understand how and why they work and until we arrive at the best version. Our television show highlights the absolute best recipes developed in the test kitchen during the past year— those recipes that our test kitchen staff makes at home time and time again. These recipes are accompanied by our most exhaustive equipment tests and our most interesting food tastings.

We start the process of testing a recipe with a complete lack of preconceptions, which means that we accept no claim, no technique, and no recipe at face value. We simply assemble as many variations as possible, test a half-dozen of the most promising, and taste the results blind. We then construct our own recipe and continue to test it, varying ingredients, techniques, and cooking times until we reach a consensus. As we like to say in the test kitchen, "We make the mistakes so you don't have to." The result, we hope, is the best version of a particular recipe, but we realize that only you can be the final judge of our success (or failure). We use the same rigorous approach when we test equipment and taste ingredients.

All of this would not be possible without a belief that good cooking, much like good music, is based on a foundation of objective technique. Some people like spicy foods and others don't, but there is a right way to sauté, there is a best way to cook a pot roast, and there are measurable scientific principles involved in producing perfectly beaten, stable egg whites. Our ultimate goal is to investigate the fundamental principles of cooking to give you the techniques, tools, and ingredients you need to become a better cook. It is as simple as that.

To see what goes on behind the scenes at America's Test Kitchen, check out our social media channels for kitchen snapshots, exclusive content, video tips, and much more. You can watch us work (in our actual test kitchen) by tuning in to *America's Test Kitchen* or *Cook's Country* on public television or on our websites. Download our award-winning podcast *Proof*, which goes beyond recipes to solve food mysteries (AmericasTestKitchen.com/proof), or listen in to test kitchen experts on public radio (SplendidTable.org) to hear insights that illuminate the truth about real home cooking. Want to hone your cooking skills or finally learn how to bake—with an America's Test Kitchen test cook? Enroll in one of our online cooking classes. And you can engage the next generation of home cooks with kid-tested recipes from America's Test Kitchen Kids.

However you choose to visit us, we welcome you into our kitchen, where you can stand by our side as we test our way to the best recipes in America.

facebook.com/AmericasTestKitchen
twitter.com/TestKitchen
youtube.com/AmericasTestKitchen
instagram.com/TestKitchen
pinterest.com/TestKitchen

AmericasTestKitchen.com
CooksIllustrated.com
CooksCountry.com
OnlineCookingSchool.com
AmericasTestKitchen.com/kids

Memories of an Italian American Kitchen

If you love food as I do, then to be born into an Italian American family is a stroke of good fortune. Of course, you might argue I love food because I am an Italian American. Whatever the answer to this chicken-or-egg question, Italian American food has shaped my identity. Red sauce runs in my veins.

My sharpest childhood memories almost always relate to my grandmother, Katherine Pizzarello. By the time I was born, she was fifty-two years old and the matriarch of a family that included her seven older brothers and one younger sister, plus all their spouses, children, and grandchildren. Her kitchen was filled with relatives I barely knew—yet I remember them all so clearly, even fifty years later. How can this be? My theory: The powerful sensory perceptions triggered by these memories keep them very much alive. Let me explain.

When I think of my grandmother's brothers Ernest Mascaro and Eddie Mascaro, my mind immediately pictures a white bakery box filled with jewel-like cookies. Ernest and Eddie were my favorite great-uncles and they always brought treats from an Italian bakery in their neighborhood—two facts that are not at all related! I liked the lacy, chocolaty Florentines best, and our recipe on page 259 is a perfect replica of this childhood memory.

If my mind turns to my great-aunt Ann Signorelli, I recall the amazing smells that greeted Sunday visitors to her home. Tomatoes, garlic, and basil were the dominant scents that mingled with meat and wine and a hint of oregano. As a kid, I imagined my grandmother and her little sister were engaged in a friendly competition that involved marinara, meatballs, and braciole. Now, that's my kind of sibling rivalry.

My best memories of my nana involve touch and sound. The oh-so-good scorch on the roof of my mouth as I gobbled up the first forkful of bubbling hot lasagna. Or the gentle tug from a just-from-the-fryer zeppole. And, most clearly, the sound of adult laughter coming from the dining room while I'm spread out on the sofa in the living room, with my pants unbuttoned, and laughing with my sister and brother (also with their pants unbuttoned).

The great waves of Italian immigration are fast receding into the history books. My Italian great-grandparents arrived in New York more than 130 years ago. Yet, in an age where everything changes in an instant, this almost ancient history feels very much alive. I firmly believe the food is responsible for keeping these memories and traditions fresh. In Italian American communities, food is family and family is food. It's that simple. I can turn my fifty-something siblings into kids again. My secret time machine? Put one baking dish of Nana's lasagna in the oven and wait for the kitchen to fill with the aroma of love.

One thing has changed over the years. I recognize that the food is about connection and I try not to overeat. I want to stick around the table talking. And for those times when I forget, I've learned a simple trick that I'm going to share with you. If you wear a belt, you can still unbutton your pants, just a bit, and stay seated at the table with the adults.

Here's to making new memories with some amazing food. As Nana said before the family would dig in: *Buon appetito.*

JACK BISHOP
Chief Creative Officer
Grandson of Roy and Katherine Pizzarello

On the Road in Italian America

Over the past few years while researching and writing the "On the Road" stories that run in *Cook's Country*, I've dined in dozens of small, family-owned, neighborhood Italian restaurants across the United States. Maybe you have too. Each one is comfortable, because it's familiar, even if you've never been there before. The bloom of garlic toasting in olive oil and the heady funk of Parmesan cheese infuse the air. The wine list is short and dominated by Chianti. The marinara is simple and ubiquitous. The scali bread, cottony light on the inside and crisp on its shell, gives up enough crumbs at first tear to make you embarrassed about the mess you're already making on the table.

Your server smiles: "Don't worry." You feel taken care of, like you're in this together, like you're old friends now. He knows everything about what you like based on the wine you ordered and the questions you asked about the ravioli, the saltimbocca, the risotto. You order too much. He asks if you want it all "family-style." Yes, you do.

This welcoming, warm energy often extends beyond the restaurant and into the surrounding neighborhood. It seems every city I've visited has, or once had, an Italian neighborhood. In Philadelphia, the green markets and butcher shops spill out onto the streets, enticing customers with fresh ingredients. On The Hill in St. Louis, Italian groceries and restaurants are peppered among middle-class homes, and it's not unusual to see the residents driving around in golf carts. The streets of Boston's North End are skinny and ancient, with narrow sidewalks that force you to jockey for room with truckers unloading food orders. On Federal Hill in Providence, Rhode Island, the highway dividing lines turn from yellow to the green, white, and red of the Italian flag. In every city, large and busy pastry shops serve as anchors, meeting places for tourists and locals alike, where the smell of toasted sugar fills the air from 100 yards out.

ABOVE Bryan discusses the ins and outs of Detroit-style pizza with Wesley Pikula, vice president of operations, at the original Conant Street location of Buddy's Pizzeria in Detroit

The markets are crowded with what seems like too many workers behind the counter, offering up samples of cheese and salami and sharing tips for how to make a perfect ragu using the beef shanks you're mulling over. Each store has a specialty: buy your Italian bread from this one; the fresh-made pasta from that one; meats and cheeses up the block. To shop in Little Italy is to play ping-pong with your meal.

For the thousands of miles I've traveled, I always come back to my favorite. Mike's Kitchen in Cranston, Rhode Island, is located in an unlikely spot: the Veterans of Foreign Wars hall. There, polenta is a light, fluffy brick laced with Pecorino Romano; the marinara carries a meaty undertone that tells you it's more than just tomatoes; and the stuffed artichoke is nearly impossible to figure out how to eat, but somehow I manage. I can spend hours at the table with friends and family reconnecting over a shared meal, tasting new dishes and relishing old favorites, laughing and arguing and reminiscing and planning our next Italian feast at home.

Home. That's the ultimate goal for any journey, really, to return home inspired and knowing more. My travels don't end when the plane touches down—far from it. Once I get back to the test kitchen, my team and I get to work creating recipes so anyone can make these dishes at home for family and friends. I hope you find inspiration in these pages to help you fill your own kitchen with those warm, welcoming aromas and warm, welcoming feelings.

BRYAN ROOF
Executive Food Editor
Cook's Country

A History of Italian America

ABOVE Italian family en route to Ellis Island, 1905

Imagine American cuisine without pasta. Without pizza. Without garlic bread and tomato sauce and tiramisu.

Unthinkable! Because the story of American food would be incomplete without the extraordinary culinary contributions of Italian immigrants and their Italian American descendants.

It's hard to believe, but there was a time when, to many Americans, "Italian" food was unfamiliar, odd. For some, suspicious. A hundred and fifty years ago, few would have imagined an American future with Italian dishes at the center of the national table.

From 1880 to 1910, over five million people immigrated to the United States from Italy, mostly from economically depressed southern Italy and Sicily. They settled in the cities, where they could find inexpensive housing and neighbors who spoke their language.

At first, most of these immigrants were men, and many—the *ritornati*—eventually returned to Italy with their savings. But millions stayed, establishing themselves in America before sending for friends and family to join them. Before long, entire extended families, and even entire villages, were making the long crossing to Ellis Island together, maintaining their traditions, habits, and hierarchies in their new homes.

Life was far from easy in an America where money was tight and not everyone was welcoming. But despite extraordinary economic and social challenges, or perhaps because of them, the spirit of cohesion proved lasting. Take lower Manhattan. There, whole buildings or blocks effectively served as resettled Italian villages with the same butcher, baker, or priest that everyone knew from back in Italy. Shops sold imported ingredients for traditional dishes. Churches celebrated feasts for village patron saints.

Soon this part of town was called Little Italy, a name that other Italian neighborhoods in other American cities eventually adopted as their own. First along the East Coast, then across the continent. As the boundaries of these neighborhoods softened and the hubs dissolved, "Little Italy" became less defined by place, and more by a state of mind, an expression of a cultural identity. Italian, yes. But American, too. And centered, as all great stories and communities are, around food.

Some dishes never diverged from their European roots, but many more adapted to American ingredients and influences. Tastes evolved and inventive cooks devised new ways to serve them. As Rudolph Valentino and Jimmy Durante helped define what it meant to be an Italian or Italian American performer in the USA, cooks in Boston, Philadelphia, New Orleans,

CLOCKWISE Clam seller, Little Italy, NYC, 1900; Mulberry Street Italian market, Little Italy, NYC, 1900; Lombardi's Pizzeria, Little Italy, NYC, 1905

CLOCKWISE Citizens of Palermo welcome U.S. tanks, 1940; Sophia Loren slices bread, 1955; Ralph and Frank Cantisano at the Ragu plant in Rochester, NY, 1957; Frank Sinatra, 1952

St. Louis, and San Francisco helped define Italian American food. Riffing on old-country underpinnings of bread, pasta, and all-day sauce, they created new, wholly American dishes: Spaghetti and meatballs. Cioppino. Scali bread.

Thousands of American servicemen and women served in Italy during and after World War II, expanding America's appreciation for the country's culinary roots and broadening our understanding of its complexity. In the post-war era, Italian Americans like Frank Sinatra and Louis Prima ruled the charts, and power brokers like New York City mayor Fiorello La Guardia increased visibility for Italian American culture and cuisine.

By the 1950s and 1960s, you could find a red sauce restaurant in Everytown, USA. Most were built on a foundation of garlic bread and basketed bottles of Chianti, maybe a baked lasagna or a special ravioli. They attracted people from all walks of life, Italian American or not, who craved simple, satisfying, and usually inexpensive meals. Connie Francis, Tony Bennett, Perry Como, and Dean Martin provided the soundtrack.

Pizza parlors and sandwich shops proliferated. Italian bakeries and groceries flourished, offering specialty ingredients and seasonal favorites. The pasta and sauce section of the grocery store started to swell. Mama Celeste and Chef Boyardee enticed customers in TV spots. In 1973, Italian American cooking instructor Marcella Hazan, based in New York, published her groundbreaking *Classic Italian Cookbook*. Soon the bookstore shelves were filled with new titles celebrating Italian, and Italian American, cuisine.

In the 1980s, restaurants began to expand beyond red sauce staples to embrace a broader, deeper interpretation of Italian fare. Suddenly, everything was "Tuscan" (even when it wasn't). Chianti shed its protective basket. Polenta emerged from the shadows. Risotto ruled. But even as so much changed, good old spaghetti and meatballs never went away.

ABOVE Mayor Fiorello H. La Guardia's last day in office, NYC, 1946

Italian American food stays vital because the food has always been magnetic and delicious. It is irresistible across generations, across political views, across economic circumstances and geographic distinctions. Everyone loves it. It's something we can all agree on. And not just because it tastes so good, but because of what it represents: perseverance, cohesion, warmth, family, life.

We wouldn't be here without it.

TUCKER SHAW
Editor in Chief
Cook's Country

APPETIZERS AND SNACKS

MARINATED OLIVES

Serves 8

Why This Recipe Works Olives are a must on any antipasto platter. Making your own marinated olives may not seem like the best use of time, especially when you can buy a wide variety of prepared olive products at the supermarket, but with just a little effort you can put together something with way more flavor and freshness than anything store-bought. The most important step when making marinated olives is to start with good olives and good olive oil. We used olives with pits (pitted olives tend to have less flavor), packed in brine, not oil. To give the dish more variety, we chose a combination of green and black olives. On top of the usual aromatics—garlic, thyme, and red pepper flakes—we added shallot, fresh oregano, and grated lemon zest for a bright citrus note. A simple variation subs cheese for the olives and mixes up the flavors. Make sure to bring the mixture to room temperature before serving or the oil will look cloudy and congealed. Serve with toothpicks and a thinly sliced baguette or crackers.

- 1 cup brine-cured green olives with pits
- 1 cup brine-cured black olives with pits
- ¾ cup extra-virgin olive oil
- 1 shallot, minced
- 2 teaspoons grated lemon zest
- 2 teaspoons minced fresh thyme
- 2 teaspoons minced fresh oregano
- 1 garlic clove, minced
- ½ teaspoon red pepper flakes
- ½ teaspoon table salt

Rinse olives thoroughly, then drain and pat dry with paper towels. Toss olives with oil, shallot, lemon zest, thyme, oregano, garlic, pepper flakes, and salt in bowl, cover, and refrigerate for at least 4 hours. Let sit at room temperature for at least 30 minutes before serving. (Olive mixture can be refrigerated for up to 4 days before serving.)

MARINATED BOCCONCINI
Serves 8

It's easy to turn little balls of fresh mozzarella (about 1 inch in diameter is ideal) into an appetizer ready for an antipasto platter. The key is to cook the marinade over low heat to bloom the flavors of the seasonings. Adding more uncooked olive oil just before serving freshens the flavor of the oil.

- ½ cup extra-virgin olive oil, divided
- 1 shallot, thinly sliced
- 1 small garlic clove, minced to a paste
- ½ teaspoon minced fresh thyme or oregano
- ½ teaspoon table salt
- ¼ teaspoon grated lemon zest
- ⅛ teaspoon red pepper flakes
- 1 pound fresh baby mozzarella cheese balls (bocconcini)

1. Combine 6 tablespoons olive oil, shallot, garlic, thyme, salt, lemon zest, and pepper flakes in small saucepan and cook over low heat until shallot is softened, about 10 minutes.

2. Meanwhile, place mozzarella cheese balls in colander, drain well, and pat dry with paper towels; transfer to medium bowl. Pour oil mixture over mozzarella and toss to combine. Cover and refrigerate until flavors have melded, at least 4 hours or up to 2 days. Bring to room temperature and stir in remaining 2 tablespoons olive oil before serving.

MARINATED ARTICHOKE HEARTS AND STUFFED PICKLED SWEET PEPPERS

Serves 8

Why This Recipe Works Stuffed peppers are a mainstay in the Italian antipasto tradition, and with good reason. They offer a bold flavor combination of salty, savory, and spicy; plus, they come together in a snap. Jarred sweet cherry peppers, rather than hot, allow you to taste the filling and ensure that the peppers don't bully other items on the platter. Tasters liked the combination of subtly tangy fontina and rich prosciutto for the filling. Pairing these peppers with the bright acidity and bite of artichoke hearts marinated with herbs and aromatics made for an easy appetizer that was wonderfully complex in its flavors. Make sure to dry the artichokes thoroughly before tossing them with the marinade or they will be watery. Sweet cherry peppers are sold in jars and at the deli counter alongside the olives. If placing the peppers on a platter, help them stand upright by using a paring knife to trim the bottom of the peppers level. Serve with store-bought thin breadsticks; grissini are ideal.

- ¼ cup minced fresh parsley or basil
- 1 shallot, minced
- ¾ teaspoon grated lemon zest plus 2 tablespoons juice
- 1 garlic clove, minced
- ¼ teaspoon table salt
- ⅛ teaspoon pepper
- ¾ cup extra-virgin olive oil
- 18 ounces frozen artichoke hearts, thawed, patted dry, and quartered if whole
- 16 ounces pickled sweet cherry peppers (25 peppers)
- 6 ounces fontina cheese, cut into ½-inch cubes
- 7 ounces thinly sliced prosciutto, cut in half lengthwise

1. Whisk parsley, shallot, lemon zest and juice, garlic, salt, and pepper together in large bowl. Whisking constantly, drizzle in oil. Measure out 2 tablespoons dressing and set aside for stuffed peppers. Gently fold artichoke hearts into remaining dressing, cover, and refrigerate until flavors meld, at least 3 hours.

2. Remove stem and core of peppers with paring knife. Rinse peppers well and pat dry with paper towels. Roll each piece of cheese inside 1 piece prosciutto and stuff inside cored peppers.

3. Transfer artichoke hearts to serving bowl and season with salt and pepper to taste. Whisk reserved dressing to re-emulsify, then drizzle over peppers. (Marinated artichokes can be refrigerated for up to 24 hours before serving. Peppers can be assembled, covered, and refrigerated for up to 24 hours. Bring to room temperature and drizzle with reserved dressing before serving.)

THE ITALIAN AMERICAN KITCHEN
A Classic Antipasto Platter

An antipasto platter is the old school way to start any Italian American meal. Some restaurants feature as many as a dozen items, but that's too much food and too many flavors. Five or six well-chosen items is plenty generous. Marinated Olives (page 10) are a must, as are one or two marinated or pickled vegetables such as cherry peppers, artichokes, sun-dried tomatoes, or *giardiniera*. Cheese is another must, with Marinated Bocconcini (page 10) or shards of fine Parmigiano-Reggiano being the classic options. Add one or two sliced cured meats—prosciutto and soppressata are favorites—and some grissini and you're ready to start the party.

CAPONATA

Makes about 3 cups

Why This Recipe Works Eggplant is a star ingredient in countless recipes with their origins in southern Italy. Sicilian caponata is boldly flavored with a sweet-and-sour finish and works just as well alongside a piece of grilled fish as it does at the start of the meal. A small bite—perhaps served on crostini—makes a perfect appetizer. To make sure the eggplant didn't turn to oil-soaked mush, we salted and microwaved it to eliminate excess moisture. For our sauce, we started with V8 juice, which delivered bright tomato flavor. Brown sugar and red wine vinegar enhanced the traditional sweet-and-sour profile. A scoopful of raisins brought additional sweetness, minced anchovies added a rich umami boost, and briny black olives offered balance. Simmering everything together for just a few minutes allowed the sauce to thicken and the flavors to meld. Although we prefer the complex flavor of V8 juice, tomato juice can be substituted. If coffee filters are not available, food-safe, undyed paper towels can be substituted when microwaving the eggplant. Be sure to remove the eggplant from the microwave immediately so that the steam can escape.

- 1 large eggplant (1½ pounds), cut into ½-inch cubes
- ½ teaspoon table salt
- ¾ cup V8 juice
- ¼ cup red wine vinegar, plus extra for seasoning
- 2 tablespoons packed brown sugar
- ¼ cup chopped fresh parsley
- 1½ teaspoons minced anchovy fillets (2 to 3 fillets)
- 1 large tomato, cored, seeded, and chopped
- ¼ cup raisins
- 2 tablespoons minced black olives
- 5–6 teaspoons extra-virgin olive oil, divided
- 1 celery rib, chopped fine
- 1 red bell pepper, stemmed, seeded, and chopped fine
- 1 small onion, chopped fine (½ cup)
- ¼ cup pine nuts, toasted

1. Toss eggplant with salt in bowl. Line entire surface of large microwave-safe plate with double layer of coffee filters and lightly spray with vegetable oil spray. Spread eggplant in even layer on coffee filters. Microwave until eggplant is dry and shriveled to one-third of its original size, 8 to 15 minutes (eggplant should not brown). Transfer eggplant immediately to paper towel–lined plate.

2. Meanwhile, whisk V8 juice, vinegar, sugar, parsley, and anchovies together in medium bowl. Stir in tomato, raisins, and olives.

3. Heat 1 tablespoon oil in 12-inch nonstick skillet over medium-high heat until shimmering. Add eggplant and cook, stirring occasionally, until edges are browned, 4 to 8 minutes, adding 1 teaspoon more oil if pan appears dry; transfer to bowl.

4. Add remaining 2 teaspoons oil to now-empty skillet and heat over medium-high heat until shimmering. Add celery, bell pepper, and onion and cook, stirring occasionally, until softened and edges are spotty brown, 6 to 8 minutes.

5. Reduce heat to medium-low and stir in eggplant and V8 juice mixture. Bring to simmer and cook until V8 juice is thickened and coats vegetables, 4 to 7 minutes. Transfer to serving bowl and let cool to room temperature. (Caponata can be refrigerated for up to 1 week; bring to room temperature before serving.) Season with extra vinegar to taste and sprinkle with pine nuts before serving.

PROSCIUTTO-WRAPPED FIGS WITH GORGONZOLA

Serves 8 to 10

Why This Recipe Works Few food pairings are more perfect than savory, salty prosciutto and sweet fresh figs. Many Italian immigrants planted fig trees in their backyards to celebrate late summer with this classic dish. Refrigerated transport means figs are widely available, even in areas where they can't be grown. Adding creamy, bold Gorgonzola cheese and a drizzle of honey brings another level of sweet-salty complexity and textural interest to this dish. We started by halving the figs to make them easier to eat. Small mounds of Gorgonzola, placed in the center of each fig before adding the honey, offered a rich, assertive counterpoint to the figs' tender flesh and sweet flavor. Briefly microwaving the honey ensured that it was easy to drizzle over the cheese-stuffed figs. Finally, we wrapped the whole thing in thin slices of prosciutto. To guarantee the ham stayed put, we stuck a toothpick through the center of each fig. Be sure to choose ripe figs for this recipe. They not only taste best, but also yield easily when mounding the cheese gently into the centers.

- 2 ounces Gorgonzola cheese
- 16 fresh figs, stemmed and halved lengthwise
- 1 tablespoon honey
- 16 thin slices prosciutto (8 ounces), cut in half lengthwise

Mound 1 teaspoon Gorgonzola into center of each fig half. Microwave honey in bowl to loosen, about 10 seconds, then drizzle over cheese. Wrap prosciutto securely around figs, leaving fig ends uncovered. Secure prosciutto with toothpick and serve. (Wrapped figs can be refrigerated for up to 8 hours; bring to room temperature before serving.)

VARIATION
Prosciutto-Wrapped Melon

Omit cheese, figs, and honey. Trim rind from 1 medium cantaloupe, cut melon in half, and scoop out seeds with spoon. Cut each half into eight crescents. Cut each crescent in half crosswise to make 32 pieces. Cut prosciutto slices in half lengthwise and wrap 1 piece around each piece of melon.

THE ITALIAN AMERICAN KITCHEN
Prosciutto

Italians have been making prosciutto for nearly 2,000 years, most notably in Parma. This city in Emilia-Romagna at the top of Italy's boot is still at it, making Italy's most famous version, Prosciutto di Parma, under the eye of an official consortium that sears Parma's five-pointed crown brand onto every approved ham. Next most renowned: Prosciutto di San Daniele, from the Friuli region in Italy's northeast, with its own consortium and brand shaped like a leg of ham. Both are designated "PDO" by the European Union—Protected Designation of Origin—meaning that they are exceptional regional products with exclusive rights to their particular names.

Prosciutto crudo ("raw ham"), as it's called in Italian, is never smoked or cooked. Producers in both regions use the same basic curing method: After slaughtering pigs, they salt and hang the legs for a minimum of 12 months. The meat's flavor concentrates with age, as prosciutto loses up to 30 percent of its weight in moisture during curing. This process gives the prosciutto its signature silky, dense texture and nutty flavor.

Not too long ago, the only way to buy prosciutto was to find an Italian market and wait while someone sliced an imported ham by hand. But since domestic producers have gotten into the game, many markets now carry grab-and-go packages. We tasted top brands and, for the most part, we were pleasantly surprised. Look for a brand that's aged at least 12 months for complex flavor and that has been sliced paper-thin to avoid chewiness. The ingredient list should include just pork and salt. Our winning brand is tender, buttery **Volpi Traditional Prosciutto.** Another advantage of presliced prosciutto is that the sealed packages can be refrigerated for several months.

ITALIAN STRAWS

Serves 4 to 6

Why This Recipe Works Italian cheese straws are always fast to disappear from a party platter, especially when they're homemade. Ours are also a cinch to prepare. We kept things simple by using frozen puff pastry, which bakes up buttery and flaky. We wanted our straws to boast bold cheese flavor, and potent Parmesan gave us a big bang for our buck. (Aged Asiago also works well.) To ensure that the cheese adhered to the pastry, we used a rolling pin to press it—along with a smattering of chopped parsley for vibrancy—into the pastry before slicing and shaping the straws. Be sure to allow enough time to defrost the puff pastry: Let it sit either in the refrigerator for 24 hours or on the counter for 30 minutes to 1 hour.

- 1 (9½ by 9-inch) sheet puff pastry, thawed
- 2 ounces Parmesan or aged Asiago cheese, grated (1 cup)
- 1 tablespoon minced fresh parsley
- ¼ teaspoon table salt
- ⅛ teaspoon pepper

1. Adjust oven rack to middle position and heat oven to 425 degrees. Line rimmed baking sheet with parchment paper.

2. Lay puff pastry on second sheet of parchment and sprinkle with Parmesan, parsley, salt, and pepper. Top with third sheet of parchment. Using rolling pin, press cheese mixture into pastry, then roll pastry into 10-inch square.

3. Remove top sheet of parchment and cut pastry into thirteen ¾-inch-wide strips with sharp knife or pizza wheel. Gently twist each strip of pastry and space about ½ inch apart on prepared baking sheet.

4. Bake until cheese straws are fully puffed and golden brown, 10 to 15 minutes. Let cheese straws cool completely on baking sheet. (Cheese straws can be wrapped in plastic wrap and stored at room temperature for up to 24 hours before serving.)

THE ITALIAN AMERICAN KITCHEN
Asiago Cheese

This cow's-milk cheese is sold at various ages. Fresh Asiago is firm like cheddar or Havarti, and the flavor is fairly mild. Aged Asiago is drier and has a much sharper, saltier flavor with buttery, nutty notes. Because of its lower price and similar flavor, aged Asiago is a common substitute for Parmesan. It is often grated over pasta, shaved for salads, or served with meats as antipasti.

RICOTTA CROSTINI WITH CHERRY TOMATOES AND BASIL

Serves 8 (Makes 24 crostini)

Why This Recipe Works Crostini, little toasts typically topped with cheese and vegetables, are a great way to start an Italian meal. To keep the vegetables in place, we made a silky-smooth ricotta topping in the food processor, using a combination of ricotta cheese, extra-virgin olive oil, salt, and pepper. We topped the ricotta with a wide variety of bite-size vegetables. We prefer to use day-old bread for this recipe because it is easier to slice. A 12-inch demi-baguette will easily yield the 24 slices needed. The crostini are best topped shortly before serving.

- 24 (¼-inch-thick) slices baguette
- 6 tablespoons extra-virgin olive oil, divided
- 6 ounces cherry tomatoes, quartered
- 1 small garlic clove, minced
- ½ teaspoon table salt, divided
- ½ teaspoon pepper, divided
- 6 ounces (¾ cup) whole-milk ricotta cheese
- ¼ cup fresh basil leaves, torn

1. Adjust oven rack to middle position and heat oven to 400 degrees. Arrange baguette slices in single layer on rimmed baking sheet. Brush tops of slices with 2 tablespoons oil. Bake until golden brown and crispy, 8 to 10 minutes. Let cool completely on sheet, about 30 minutes.

2. Combine tomatoes, garlic, ¼ teaspoon salt, ¼ teaspoon pepper, and 2 tablespoons oil in bowl; set aside.

3. Process ricotta, remaining ¼ teaspoon salt, and remaining ¼ teaspoon pepper in food processor until smooth, about 10 seconds. With processor running, slowly add remaining 2 tablespoons oil until incorporated; transfer to bowl. Spread ricotta mixture evenly on toasted baguette slices. Spoon tomato mixture over ricotta and sprinkle with basil.

VARIATIONS

Ricotta Crostini with Asparagus and Radishes
Substitute 2 ounces asparagus, trimmed and sliced thin on bias, for tomatoes. Add 4 radishes, trimmed and sliced thin; ¼ cup minced fresh chives; 1 tablespoon lemon juice; and 1 minced anchovy fillet to asparagus mixture. Omit basil.

Ricotta Crostini with Olives and Sun-Dried Tomatoes
Substitute ¾ cup pitted kalamata olives, chopped coarse, for tomatoes. Add ½ cup oil-packed sun-dried tomatoes, patted dry and chopped coarse, and 1 teaspoon red wine vinegar to olive mixture. Process ½ teaspoon grated orange zest with ricotta mixture. Substitute ¼ cup toasted pine nuts, chopped, for basil.

Ricotta Crostini with Peas and Mint
Substitute 1 cup thawed frozen peas for tomatoes, 1 minced small shallot for garlic, and torn fresh mint leaves for basil. Add 2 teaspoons red wine vinegar to pea mixture.

Ricotta Crostini with Roasted Red Peppers and Capers
Substitute 1 cup jarred roasted red peppers, patted dry and chopped fine, for tomatoes. Reduce salt to ⅛ teaspoon in red pepper mixture and add ¼ cup chopped fresh parsley and 2 tablespoons capers, rinsed and minced. Process ½ teaspoon grated lemon zest with ricotta mixture. Omit basil.

BRUSCHETTA

Serves 8 to 10

Why This Recipe Works Bruschetta are larger than crostini. The warm toasts can be served as is, simply rubbed with a raw garlic clove to impart flavor, then brushed with extra-virgin olive oil and sprinkled with salt. Of course, adding toppings makes them even more appealing. One problem that consistently plagues bruschetta recipes is soggy bread, especially once you add substantial toppings. Bread choice is key to fixing this—we use a crusty loaf of country-style bread with a tight crumb so the toppings don't fall through, and we cut the bread into thick slices for maximum support.

1 loaf country bread, ends discarded, sliced crosswise into ¾-inch-thick pieces

½ garlic clove, peeled

Extra-virgin olive oil

Adjust oven rack 4 inches from broiler element and heat broiler. Place bread on aluminum foil–lined baking sheet. Broil until bread is deep golden, 1 to 2 minutes per side. Flip and repeat on second side. Lightly rub 1 side of each slice with garlic and brush with oil. Season with kosher salt to taste.

VARIATIONS

Black Olive Pesto, Ricotta, and Basil Topping

Process ½ cup pitted kalamata olives, 1 minced small shallot, 2 tablespoons extra-virgin olive oil, 1½ teaspoons lemon juice, and 1 minced garlic clove in food processor until uniform paste forms, about 10 seconds. Season 12 ounces whole-milk ricotta cheese with salt and pepper to taste. Spread olive pesto evenly on toasts. Carefully spread ricotta over pesto. Drizzle with additional extra-virgin olive oil to taste, sprinkle with 2 tablespoons shredded fresh basil, and serve.

Grape Tomato, White Bean Puree, and Rosemary Topping

Combine 12 ounces grape tomatoes, quartered; ½ teaspoon table salt; and ¼ teaspoon sugar in bowl and let sit for 30 minutes. Spin tomatoes in salad spinner until excess liquid has been removed, 45 to 60 seconds, redistributing tomatoes several times during spinning. Return to bowl and toss with 3 tablespoons extra-virgin olive oil, 1 tablespoon red wine vinegar, and ¼ teaspoon pepper. Process 1 (15-ounce) can cannellini beans, rinsed, with 2 tablespoons water, ½ teaspoon table salt, and ¼ teaspoon pepper in food processor until smooth, about 1 minute. With processor running, slowly add 3 tablespoons extra-virgin olive oil until incorporated. Spread bean mixture evenly on toasts. Top with tomatoes and 1 ounce Parmesan cheese, shaved, and sprinkle with 2 teaspoons minced fresh rosemary. Serve.

Artichoke and Parmesan Topping

Pulse 1 (14-ounce) can artichoke hearts packed in water, rinsed and patted dry; 2 tablespoons extra-virgin olive oil; 2 tablespoons chopped fresh basil; 2 teaspoons lemon juice; 1 minced garlic clove; ¼ teaspoon table salt; and ¼ teaspoon pepper in food processor until coarsely pureed, about 6 pulses, scraping down bowl once during pulsing. Add ½ cup finely grated Parmesan cheese and pulse to combine, about 2 pulses. Spread artichoke mixture evenly on toasts. Top toasts with 1 ounce Parmesan cheese, shaved, season with pepper to taste, and drizzle with additional extra-virgin olive oil to taste. Serve.

STUFFED MUSHROOMS

Serves 4 to 6

Why This Recipe Works Forget about leathery, dried-out stuffed mushrooms with bland, watery filling; these are meaty bites full of great savory flavor. To get rid of excess moisture before stuffing, we roasted the mushrooms gill side up until their juice was released and they were browned; we then flipped them gill side down to let the liquid evaporate. To create the filling, we chopped the mushroom stems in the food processor and sautéed them with garlic and wine. Cheese bound the filling together, and a final hit of acid brightened the earthy, savory flavor.

- 24 large white mushrooms (1¾ to 2 inches in diameter), stems removed and reserved
- ¼ cup extra-virgin olive oil, divided
- ¼ teaspoon table salt
- ¼ teaspoon pepper, divided
- 1 small shallot, minced
- 2 garlic cloves, minced
- ¼ cup dry white wine
- 1 ounce Parmesan cheese, grated (½ cup)
- 1 teaspoon minced fresh thyme
- 1 teaspoon lemon juice
- 1 teaspoon minced fresh parsley

1. Adjust oven rack to middle position and heat oven to 425 degrees. Line rimmed baking sheet with aluminum foil. Toss mushroom caps with 2 tablespoons oil, salt, and ⅛ teaspoon pepper in large bowl. Arrange caps gill side up on prepared sheet and roast until juice is released, about 20 minutes. Flip caps and roast until well browned, about 10 minutes; set aside.

2. Meanwhile, pulse reserved stems, shallot, garlic, and remaining ⅛ teaspoon pepper in food processor until finely chopped, 10 to 14 pulses. Heat remaining 2 tablespoons oil in 8-inch nonstick skillet over medium heat until shimmering. Add stem mixture to skillet and cook until golden brown and moisture has evaporated, about 5 minutes. Add wine and cook until nearly evaporated and mixture thickens slightly, about 1 minute. Transfer to bowl and let cool slightly, about 5 minutes. Stir in Parmesan, thyme, and lemon juice. Season with salt and pepper to taste.

3. Flip caps gill side up. Divide stuffing evenly among caps. Return caps to oven and bake until stuffing is heated through, 5 to 7 minutes. Sprinkle with parsley and serve. (Stuffed caps can be refrigerated for 24 hours before baking. Increase baking time to 10 to 15 minutes.)

VARIATION
Stuffed Mushrooms with Olives and Goat Cheese
Substitute ¼ cup crumbled goat cheese for Parmesan, 1 teaspoon chopped fresh oregano for thyme, and red wine vinegar for lemon juice. Add 3 tablespoons chopped pitted kalamata olives to cooked stuffing.

FRIED ASPARAGUS

Serves 4 to 6

Why This Recipe Works These snappy spears are a decidedly American invention with Italian roots. For the crispiest coating, we relied on the tried-and-true bound breading technique but found that the coating wasn't adhering as steadfastly as we wanted. To get around this, we rinsed the spears under cold running water before dipping them in the flour. The residual moisture was just enough to help the flour (and the coating) stick. We used fresh bread to amplify the sweetness of the crumbs. A bright yet creamy sauce made with sour cream, lemon juice, and mustard was the perfect accompaniment. Do not use asparagus that is thinner than ½ inch here. The bottom 1½ inches or so of asparagus is woody and needs to be trimmed. To know where to cut the spears, grip one spear about halfway down; with your other hand, hold the stem between your thumb and index finger about 1 inch from the bottom and bend the spear until it snaps. Using this spear as a guide, cut the remaining spears with your knife.

½ cup sour cream

1 tablespoon lemon juice

1 tablespoon Dijon mustard

1½ teaspoons table salt, divided

¾ teaspoon pepper, divided

¼ cup plus 3 tablespoons all-purpose flour, divided

3 large eggs

4 slices hearty white sandwich bread, torn into 1-inch pieces

1 pound (½-inch-thick) asparagus, trimmed

1 quart peanut or vegetable oil

1. Combine sour cream, lemon juice, mustard, ½ teaspoon salt, and ¼ teaspoon pepper in bowl; set aside sauce.

2. Place ¼ cup flour in shallow dish. Beat eggs in second shallow dish. Process bread, remaining 1 teaspoon salt, remaining ½ teaspoon pepper, and remaining 3 tablespoons flour in food processor until finely ground, about 1 minute. Transfer bread-crumb mixture to 13 by 9-inch baking dish.

3. Place asparagus in colander and rinse under cold running water. Shake colander to lightly drain asparagus (asparagus should still be wet). Transfer one-third of asparagus to flour and toss to lightly coat; dip in egg, allowing excess to drip off; then transfer to bread-crumb mixture and press lightly to adhere. Transfer breaded asparagus to baking sheet. Repeat with remaining asparagus in 2 batches.

4. Line large plate with paper towels. Heat oil in large Dutch oven over medium-high heat to 350 degrees. Carefully add one-third of asparagus to hot oil and cook until golden brown, 1 to 2 minutes. Transfer to prepared plate. Repeat with remaining asparagus in 2 batches. Serve with sauce.

FRIED CALAMARI

Serves 6 to 8

Why This Recipe Works This Italian American restaurant favorite is too good to enjoy just when eating out. We wanted to develop a foolproof way to make this perennial seafood favorite at home. Without the advantage of a restaurant-grade deep-fryer, it can be tricky to get both the squid and the breading to finish cooking at the same time. In our tests, by the time the squid was perfectly cooked, the breading was only light brown, not the golden-brown we were looking for. Boosting the oil temperature improved browning, but the rings were still on the pale side. To improve the coating's color, we added cornmeal to the flour. Although cornmeal is not a traditional Italian ingredient in fried calamari recipes, we liked the color, flavor, and crunch it contributed. Cayenne pepper also helped, and the spiciness sharpened the squid's mild flavor. This recipe still yields calamari that is slightly lighter in color than most restaurant versions, so keep that in mind when frying. Follow the cooking time, not the color, and you will have perfectly cooked squid. Before slicing the squid, check the bodies for beaks the fishmonger might have missed. They look and feel like pieces of transparent plastic. Use a Dutch oven that holds 6 quarts or more for this recipe. For the best results, clip a candy/deep-fry thermometer to the side of the Dutch oven to monitor the temperature of the oil. Do not use stone-ground cornmeal in this recipe; it will make the texture too gritty. Serve with marinara sauce (see recipe on page 102) or lemon wedges.

1¼ cups unbleached all-purpose flour

¼ cup cornmeal

½ teaspoon table salt

½ teaspoon pepper

½ teaspoon cayenne pepper

2 large egg whites

1 pound squid, bodies sliced crosswise into ½-inch-thick rings, tentacles left whole, divided

1 quart vegetable oil

1. Thoroughly combine flour, cornmeal, salt, pepper, and cayenne in medium bowl. In second medium bowl, beat egg whites with fork until frothy, about 10 seconds. Add half of squid to bowl with egg whites, toss to coat, and remove with slotted spoon or your hands, allowing excess whites to drip back into bowl. Add squid to bowl with seasoned flour and, using your hands or large rubber spatula, toss to coat. Place coated squid in single layer on wire rack set in rimmed baking sheet, allowing excess flour to fall free of squid. Repeat with remaining squid.

2. Meanwhile, add oil to large Dutch oven until it measures about ¾ inch deep and heat over medium-high heat to 400 degrees. Carefully add one-quarter of squid and fry until light golden (do not let coating turn golden brown, or squid will toughen), about 1½ minutes, adjusting heat as necessary to maintain temperature of 380 to 400 degrees. With slotted spoon or mesh skimmer, transfer fried squid to paper towel–lined plate. Fry remaining batches of squid and add them to plate. Season with salt to taste and serve immediately.

MOZZARELLA STICKS

Serves 4 to 6

Why This Recipe Works To make this restaurant classic at home, we needed one important piece of equipment: the freezer. We cut the block mozzarella into planks and then sticks, dredged them in flour, dipped them in egg, and coated them with panko bread crumbs. After a stint in the freezer (at least 1 but no more than 2 hours), the cheese stayed intact during frying. Unfortunately, we learned the hard way that if we didn't freeze the mozzarella sticks prior to frying, the cheese exploded and leaked out. Serve with marinara sauce (see recipe on page 102) or lemon wedges.

1   pound whole-milk mozzarella cheese

½   cup all-purpose flour

2   large eggs

2   cups panko bread crumbs

½   teaspoon table salt

½   teaspoon pepper

¼   teaspoon dried oregano

¼   teaspoon garlic powder

2   quarts peanut or vegetable oil

1. Set wire rack in rimmed baking sheet and line half of rack with triple layer of paper towels. Slice mozzarella crosswise into six ½-inch-wide planks. Cut each plank lengthwise into 3 equal sticks. (You will have 18 pieces.)

2. Spread flour in shallow dish. Beat eggs in second shallow dish. Pulse panko, salt, pepper, oregano, and garlic powder in food processor until finely ground, about 10 pulses; transfer to third shallow dish.

3. Working with 1 piece at a time, coat sticks with flour, shaking to remove excess; dip in eggs, allowing excess to drip off; and dredge in panko mixture, pressing to adhere. Transfer to plate. Freeze sticks until firm, at least 1 hour or up to 2 hours.

4. Add oil to large Dutch oven until it measures about 1½ inches deep and heat over medium-high heat to 400 degrees. Add 6 sticks to hot oil and fry until deeply browned on all sides, about 1 minute. Adjust burner as necessary to maintain oil temperature between 375 and 400 degrees.

5. Transfer sticks to paper towel–lined side of prepared rack to drain for 30 seconds, then move to unlined side of rack. Return oil to 400 degrees and repeat frying in 2 more batches with remaining 12 sticks.

TO MAKE AHEAD
Mozzarella sticks can be prepared through step 3 and frozen for up to 1 month in zipper-lock bag or airtight container. After frying (do not thaw sticks), let sticks rest for 3 minutes before serving to allow residual heat to continue to melt centers.

THE ITALIAN AMERICAN KITCHEN
Bread Crumbs

Italian-style bread crumbs flavored with dried herbs are a staple of Italian American cooking. But this American invention (in Italy home cooks traditionally use leftover bread) is ready for retirement—fine Italian-style crumbs have a dusty texture and stale flavor. Good bread crumbs should be mildly wheaty but neutral in flavor (no herbs, thanks). What really matters is that they be ultracrunchy and have excellent coating abilities. Japanese-style panko bread crumbs create craggy texture and excellent crunch on most foods—from mozzarella sticks to chicken cutlets. Our favorite is **Ian's Panko Breadcrumbs, Original Style,** which provide the best balance between maximum coating and ultimate crunch.

TODAY'S FEATURE
n Homemade
Plant Rollatini
pinach, mozz,
a is so good...

Boar's Head

TODAY'S FEATURE
Fresh Homemade
Roast Beef
made fresh daily

Boar's Head

TODAY'S FEATURE
Italian Combo hero
Named the best
Sandwhich in Brooklyn

Boar's Head

TODAY'S FEATURE
Fresh
* Chicken Cutle
* Chicken Grill
* Whole chickens

Boar's Head

SANDWICHES, SOUPS, AND SALADS

NEW ORLEANS MUFFULETTA

Serves 8

Why This Recipe Works This hefty round of seeded bread stuffed with Italian meats, cheeses, and olive spread is the signature—and only—sandwich served at the Central Grocery on Decatur Street in New Orleans. In 1906, Salvatore Lupo, the owner of Central Grocery, noticed Sicilian immigrants on their lunch breaks eating meals of meats, cheeses, olives, and bread. The enterprising grocer decided to save the workers some trouble by combining all the components in a sandwich. Thus was born the muffuletta, named after the round Sicilian bread it's made on and served at Central Grocery—and elsewhere all over the city—ever since. For our cold cuts, we layered the provolone with three standards: salami, mortadella, and capicola. Our olive salad combined green and black olives, *giardiniera* (see page 42), garlic, and capers; rinsing the capers and using more green olives than black controlled the salad's salty taste. To infuse our salad with more zest, we added red wine vinegar, oregano, and thyme. For easy muffuletta bread, we used a double batch of our Simple Pizza Dough (page 97), but store-bought pizza dough works well. Just make sure to shape the dough into rounds and sprinkle them with sesame seeds before baking. After slicing the bread in half, we spread the salad on the cut sides and layered the meats and cheese. We wrapped the sandwiches in plastic wrap and pressed them under a weighted baking sheet for compact, sliceable muffulettas. You will need one 16-ounce jar of giardiniera to yield 2 cups drained.

- 2 recipes Simple Pizza Dough (page 97) or 2 pounds store-bought pizza dough
- 2 cups drained jarred giardiniera
- 1 cup pimento-stuffed green olives
- ½ cup pitted kalamata olives
- 2 tablespoons capers, rinsed
- 1 tablespoon red wine vinegar
- 1 garlic clove, minced
- ½ teaspoon dried oregano
- ¼ teaspoon red pepper flakes
- ¼ teaspoon dried thyme
- ½ cup extra-virgin olive oil
- ¼ cup chopped fresh parsley

- 1 large egg, lightly beaten
- 5 teaspoons sesame seeds
- 4 ounces thinly sliced Genoa salami
- 6 ounces thinly sliced aged provolone cheese
- 6 ounces thinly sliced mortadella
- 4 ounces thinly sliced hot capicola

1. Form dough balls into 2 tight round balls on oiled baking sheet, cover loosely with greased plastic wrap, and let sit at room temperature for 1 hour.

2. Meanwhile, pulse giardiniera, green olives, kalamata olives, capers, vinegar, garlic, oregano, pepper flakes, and thyme in food processor until coarsely chopped, about 6 pulses, scraping down sides of bowl as needed. Transfer to bowl and stir in oil and parsley. Let sit at room temperature for 30 minutes. (Olive salad can be refrigerated for up to 1 week.)

3. Adjust oven rack to middle position and heat oven to 425 degrees. Keeping dough balls on sheet, flatten each into 7-inch disk. Brush tops of disks with egg and sprinkle with sesame seeds. Bake until golden brown and loaves sound hollow when tapped, 18 to 20 minutes, rotating sheet halfway through baking. Transfer loaves to wire rack and let cool completely, about 1 hour. (Loaves can be wrapped in plastic and stored at room temperature for up to 24 hours.)

4. Slice loaves in half horizontally. Spread one-fourth of olive salad on cut side of each loaf top and bottom, pressing firmly with rubber spatula to compact. Layer 2 ounces salami, 1½ ounces provolone, 3 ounces mortadella, 1½ ounces provolone, and 2 ounces capicola in order on each loaf bottom. Cap with loaf tops and individually wrap sandwiches tightly in plastic.

5. Place baking sheet on top of sandwiches and weigh down with heavy Dutch oven or two 5-pound bags of flour or sugar for 1 hour, flipping sandwiches halfway through pressing. Unwrap and slice each sandwich into quarters and serve. (Pressed, wrapped sandwiches can be refrigerated for up to 24 hours. Bring to room temperature before serving.)

ROASTED EGGPLANT AND MOZZARELLA PANINI

Serves 4

Why This Recipe Works With such a simple ingredient list, this sandwich should be easy to make. But most versions are greasy and lack flavor. To cut back on greasiness, we broiled the eggplant instead of pan-frying it. Traditionally, the eggplant is layered with fresh tomatoes, mozzarella, and basil. But since we were broiling the eggplant, we opted to broil grape tomatoes as well, along with some garlic. We then mashed the charred tomatoes with the roasted garlic and red wine vinegar. We layered the broiled eggplant with the tomato sauce, shredded mozzarella, and chopped fresh basil to make a bold, balanced eggplant panini that's even better than the classic.

- 1 pound eggplant, sliced into ½-inch rounds
- 10 ounces grape tomatoes
- 2 garlic cloves, peeled
- 5 tablespoons extra-virgin olive oil, divided
- 1 teaspoon table salt, divided
- ½ teaspoon pepper, divided
- 1 tablespoon red wine vinegar
- 8 (½-inch-thick) slices crusty bread
- 6 ounces mozzarella cheese, shredded (1½ cups)
- ½ cup coarsely chopped fresh basil

1. Adjust 1 oven rack 4 inches from broiler element and second rack to middle position, and heat broiler. Line rimmed baking sheet with aluminum foil and spray with vegetable oil spray. Spread eggplant, tomatoes, and garlic evenly over baking sheet and drizzle with 3 tablespoons oil. Sprinkle with ½ teaspoon salt and ¼ teaspoon pepper. Broil until vegetables are browned and tomatoes have split open, 8 to 10 minutes, flipping eggplant once during broiling.

2. Transfer tomatoes to small bowl and mash with fork. Mince roasted garlic and stir into tomatoes. Stir in vinegar, remaining ½ teaspoon salt, and remaining ¼ teaspoon pepper.

3. Reduce oven temperature to 200 degrees. Set wire rack in clean rimmed baking sheet. Brush remaining 2 tablespoons oil evenly over 1 side of each slice of bread. Assemble 4 sandwiches by layering ingredients as follows between prepared bread (with oiled sides outside sandwich): half of mozzarella, tomato sauce, eggplant, basil, and remaining mozzarella. Press gently on sandwiches to set.

4. Heat 12-inch nonstick grill pan over medium heat for 1 minute. Place 2 sandwiches in pan, place Dutch oven on top, and cook until bread is golden and crisp on first side, about 4 minutes. Flip sandwiches, replace Dutch oven, and cook until second side is crisp and cheese is melted, about 4 minutes.

5. Transfer sandwiches to prepared wire rack and keep warm in oven. Wipe out grill pan with paper towels and cook remaining 2 sandwiches. Serve.

THE ITALIAN AMERICAN KITCHEN
Mozzarella

Most of the mozzarella you see—blocks, shredded, slices—is an Italian American invention, created in the early 1900s by immigrants who wanted a cheese with a longer shelf life. It's made much like traditional Italian mozzarella (aka "fresh" mozzarella), but the curds are cooked and stirred longer before stretching, resulting in a low-moisture cheese with more longevity that grates easily and melts beautifully.

We prefer whole-milk mozzarella to park-skim and avoid shredded cheeses, which are dry and don't melt as well. Avoid cheeses labeled "low-moisture"—they tend to be firm and rubbery.  Our top-rated brand is **Polly-O Whole Milk Mozzarella Cheese,** which approximates the rich, milky flavor we love in fresh mozzarella while maintaining a springy, shreddable texture that melts effortlessly.

MEATBALL SUBS

Serves 4

Why This Recipe Works Submarine sandwiches are a staple at most Italian American delis. Until the late 19th century, the American sandwich was a between-two-slices affair. But in 1893 at the Chicago World's Fair, the "Columbia roll"—basically a whole loaf of bread, so named because the Fair's formal name was the World's Columbia Exposition—made its debut. When this was married to the Italian cold cut sandwich popularized by Italian immigrants in the late 19th century, the sub was born. It soon spread throughout the United States, acquiring different names as it went. We found some 15 names for it, from relatively widespread ones like the hero to more intensely regional names like the bomber (upstate New York); the Garibaldi (Madison, Wisconsin—named for the Italian patriot); the torpedo (New Jersey, New York, and parts of the Midwest); the grinder (New England slang for workers who ground the hulls of ships before repainting); the zeppelin (eastern Pennsylvania); the gondola (central Illinois); the hoagie (Philadelphia—from Hog Island Shipyard workers in World War II); and the wedgie (southeastern New York). Whatever the name, saucy meatballs and melted cheese are a classic filling. To keep things simple, this entire recipe—from making the meatballs to heating the sauce and melting the cheese—happens in the oven, avoiding stovetop splatter. While we don't typically call for dried bread crumbs, in this recipe they are a fast way to build flavor and their dusty texture is well hidden inside the meatballs. And while we usually prefer to make our own tomato sauce for pasta, a good jarred sauce makes perfect sense for a meal like this—so make or buy sauce, as you like.

1 tablespoon extra-virgin olive oil

1¼ pounds 85 percent lean ground beef

¾ cup dried bread crumbs with Italian seasonings

2 large eggs, lightly beaten

1 teaspoon garlic powder

1 teaspoon table salt

½ teaspoon pepper

4 (6-inch) Italian sub rolls, split lengthwise

1⅓ cups Classic Marinara (page 102) or jarred pasta sauce

4 thin slices deli provolone cheese (4 ounces)

1. Adjust oven rack to middle position and heat oven to 400 degrees. Grease rimmed baking sheet with oil. Mix beef, bread crumbs, eggs, garlic powder, salt, and pepper in bowl until well combined. Form mixture into twelve 2-inch meatballs, place on prepared sheet, and bake until browned and meat registers 160 degrees, about 15 minutes. Transfer meatballs to plate; discard accumulated grease on sheet.

2. Carefully line now-empty sheet with parchment paper. Place rolls on sheet and lay 3 meatballs inside each roll. Top meatballs on each sandwich with ⅓ cup marinara sauce and 1 slice provolone. Bake until cheese is melted and sauce is heated through, about 5 minutes. Serve.

THE ITALIAN AMERICAN KITCHEN
Jarred Pasta Sauce

Though the ingredient list can be simple—tomatoes, oil, and spices—choosing a jarred pasta sauce at the supermarket is not. Some manufacturers offer more than a dozen sauces. For our taste test, we eliminated sauces containing cheese, meat, vegetables, cream, or wine and instead focused on simple sauces from the 10 best-selling national manufacturers.

We found striking differences in the products. Half were "borderline inedible." They were cloying like "bad barbecue sauce" or inundated with herb flavors reminiscent of "air freshener." In the end, we could fully recommend only two sauces. What set these apart?

No added sugar was a good start. Lackluster sauces were made primarily from reconstituted tomato paste with some diced tomatoes thrown in for texture. Our favorite sauces started with whole tomatoes. Our favorites also had lots of fat in the form of olive oil. Those with less fat were dull on pasta, whereas sauces with more fat tasted rich. Our winner, **Rao's Homemade Marinara Sauce,** and runner-up, **Victoria Fine Foods Premium Marinara Sauce**, are good stand-ins for homemade.

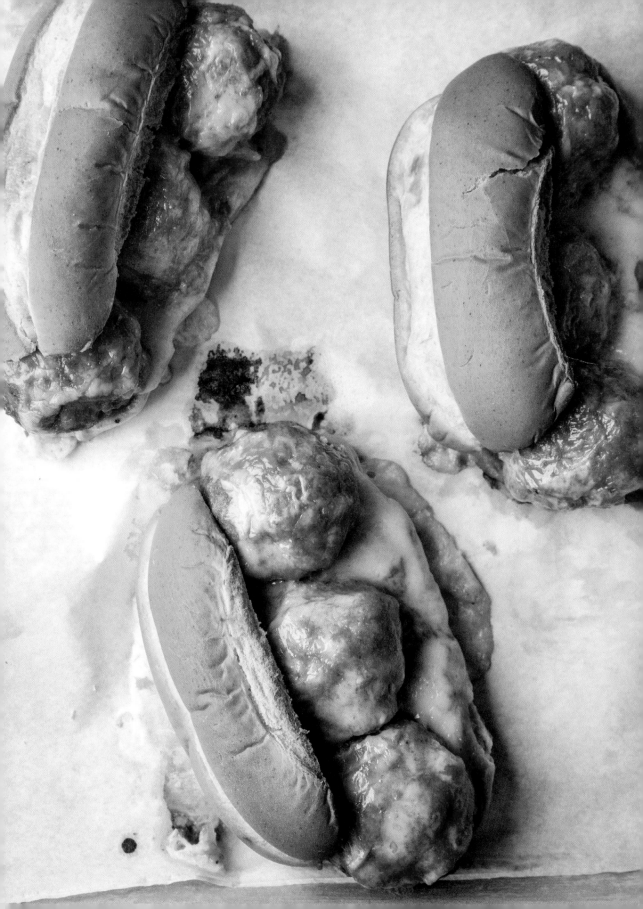

GRILLED SAUSAGE SUBS WITH BELL PEPPERS AND ONIONS

Serves 6

Why This Recipe Works The influence of Italian American cuisine extends to the ballpark, where fans typically watch the national pastime while enjoying fennel-laced Italian sausages nestled in a bun with sautéed bell peppers and onions. This Italian American creation is perfectly matched with ice-cold beer and plenty of sunshine. To translate this sandwich for the backyard grill, we discovered that we needed to stagger the cooking process. We cooked the sausages gently on the cooler side of the grill until they were nearly done and then moved them to the hotter side to develop nice grill marks and a slight char. For the vegetables, we relied on the microwave to jump-start their cooking. We then transferred them to a disposable aluminum pan set on the hotter side of the grill, which acted as our makeshift ballpark flat-top grill. We seasoned the vegetables with vinegar, salt, and pepper, and they reached perfect tenderness just as the sausages finished cooking. Just before serving, we transferred the sausages to the disposable pan, covered it with aluminum foil, and let everything rest for a few minutes before serving. You can substitute hot Italian sausages for sweet, if desired. Minor flare-ups are to be expected when grilling the sausages on the hotter side of the grill; they give the sausages color and flavor.

- 3 red bell peppers, stemmed, seeded, and cut into ¼-inch-wide strips
- 2 onions, halved and sliced ¼ inch thick
- 3 tablespoons distilled white vinegar
- 2 tablespoons sugar
- 1 tablespoon vegetable oil
- ½ teaspoon table salt
- ½ teaspoon pepper
- 1 (13 by 9-inch) disposable aluminum pan
- 2 pounds sweet Italian sausage
- 12 (6-inch) Italian sub rolls

1. Toss bell peppers, onions, vinegar, sugar, oil, salt, and pepper together in bowl. Microwave, covered, until vegetables are just tender, about 6 minutes. Pour vegetable mixture and any accumulated juices into disposable pan.

2A. For a charcoal grill Open bottom vent completely. Light large chimney starter filled with charcoal briquettes (6 quarts). When top coals are partially covered with ash, pour evenly over half of grill. Set cooking grate in place, cover, and open lid vent completely. Heat grill until hot, about 5 minutes.

2B. For a gas grill Turn all burners to high, cover, and heat grill until hot, about 15 minutes. Leave primary burner on high and turn off other burner(s). (Adjust primary burner [or, if using three-burner grill, primary burner and second burner] as needed to maintain grill temperature between 375 and 400 degrees.)

3. Clean and oil cooking grate. Place disposable pan on hotter side of grill (over primary burner if using gas). Cover and cook for 20 minutes.

4. Place sausages on cooler side of grill and stir vegetable mixture; cover and cook for 8 minutes. Flip sausages and stir vegetable mixture again; cover and cook until sausages register 150 degrees and vegetables are softened and beginning to brown, about 8 minutes.

5. Transfer sausages to disposable pan with vegetables; slide disposable pan to cooler side of grill, then transfer sausages from disposable pan to hotter side of grill. Cook sausages, uncovered, turning often, until well browned and registering 160 degrees, 2 to 3 minutes (there may be flare-ups).

6. Return sausages to disposable pan with vegetables. Remove disposable pan from grill, tent with aluminum foil, and let rest for 5 minutes. Divide sausages and vegetables among rolls. Serve.

CHICAGO-STYLE ITALIAN BEEF SANDWICHES

Serves 4

Why This Recipe Works Italian beef sandwiches are a Chicago specialty that you simply won't find anywhere else. From the spicy *giardiniera* to the jus-soaked roll, the flavors are bright, bold, and well equipped to stand up to juicy, generously seasoned Chicago-Style Italian Roast Beef (page 172). To quickly marry the sandwich's flavors, we simmered the meat, jus, and giardiniera brine until the beef was no longer pink. For a rich, spicy relish that stayed put and didn't turn our bread soggy, we pulsed the drained giardiniera in the food processor with mayonnaise and red pepper flakes. Brushing the sub rolls with oil and toasting them under the broiler made for a sturdy sandwich, ready to sop up the flavorful jus. Our kitchen may not have the same charm as the Little Italy eateries that made these sandwiches famous, but our take on their spicy claim to fame tasted like the real deal. If you don't have enough leftover jus, make our Quick Jus (recipe follows).

4 (6-inch) Italian sub rolls, partially split lengthwise

1 tablespoon vegetable oil

4 cups thinly sliced leftover roast beef

1½ cups leftover jus

1 (16-ounce) bottle giardiniera, drained, 1 tablespoon brine reserved

1 tablespoon mayonnaise

¼ teaspoon red pepper flakes

1. Adjust oven rack to upper-middle position and heat broiler. Brush interior of rolls with oil and arrange, oiled side up, on baking sheet. Broil until golden brown, about 1 minute.

2. Combine beef, jus, and giardiniera brine in 12-inch skillet and simmer over medium heat until meat is no longer pink, about 6 minutes. Meanwhile, pulse giardiniera, mayonnaise, and pepper flakes in food processor until finely chopped.

3. Arrange beef on toasted rolls, drizzle with jus, and top with giardiniera mixture. Serve.

QUICK JUS
Makes 1 cup

For this recipe, we enriched canned beef broth with browned scraps of beef, then thickened the broth with a little flour.

1 teaspoon extra-virgin olive oil

1 cup leftover roast beef trimmings

¼ cup finely chopped onion

1 teaspoon all-purpose flour

2 cups beef broth

Heat oil in 10-inch skillet over medium-high heat until just smoking. Add beef and cook until dark brown, about 1 minute. Reduce heat to medium, add onion, and cook until slightly softened, about 1 minute. Add flour and cook, stirring constantly, until fragrant and toasty, about 1 minute. Whisk in broth, scraping up browned bits. Simmer until liquid is reduced by half, about 10 minutes. Pour through fine-mesh strainer and serve.

THE ITALIAN AMERICAN KITCHEN
Giardiniera

In Italy, giardiniera refers to pickled vegetables that are typically eaten as an antipasto. But here in the United States, it's most recognized as a combination of pickled cauliflower, carrots, celery, and sweet and hot peppers that is served alongside sandwiches or other lunch fare. Our favorite product is from **Pastene**. It includes a good mix of crunchy vegetables and boasts a "sharp, vinegary tang."

Meet Philly's Other Sandwich

You hear Philadelphia, you think cheesesteak. But Italian Americans in Philly have their own claim to fame. If you're ordering the house special hot roast pork sandwich at John's Roast Pork in South Philadelphia, you don't have to wait in line; that deeply satisfying sandwich of roasted pork, braised spinach, and a noticeable kick of red peppers can be made in short order, and you're allowed to weave through the lunch-rush crowd and up to the counter. At midday, John's is a noisy place, thanks mostly to the yelling between the cashiers, line cooks, and back kitchen staff all jammed into a tiny shoebox of a building.

By contrast, the cavernous Reading Terminal Market across town delivers a much bigger, nearly overwhelming sensory experience with its butchers and grocers and gift shops and bakeries selling freshly fried doughnuts. It's packed to the brim with a mix of tourists and locals and, despite the

neon signs, there's an air of antiquity and comfort to the place, a sit-and-stay-awhile kind of vibe. This is no surprise: The building made its debut as a civic marketplace more than 100 years ago and has become an indelible part of the city's cultural fabric.

That fabric includes Tommy DiNic's, a Reading Terminal Market standby since 1980. DiNic's draws a huge and reliable lunchtime crowd, weekdays and weekends alike. Cooks pile garlicky broccoli rabe atop the thin slices of seasoned pork, along with sharp provolone cheese. Fresh bread, crunchy on the outside and soft inside, soaks up the juices and keeps everything in place. Most of the time, anyway.

PHILADELPHIA PORK SANDWICHES

Serves 8

Why This Recipe Works A Philadelphia roast pork sandwich is a glorious beast: thinly sliced seasoned pork; bitter, garlicky greens; a rich, herby jus; and sharp provolone cheese melted onto a fluffy roll (not to mention the optional hot peppers). It's not a shy sandwich, boasting a bold personality full of different flavors. It is a local triumph and a point of pride. To re-create these famous Philly sandwiches at home, we opted for a boneless pork butt roast and braised it in chicken broth. This made tender and flavorful pork, and the juices from the pork mingled with the chicken broth during cooking to create an ultrasavory jus. Letting the roast cool and cutting it in half made it easier to slice paper-thin. We then rewarmed the pork before shingling the thin slices on warm Italian rolls with garlicky broccoli rabe and sharp provolone cheese. You need to let the pork cool for 1 hour and then refrigerate it for at least 1 hour to make slicing easier. Sharp provolone is often labeled "Provolone Picante," but you can use standard deli provolone, too. If you're using table salt, cut the amounts in half. Serve with jarred hot cherry peppers, if desired.

Pork and Jus

- 1 tablespoon kosher salt
- 2 teaspoons minced fresh rosemary
- 2 teaspoons dried thyme
- 2 teaspoons dried oregano
- 2 teaspoons fennel seeds
- 1 teaspoon red pepper flakes
- 1 (4-pound) boneless pork butt roast, trimmed
- 2 cups chicken broth, plus extra as needed
- 8 garlic cloves, peeled and smashed

Broccoli Rabe

- 2 tablespoons extra-virgin olive oil
- 3 garlic cloves, sliced thin
- 1 pound broccoli rabe, trimmed and cut into ½-inch pieces
- 2 teaspoons kosher salt
  Pinch red pepper flakes

Sandwiches

- 8 (8-inch) Italian sub rolls, split lengthwise
- 12 ounces sliced sharp provolone cheese

1. For the pork and jus Adjust oven rack to lower-middle position and heat oven to 300 degrees. Combine salt, rosemary, thyme, oregano, fennel seeds, and pepper flakes in bowl. Tie pork with kitchen twine at 1-inch intervals. Sprinkle pork with salt mixture and transfer to large Dutch oven. Pour broth around pork and add garlic to pot. Cover, transfer to oven, and cook until meat registers 190 degrees, 2½ to 3 hours.

2. Transfer pork to large plate. Transfer braising liquid to 4-cup liquid measuring cup; add extra broth, if necessary, to equal 3 cups. Let pork and liquid cool completely, about 1 hour. Cover and refrigerate both for at least 1 hour or up to 2 days.

3. For the broccoli rabe Heat oil and garlic in Dutch oven over medium heat until garlic is golden brown, 3 to 5 minutes. Add broccoli rabe, salt, and pepper flakes and cook, stirring occasionally, until tender, 4 to 6 minutes. Transfer to bowl.

4. About 20 minutes before serving, adjust oven rack to middle position and heat oven to 450 degrees. Remove twine and cut cooled pork in half lengthwise to make 2 even-size roasts. Position roasts cut side down and slice each crosswise as thin as possible.

5. Spoon solidified fat off cooled jus and discard. Transfer jus to Dutch oven and bring to boil over high heat. Reduce heat to low, add pork, cover, and cook until pork is heated through, about 3 minutes, tossing occasionally. Cover and keep warm.

6. For the sandwiches Arrange rolls on 2 rimmed baking sheets (4 rolls per sheet). Divide provolone evenly among rolls. Bake, 1 sheet at a time, until cheese is melted and rolls are warmed, about 3 minutes. Using tongs, divide pork and broccoli rabe evenly among rolls (about 1 cup pork and ⅓ cup broccoli rabe per roll). Serve, passing any remaining jus separately.

IRON RANGE PORKETTA SANDWICHES

Serves 8

Why This Recipe Works Porketta sandwiches are as ubiquitous as hamburgers in Minnesota's Iron Range but barely known outside the region. These sandwiches are all about the meat: roasted, shredded pork seasoned with fennel, garlic, salt, and pepper and served on crusty rolls. They are a simplified take on Italian "porchetta," which was brought to the Iron Range by Italian iron miners around the turn of the 20th century. Nearly every restaurant and sandwich shop in Hibbing, home to the world's largest iron ore mine, has it on the menu. Local grocery stores even sell seasoned roasts and premixed spice packets for the dish. Hoping to introduce this heavily seasoned shredded pork specialty to a wider audience, we started by infusing a boneless pork butt roast with the signature porketta spices—fennel and garlic. To maximize the seasoning's penetration and to shorten the roast's cooking time, we butterflied the meat and cut a crosshatch pattern into both sides. We rubbed a mixture of cracked fennel seeds, salt, pepper, and granulated garlic into the meat before wrapping it in plastic wrap and refrigerating it for 6 hours. The pork butt's licorice flavor was reinforced when we spread chopped fresh fennel over its surface just before roasting. The roast was tender and ready for shredding in about 3 hours, and after we tossed the bite-size pieces of meat with some of the drippings, our flavor-packed porketta was fit to serve. Pork butt roast is often labeled "Boston butt" in the supermarket. This recipe calls for granulated garlic, which has a well-rounded garlic flavor. It is golden and has the texture of table salt. Garlic powder is paler, with the texture of flour, and can be acrid. Don't confuse the two or substitute garlic powder in this recipe. To crack the fennel seeds, spread them on a cutting board, place a skillet on top, and press down firmly with both hands. The porketta tastes best when the raw meat sits in the refrigerator for a full 24 hours with the spices.

3 tablespoons fennel seeds, cracked

1 tablespoon table salt

2 teaspoons pepper

2 teaspoons granulated garlic

1 (5-pound) boneless pork butt roast, trimmed

1 fennel bulb, stalks discarded, bulb halved, cored, and chopped

8 crusty sandwich rolls

1. Combine fennel seeds, salt, pepper, and granulated garlic in bowl. Slice through pork parallel to counter, stopping 1/2 inch from edge, then open meat flat like a book. Cut 1/4-inch-deep slits, spaced 1 inch apart, in crosshatch pattern on both sides of roast. Rub roast all over with spice mixture, taking care to work spices into crosshatch. Wrap roast tightly with plastic wrap and refrigerate for at least 6 hours or up to 24 hours.

2. Adjust oven rack to middle position and heat oven to 325 degrees. Unwrap meat and place in roasting pan, fat side down. Spread chopped fennel evenly over top of roast. Cover roasting pan tightly with aluminum foil. Roast until meat registers 200 degrees and fork slips easily in and out of meat, 3 to 4 hours.

3. Transfer pork to carving board and let rest for 30 minutes. Strain liquid in roasting pan through fine-mesh strainer into fat separator; discard solids. Shred pork into bite-size pieces, return to pan, and toss with 1/2 cup defatted cooking liquid. Season with salt and pepper to taste. Divide meat among rolls and serve.

HEARTY MINESTRONE

Serves 6 to 8

Why This Recipe Works You can almost always take the measure of an Italian American restaurant by trying its minestrone. A good one captures the fleeting flavors of summer vegetables in a bowl and tastes like it has layers and layers of flavor. This recipe squeezes every last ounce of flavor out of the vegetables and features creamy dried beans and a surprisingly rich broth. Sautéing pancetta and then cooking the vegetables in the rendered fat gave our soup layers of flavor, while a Parmesan rind added richness. Starch from simmering beans thickened the soup. The last component we considered for our perfect minestrone was the liquid, settling on just the right combination of chicken broth, water, and V8 juice (which added a big wallop of vegetable flavor). We prefer cannellini beans, but navy or great Northern beans can be used. We prefer pancetta, but bacon can be used. For a spicier dish, use the larger amount of red pepper flakes. To make this soup vegetarian, substitute 2 teaspoons of olive oil for the pancetta and vegetable broth for the chicken broth. The Parmesan rind can be replaced with a 2-inch chunk of Parmesan cheese. For the starch from the beans to thicken the soup, it's important to maintain a vigorous simmer in step 3. You must brine the beans for at least 8 hours or up to 24 hours before making the soup. If you're pressed for time, you can use our quick-salt-soak method: In step 1, combine the salt, water, and beans in a Dutch oven and bring them to a boil over high heat. Remove the pot from the heat, cover, and let stand for 1 hour. Drain and rinse the beans and proceed with step 2.

½ teaspoon table salt, plus salt for brining beans

8 ounces (1¼ cups) dried cannellini beans, picked over and rinsed

1 tablespoon extra-virgin olive oil, plus extra for serving

3 ounces pancetta, cut into ¼-inch pieces

2 celery ribs, cut into ½-inch pieces

2 small onions, cut into ½-inch pieces

1 carrot, peeled and cut into ½-inch pieces

1 zucchini, cut into ½-inch pieces

½ small head green cabbage, halved, cored, and cut into ½-inch pieces (2 cups)

2 garlic cloves, minced

⅛–¼ teaspoon red pepper flakes

2 cups chicken broth

1 Parmesan cheese rind, plus grated Parmesan for serving

1 bay leaf

1½ cups V8 juice

½ cup chopped fresh basil

1. Dissolve 1½ tablespoons salt in 2 quarts water in large container. Add beans and soak at room temperature for at least 8 hours or up to 24 hours. Drain and rinse well.

2. Heat oil and pancetta in Dutch oven over medium-high heat. Cook, stirring occasionally, until pancetta is lightly browned and fat has rendered, 3 to 5 minutes. Add celery, onions, carrot, and zucchini and cook, stirring frequently, until vegetables are softened and lightly browned, 5 to 9 minutes. Stir in cabbage, garlic, ½ teaspoon salt, and pepper flakes and continue to cook until cabbage starts to wilt, 1 to 2 minutes. Transfer vegetables to rimmed baking sheet and set aside.

3. Add soaked beans, 8 cups water, broth, Parmesan rind, and bay leaf to pot and bring to boil over high heat. Reduce heat and simmer vigorously, stirring occasionally, until beans are fully tender and liquid begins to thicken, 45 minutes to 1 hour.

4. Add reserved vegetables and V8 juice to pot and cook until vegetables are soft, about 15 minutes. Discard bay leaf and Parmesan rind, stir in basil, and season with salt and pepper to taste. Serve with extra oil and grated Parmesan. (Soup can be refrigerated for up to 2 days. Reheat gently and add basil just before serving.)

PITTSBURGH WEDDING SOUP

Serves 6 to 8

Why This Recipe Works Tender meatballs, pasta, and greens match up perfectly in this western Pennsylvania favorite. We wanted a soup that tasted as if it had taken all day to make—but we also wanted it to be quick and easy. To start, we punched up the broth by mixing garlic and red pepper flakes cooked in olive oil into store-bought chicken broth. We turned to meatloaf mix (a tasty combination of beef, pork, and veal) for our meatballs. Poaching them in the broth saved time and added extra flavor to the base. Many recipes call for spinach or escarole but we found them a bit bland. Chopped kale held its own in the hot liquid, adding great texture and flavor without losing its hearty crunch, and orzo proved the right size for spooning up with the meatballs and greens. If meatloaf mix isn't available, substitute 1 pound of 85-percent-lean ground beef. Using the large end of a melon baller guarantees uniform meatballs that cook evenly. Serve with extra Parmesan cheese and a drizzle of extra-virgin olive oil.

Meatballs

- 2 slices hearty white sandwich bread, torn into pieces
- 1/2 cup milk
- 1 large egg yolk
- 1 ounce Parmesan cheese, grated (1/2 cup)
- 3 tablespoons chopped fresh parsley
- 3 garlic cloves, minced
- 3/4 teaspoon table salt
- 1/2 teaspoon pepper
- 1/2 teaspoon dried oregano
- 1 pound meatloaf mix

Soup

- 1 tablespoon extra-virgin olive oil
- 2 garlic cloves, minced
- 1/4 teaspoon red pepper flakes
- 3 quarts chicken broth
- 1 large head kale or Swiss chard, stemmed, leaves chopped
- 1 cup orzo
- 3 tablespoons chopped fresh parsley

1. For the meatballs Using potato masher, mash bread and milk together in large bowl until smooth. Add remaining ingredients, except meatloaf mix, and mash to combine. Add meatloaf mix and knead by hand until well combined. Form mixture into 1-inch meatballs (you should have about 55 meatballs) and arrange in rimmed baking sheet. Cover with plastic wrap and refrigerate until firm, at least 30 minutes. (Meatballs can be made up to 24 hours in advance.)

2. For the soup Heat oil in Dutch oven over medium-high heat until shimmering. Cook garlic and pepper flakes until fragrant, about 30 seconds. Add broth and bring to boil. Stir in kale and simmer until softened, 10 to 15 minutes. Stir in meatballs and orzo, reduce heat to medium, and simmer until meatballs are cooked through and pasta is tender, about 10 minutes. Stir in parsley and salt and pepper to taste. Serve.

THE ITALIAN AMERICAN KITCHEN
Chicken Broth

Thrifty Italian grandmothers would certainly save chicken backs and wings to make stock, but many modern Italian American cooks rely on store-bought broth. That's fine if you buy the right one. But pick the wrong brand and you can ruin a simple soup this like one. Bad broths can be simply meek-flavored, but they can also be unpalatably salty or have funky off-flavors. On the other end of the spectrum is our favorite broth, **Swanson Chicken Stock,** which our tasters lauded for its "rich," "meaty" flavor. It's worth seeking out.

WHITE BEAN SOUP

Serves 6 to 8

Why This Recipe Works This classic soup is comprised of only two components: tender, creamy beans and a broth perfumed with garlic and rosemary. Adding onion, garlic, bay leaf, and pancetta to the broth gave the soup a welcome depth of flavor. For a heartier soup, place a small slice of lightly toasted Italian bread in the bottom of each bowl and ladle the soup over it. To make this soup vegetarian, omit the pancetta and add a piece of Parmesan cheese rind to the pot with the onion and garlic in step 2. We do not recommend freezing this soup as the beans become mushy. You must brine the beans for at least 8 hours or up to 24 hours. If you're pressed for time, you can use our quick-salt-soak method: In step 1, combine the salt, water, and beans in a Dutch oven and bring them to a boil over high heat. Remove the pot from the heat, cover, and let stand for 1 hour. Drain and rinse the beans and proceed with step 2.

- 1 teaspoon table salt, plus salt for brining beans
- 1 pound (2½ cups) dried cannellini beans, picked over and rinsed
- 6 ounces pancetta, cut into 1-inch pieces
- 1 large onion, unpeeled and halved, plus 1 small onion, chopped, divided
- 7 garlic cloves (4 unpeeled, 3 minced), divided
- 1 bay leaf
- ¼ cup extra-virgin olive oil, plus extra for serving
- 1 sprig fresh rosemary
  Balsamic vinegar

1. Dissolve 3 tablespoons salt in 4 quarts cold water in large container. Add beans and soak at room temperature for at least 8 hours or up to 24 hours. Drain and rinse well.

2. Adjust oven rack to lower-middle position and heat oven to 250 degrees. Cook pancetta in Dutch oven over medium heat until just golden, 8 to 10 minutes. Add 12 cups water, beans, halved onion, unpeeled garlic cloves, bay leaf, and 1 teaspoon salt and bring to boil over medium-high heat. Cover pot, transfer to oven, and cook until beans are tender, 1¼ to 1½ hours.

3. Drain beans in colander set over medium bowl, reserving 5 cups bean cooking liquid (if you don't have enough bean cooking liquid, add water to equal 5 cups). Discard pancetta, onion, unpeeled garlic cloves, and bay leaf. Spread beans in even layer on rimmed baking sheet and let cool.

4. Meanwhile, heat oil in now-empty pot over medium heat until shimmering. Add chopped onion and cook, stirring occasionally, until softened, 5 to 6 minutes. Stir in minced garlic and cook until fragrant, about 30 seconds. Add cooled beans and reserved cooking liquid. Increase heat to medium-high and bring to simmer.

5. Off heat, submerge rosemary in soup, cover, and let stand until fragrant, about 15 minutes. Discard rosemary sprig and season soup with salt and pepper to taste. Ladle soup into bowls, drizzling individual portions with vinegar and additional oil. (Soup can be refrigerated for up to 3 days.)

THE ITALIAN AMERICAN KITCHEN
Pancetta

Made from the belly of the pig, this Italian staple adds flavor and meaty depth to many soups and stews. Sometimes called Italian bacon, the fatty cut is also used to make American bacon. However, while American bacon is salted, (usually) sugared, and smoked, pancetta is treated with salt, black pepper, and spices and rolled into a cylinder. It is never smoked.

To use bacon in place of pancetta, blanch the bacon in boiling water to mellow its smoky flavor. Because blanching also removes fat from the bacon, you may need to supplement with additional oil. While the bacon may still impart subtle smokiness, it is an acceptable substitute.

PASTA E FAGIOLI

Serves 4 to 6

Why This Recipe Works From type of bean to shape of pasta, the iterations of this Italian American pasta-and-bean soup are endless. One rendition from a restaurant in New Jersey, studded with creamy beans and soft little pieces of pasta, was the inspiration for our version. Starting with a base of pancetta, finely chopped vegetables, plenty of garlic, and a small but powerful punch from tomato paste, we built a rich and flavorful broth as a backdrop for our soup. To thicken it, we pureed half the cannellini beans that we were adding to the soup. For ease, rather than boiling the pasta in a separate pot, we added little ditalini right into the simmering soup to cook in the last moments before serving. Some grated Parmesan cheese for extra richness and seasoning and a big handful of fresh basil for a blast of fragrant freshness was all that was needed to finish the dish. You can use any small pasta shape, such as tubettini, elbow macaroni, or small shells, in place of the ditalini. To make this soup vegetarian, omit the pancetta and substitute vegetable broth for the chicken broth. If you do not have a food processor, you can use a blender to process the beans and water in step 1.

2 (15-ounce) cans cannellini beans, rinsed, divided

1 cup water

2 tablespoons extra-virgin olive oil, plus extra for drizzling

2 onions, chopped fine

2 carrots, peeled and chopped fine

1 celery rib, chopped fine

2 ounces pancetta, chopped fine

¾ teaspoon table salt

½ teaspoon pepper

2 tablespoons tomato paste

4 garlic cloves, minced

¼ teaspoon red pepper flakes (optional)

4 cups chicken broth

4 ounces (1 cup) ditalini

2 ounces Parmesan cheese, grated (1 cup), plus extra for serving

½ cup finely chopped fresh basil

1. Process 1 can of beans and water in food processor until smooth, about 30 seconds. Set aside.

2. Heat oil in large saucepan over medium heat until shimmering. Add onions, carrots, celery, pancetta, salt, and pepper and cook until vegetables are softened, about 10 minutes.

3. Add tomato paste, garlic, and pepper flakes, if using, and cook until fragrant, about 2 minutes. Stir in broth, remaining can of beans, and pureed bean mixture. Bring to boil, reduce heat to medium-low, and simmer, stirring occasionally, until flavors have melded, about 10 minutes. (Soup can be refrigerated for up to 2 days or frozen for up to 1 month. Thaw soup, if necessary, and reheat before proceeding with step 4.)

4. Increase heat to medium and bring to boil. Add pasta and cook, stirring occasionally, until pasta is al dente, about 12 minutes. Off heat, stir in Parmesan and basil. Serve, drizzled with extra oil and passing extra Parmesan separately.

THE ITALIAN AMERICAN KITCHEN
Canned Cannellini Beans

We go through a lot of cannellini beans in the test kitchen. Their creamy texture and mildly nutty flavor round out soups, casseroles, pasta dishes, and salads alike. Modern canning practices generally call for cleaning, sorting, and blanching the beans before sealing them in their cans with water and, often, salt, which flavors the beans and tenderizes the skins. All but one of the products we tasted add calcium chloride, which maintains firmness and prevents splitting, and calcium disodium EDTA, a preservative that binds iron in the water and prevents white beans from turning brown. Sampling the beans plain, in dip, and in soup, we found that saltiness ended up playing the biggest role in our results: Our winning can, made by **Goya**, was the saltiest in the bunch, while our last-place contender was a no-salt-added product.

Phil's Fish Story

If it weren't for the line of people snaking through the parking lot to the front door of Phil's Fish Market & Eatery in Moss Landing, California, you could easily drive right by it. The tin-sided combination of seafood market and restaurant blends into its industrial port surroundings, camouflaged by stacks of wooden pallets, rusted shipping containers, and dry-docked boats. The building was once a squid processing plant, one of many now-defunct fish processing facilities in the area (John Steinbeck's famous novel *Cannery Row* was set in Monterey, just a short drive down the coast from Phil's).

Owner Phil DiGirolamo expected to feed 3,500 customers on the day that we arrived. The place is loud, owing in part to the polished concrete floor, intended for high traffic and easy cleanup. "It's not for everybody," DiGirolamo explains. "I play to families."

DiGirolamo grew up along this stretch of coast, one of 13 kids who pitched in at the family seafood restaurant. "We wanted to be managers, but my uncles had those jobs." Instead, DiGirolamo stuck to the kitchen, where he learned his grandmother's cooking secrets, measuring her handfuls of ingredients so he could re-create the recipes.

The most popular item on the menu is cioppino, which DiGirolamo claims gets its name from everyone "chipping in" to the pot depending on what came in from the sea that day. His version contains scallops, prawns, calamari, mussels, fish, clams, and a cluster of Dungeness crab legs poking out of the top. Servers deliver gadgets for cracking shells and prying meat along with cheap plastic bibs that, while not stylish, do keep your clothes safe from stains.

MONTEREY BAY CIOPPINO

Serves 6 to 8

Why This Recipe Works Cioppino is an Italian American fish stew from San Francisco featuring an abundance of seafood in a garlicky broth of tomatoes, stock, and wine. It's a treasured dish, a staple in Bay Area restaurants. But on a recent visit to Phil's Fish Market & Eatery in Moss Landing, a 90-minute drive away, we were inspired by a slightly sweeter, more herby version that locals and visitors alike line up for. This cioppino is richer, darker, and more complex than more-common renditions. To create a home recipe inspired by the cioppino served up at Phil's, we started by making a tomatoey marinara base that relied on pantry staples and came together quickly, bolstering the mix with bottled clam juice and, for a bit of sweetness, dry sherry. Instead of breaking out the food processor to make a traditional pesto to flavor our stew as Phil does, we simply added pesto's key ingredients (olive oil, basil, and garlic) to the mix. Phil's soup is brimming with a wide range of seafood, but we wanted to tighten the roster for our version, so we bypassed clams and calamari, opting instead for easy-to-find shrimp, scallops, sea bass, and mussels. Adding our seafood to the pot in stages and finishing the cooking off the heat ensured that each component was perfectly cooked. We recommend buying "dry" scallops, which don't have chemical additives and taste better than "wet" scallops. Dry scallops will look ivory or pinkish; wet scallops are bright white. If you can't find fresh dry scallops, you can substitute thawed frozen scallops. If you can't find sea bass, you can substitute cod, haddock, or halibut fillets.

Marinara

- 3 tablespoons extra-virgin olive oil
- 1 large onion, halved and sliced thin
- 3 garlic cloves, sliced thin
- ¾ teaspoon table salt
- 1 (15-ounce) can tomato sauce
- 1 cup canned tomato puree
- ½ cup chopped fresh basil
- 1 tablespoon packed light brown sugar
- 1½ teaspoons Worcestershire sauce
- ¼ teaspoon ground cinnamon

Cioppino

- 1½ pounds skinless sea bass fillets, 1 to 1½ inches thick, cut into 1½-inch pieces
- 12 ounces extra-large shrimp (21 to 25 per pound), peeled, deveined, and tails removed
- 12 ounces large scallops, tendons removed, cut in half horizontally
-     Table salt and pepper
- 3 tablespoons extra-virgin olive oil
- 1 pound mussels, scrubbed and debearded
- ½ cup chopped fresh basil
- ¼ cup dry sherry
- 3 garlic cloves, minced
- 1 teaspoon Worcestershire sauce
- ½ teaspoon saffron threads, crumbled
- 2 (8-ounce) bottles clam juice
- 1 (12-inch) baguette, sliced and toasted
-     Lemon wedges

1. For the marinara Heat oil in large saucepan over medium heat until shimmering. Add onion, garlic, and salt and cook until onion is softened and just beginning to brown, about 8 minutes. Add tomato sauce, tomato puree, basil, sugar, Worcestershire, and cinnamon and bring to boil. Reduce heat to medium-low and simmer until marinara is slightly thickened, 10 to 12 minutes. Remove from heat, cover, and set aside.

2. For the cioppino Season sea bass, shrimp, and scallops with salt and pepper; set aside. Heat oil in Dutch oven over medium-high heat until shimmering. Add mussels, basil, sherry, garlic, Worcestershire, saffron, and ½ teaspoon salt. Cover and cook until mussels start to open, about 2 minutes.

3. Stir in clam juice and marinara until combined. Nestle sea bass and scallops into pot and bring to boil. Reduce heat to medium, cover, and simmer until seafood is just turning opaque, about 2 minutes. Nestle shrimp into pot and return to simmer. Cover and cook until all seafood is opaque, about 3 minutes. Remove from heat and let sit, covered, for 5 minutes. Serve with baguette slices and lemon wedges.

ULTIMATE CAESAR SALAD

Serves 4

Why This Recipe Works This Italian American invention dates back to the 1920s when restaurateur Caesar Cardini first served a novel concoction at his restaurant in Tijuana. Cardini lived in San Diego, but for a time operated his restaurant south of the border to avoid Prohibition restrictions. His restaurant was frequented by early Hollywood movie stars who popularized his salad. It was made tableside and famously enjoyed by Julia Child during her California childhood. There are precious few salads as popular as the classic Caesar, and when you have a good one, it's easy to see why. To create a recipe for a Caesar salad that could truly live up to the hype, we threw it back to the classic method, slowly whisking extra-virgin olive oil into a pungent mix of egg yolk, lemon juice, Dijon mustard, minced anchovies, and Worcestershire sauce to create a luscious, creamy dressing. For the perfect buttery, crisp garlic-flavored croutons, we cut ciabatta bread into ½-inch cubes and tossed them in garlic oil before baking them until crisp and golden. To infuse the entire salad with savory Parmesan cheese, we stirred finely grated Parmesan into the dressing and tossed coarsely shredded Parmesan into the salad. When it all came together with the crunchy, lightly sweet romaine lettuce, we remembered why everyone knows the name Caesar. Use a rasp-style grater or the fine holes of a box grater to grate the Parmesan. To shred it, use the large holes of a box grater. The size of the lettuce is important here. To cut the lettuce into 1-inch pieces, first cut off the cores and then cut each romaine heart in half lengthwise. Cut the halves in half lengthwise. Finally, cut crosswise into 1-inch pieces.

¾ cup extra-virgin olive oil, divided

2 garlic cloves, minced, divided

½ teaspoon table salt, divided

½ teaspoon pepper, divided

4 ounces ciabatta, cut into ½-inch cubes (4 cups)

1 large egg yolk

1 tablespoon lemon juice

2 teaspoons Worcestershire sauce

2 teaspoons Dijon mustard

2 anchovy fillets, rinsed and minced, plus extra fillets for serving (optional)

¼ cup grated Parmesan cheese, plus 1½ ounces shredded (½ cup)

2 romaine lettuce hearts (12 ounces), cut into 1-inch pieces

1. Adjust oven rack to middle position and heat oven to 350 degrees. Stir ¼ cup oil, half of garlic, ¼ teaspoon salt, and ¼ teaspoon pepper together in large bowl. Add bread and toss to combine. Transfer bread to rimmed baking sheet and bake until light golden, about 18 minutes, stirring halfway through baking. Let cool completely. Wipe bowl clean with paper towels.

2. Form damp dish towel into ring shape on counter. Set now-empty bowl on towel to stabilize. Whisk egg yolk, lemon juice, Worcestershire, mustard, anchovies, remaining ¼ teaspoon salt, remaining ¼ teaspoon pepper, and remaining garlic together in bowl. Whisking constantly, slowly drizzle in remaining ½ cup oil until emulsified. Whisk in grated Parmesan.

3. Add lettuce, croutons, and shredded Parmesan to bowl with dressing and toss to combine. Season with salt and pepper to taste. Serve, garnished with extra anchovies, if using.

CHOPPED CAPRESE SALAD

Serves 4 to 6

Why This Recipe Works Reinvention is the hallmark of Italian American cooking. Start with something Italian and then make it bigger. This salad, which follows in that tradition, was inspired by the Italian classic salad of sliced mozzarella shingled with sliced tomatoes and basil leaves. Adding chopped romaine lettuce transforms an appetizer into a hearty tossed salad. Chopped globe tomatoes turned the salad watery, but halved grape tomatoes provide a pop of color and sweet, year-round tomato flavor. To further guard against watery salad, we toss the tomatoes with salt ahead of time to season them and draw out excess liquid. A potent mix of olive oil, garlic, basil, and shallot seasons the cheese, and the same mix, along with red wine vinegar, becomes the dressing for the salad. You can use cherry tomatoes in place of grape tomatoes.

- 8 ounces fresh mozzarella, cut into ½-inch pieces
- 3 tablespoons extra-virgin olive oil
- 2 tablespoons minced shallot
- 1 garlic clove, minced
- 1¼ teaspoons table salt, divided
- ¼ teaspoon pepper
- ½ cup fresh basil leaves, divided
- 1½ pounds grape tomatoes, cut in half lengthwise
- 2 romaine hearts (12 ounces), quartered lengthwise and cut into ½-inch pieces
- ¼ cup pitted kalamata olives, chopped
- 3 tablespoons red wine vinegar

1. Combine mozzarella, oil, shallot, garlic, ¼ teaspoon salt, and pepper in bowl. Coarsely chop half of basil leaves and add to mozzarella mixture; set aside while preparing tomatoes. Combine tomatoes and remaining 1 teaspoon salt in separate bowl; transfer to colander set in sink; and let drain for 15 minutes, stirring occasionally. (Tomatoes can be prepared up to 1 hour in advance.)

2. Tear remaining basil leaves into ½-inch pieces. Gently toss mozzarella mixture, tomatoes, torn basil, romaine, olives, and vinegar together in large bowl. Season with salt and pepper to taste and serve.

THE ITALIAN AMERICAN KITCHEN
Fresh Mozzarella

For centuries, fresh mozzarella has been made in Italy using buffalo's milk. But since buffalo mozzarella is not aged and is usually produced with unpasteurized milk, its shelf life is only four to five days, making the cheese difficult to export to the United States. While there are a few buffalo mozzarella producers in the United States, most domestic "fresh" mozzarella is made from pasteurized cow's milk. The term "fresh mozzarella" is not recognized by the U.S. Food and Drug Administration, but cheesemakers use it to denote a style of mozzarella that is higher in moisture and is eaten raw ("fresh") rather than cooked (with a few exceptions, such as when it's used to top pizza margherita).

With this in mind, we set out to find our favorite fresh mozzarella, focusing on cheeses labeled "fresh" and sold in shrink-wrapped balls or packed in brine. We rounded up eight nationally available products and tasted them plain, in salad, and melted onto miniature toasts. We didn't notice much difference in the cheeses when they were melted; however, flavor and texture differences were apparent in the plain and salad tastings. Our favorite cheese was **BelGioioso Fresh Mozzarella** (packaged in a vacuum-sealed ball), which had moderate tang, moderate sodium, and high moisture. These attributes combined to create a cheese with a savory, buttery richness; a tender curd; and clean, milky flavor.

SIMPLE TOMATO SALAD

Serves 4

Why This Recipe Works The tomato is the start of countless Italian salads. This is one recipe that Italian Americans have left pretty much alone. The point of the salad is simplicity itself so you can appreciate the freshness and complexity of the tomatoes. Because tomatoes are already fairly acidic, we found that a dressing made with the typical 3:1 ratio of oil to acid was too sharp. Adjusting the amount of lemon juice to minimize the acidity perfectly balanced the salad. A minced shallot added just a bit of sweetness and crunch, while torn basil leaves completed the salad with a fresh note. Start with the ripest tomatoes you can find, either from the farmers' market or the grocery store (or, better yet, your backyard garden). Don't make the recipe with anything other than peak-of-the-season tomatoes. Serve with crusty bread to sop up the dressing.

1½   pounds mixed ripe tomatoes, cored and sliced ¼ inch thick

3   tablespoons extra-virgin olive oil

1   tablespoon minced shallot

1   teaspoon lemon juice

½   teaspoon table salt

¼   teaspoon pepper

2   tablespoons pine nuts, toasted

1   tablespoon torn fresh basil leaves

Arrange tomatoes on large, shallow platter. Whisk oil, shallot, lemon juice, salt, and pepper together in bowl. Spoon dressing over tomatoes. Sprinkle with pine nuts and basil. Serve immediately.

VARIATIONS
Simple Tomato Salad with Capers and Parsley
Add 1 tablespoon rinsed capers, 1 rinsed and minced anchovy fillet, and ⅛ teaspoon red pepper flakes to dressing. Omit pine nuts. Substitute coarsely chopped fresh parsley for basil.

Simple Tomato Salad with Pecorino Romano and Oregano
Add ½ teaspoon grated lemon zest and ⅛ teaspoon red pepper flakes to dressing. Omit pine nuts. Substitute 2 teaspoons coarsely chopped fresh oregano for basil. Sprinkle salad with 1 ounce shaved Pecorino Romano cheese.

THE ITALIAN AMERICAN KITCHEN
Premium Extra-Virgin Olive Oil

A simple salad like this is the perfect way to highlight the flavor of an expensive premium extra-virgin olive oil. Of course, extra-virgin olive oil, the lush, vibrant product of fresh olives, is premium by definition—or it should be. But most of what you'll find at the supermarket doesn't deserve that label. The oils are often mislabeled as a higher grade, mishandled so their flavor turns rancid, or even occasionally fraudulently blended with other, cheaper oils and passed off as the real deal.

We rounded up 10 premium oils priced from $0.94 to $2.13 per ounce (plus shipping) from France, Italy, Spain, Greece, Tunisia, Portugal, and the United States. Our first step was to sample the oils plain. As we then tasted them tossed with butter lettuce and a little salt and finally drizzled over a bowl of warm cannellini beans, we marveled at how distinct each oil was. Ultimately we recommended them all and classified them by flavor profile, from mild to robust, but our crowd-pleasing favorite was **Gaea Fresh Extra Virgin Olive Oil,** which tasters described as "buttery," "smooth," and "nicely balanced."

MARINATED ANTIPASTO SALAD

Serves 6 to 8

Why This Recipe Works Antipasto salad, an Italian American take on chef's salad, is a staple of red-sauce restaurants and pizzerias. The best ones highlight cured meats, marinated vegetables, cheese, olives, and crisp lettuce with a potent dressing to unite the components. For a salad that wouldn't be overloaded but still had good fresh-briny balance, we decided on salami, provolone, olives, red onion, artichoke hearts, pepperoncini, cherry tomatoes, and basil to go with neutral-flavored romaine lettuce. Surprisingly, this was showing restraint, as many recipes call for far more. Jarred marinated vegetables were greasy and raw onions were too pungent, so we simmered both in a combination of vinegar, water, garlic, and dried oregano, essentially quick-pickling them, and then added a modest amount of olive oil for balance. Using the leftover pickling liquid in the vinaigrette tied all the flavors together. If you buy whole frozen artichoke hearts, quarter them through the stem after thawing. The drained marinated vegetables and vinaigrette can be refrigerated separately for up to one day. Dress the salad just before serving.

2/3 cup red wine vinegar

1/4 cup water

2 garlic cloves, minced

2 teaspoons dried oregano

1 teaspoon table salt

1 red onion, halved and sliced 1/4 inch thick

9 ounces frozen artichoke hearts, thawed and patted dry

1/3 cup jarred sliced pepperoncini

2 tablespoons extra-virgin olive oil, divided

2 romaine lettuce hearts (12 ounces), chopped

12 ounces cherry tomatoes, halved

3 (1/4-inch-thick) slices provolone cheese (6 ounces), cut into 1-inch-long matchsticks

3 (1/4-inch-thick) slices salami (6 ounces), cut into 1-inch-long matchsticks

1/3 cup pitted kalamata olives

1/4 cup chopped fresh basil

1. Bring vinegar, water, garlic, oregano, and salt to boil in small saucepan over medium-high heat. Add onion, reduce heat to medium-low, and simmer, stirring occasionally, until onion is nearly tender, 5 to 7 minutes. Stir in artichokes and cook until tender, about 3 minutes. Off heat, add pepperoncini, transfer mixture to bowl, and refrigerate until cool, about 20 minutes.

2. Drain marinated vegetables through fine-mesh strainer into bowl; reserve 1/4 cup vinegar mixture. Toss marinated vegetables with 1 tablespoon oil in bowl. Whisk remaining 1 tablespoon oil into reserved vinegar mixture until thoroughly incorporated. Toss romaine, tomatoes, provolone, and salami with vinaigrette in large bowl. Season with salt and pepper to taste. Transfer salad mixture to platter and top with marinated vegetables, olives, and basil. Serve.

ITALIAN PASTA SALAD

Serves 8 to 10 as a side dish

Why This Recipe Works Pasta salad, loaded with meats and cheeses and served cold at summertime cookouts, is a decidedly Italian American invention. For a better, more worthwhile pasta salad, we used corkscrew-shaped fusilli, which had plenty of surface area for capturing dressing. We cooked the pasta until it was a little too soft so that as it cooled and firmed up, it would have just the right tender texture. Rather than toss raw vegetables into the mix, we took inspiration from Italian antipasto platters and used intensely flavored jarred ingredients: Sun-dried tomatoes, kalamata olives, and pepperoncini offered a mix of textures that didn't overshadow the pasta. For heartiness, we included salami, and to balance the salt and tang, we added chunks of creamy mozzarella, fresh basil, and peppery arugula. To ensure that the pasta itself was just as flavorful as the rest of the dish, we made a thick, punchy dressing by processing some of the salad ingredients themselves—capers and pepperoncini plus some of the tangy pepperoncini brine—with olive oil infused with garlic, red pepper flakes, and anchovies. The pasta firms as it cools, so overcooking is key to ensuring the proper texture. We prefer a small, individually packaged, dry Italian-style salami such as Genoa or soppressata, but unsliced deli salami can be used. If the salad is not being served right away, don't add the arugula and basil until right before serving.

1 pound fusilli

   Table salt for cooking pasta

¼ cup extra-virgin olive oil

3 garlic cloves, minced

3 anchovy fillets, rinsed, patted dry, and minced

¼ teaspoon red pepper flakes

1 cup pepperoncini, stemmed, divided, plus 2 tablespoons brine

2 tablespoons capers, rinsed

2 ounces (2 cups) baby arugula

1 cup chopped fresh basil

½ cup oil-packed sun-dried tomatoes, sliced thin

½ cup pitted kalamata olives, quartered

8 ounces salami, cut into ⅜-inch dice

8 ounces fresh mozzarella cheese, cut into ⅜-inch dice and patted dry

1. Bring 4 quarts water to boil in large pot. Add pasta and 1 tablespoon salt and cook, stirring often, until pasta is tender throughout, 2 to 3 minutes past al dente. Drain pasta and rinse under cold water until chilled. Drain well and transfer to large bowl.

2. Meanwhile, combine oil, garlic, anchovies, and pepper flakes in liquid measuring cup. Cover and microwave until bubbling and fragrant, 30 to 60 seconds. Set aside.

3. Slice half of pepperoncini into thin rings and set aside. Transfer remaining pepperoncini to food processor. Add capers and pulse until finely chopped, 8 to 10 pulses, scraping down sides of bowl as needed. Add pepperoncini brine and warm oil mixture and process until combined, about 20 seconds.

4. Add dressing to pasta and toss to combine. Add arugula, basil, tomatoes, olives, salami, mozzarella, and reserved pepperoncini and toss well. Season with salt and pepper to taste. Serve. (Salad can be refrigerated without the arugula and basil for up to 3 days. Let come to room temperature and add arugula and basil before serving.)

THE ITALIAN AMERICAN KITCHEN
Sun-Dried Tomatoes

Sun-dried plum tomatoes are valued for their chewy texture and concentrated flavor. Most products are imported from Italy or Turkey and are sold either dry-packed in plastic containers or bags, or oil-packed in jars. We prefer oil-packed; the dry-packed variety is often leathery.

PANZANELLA

Serves 4

Why This Recipe Works Italian cooks are known for their clever use of leftovers. In this recipe, stale bread is matched with tomatoes and cucumbers to create a summertime classic worth making even when there is no leftover bread. When this rustic salad is done well, the sweet juice of the tomatoes mixes with a bright-tasting vinaigrette, moistening chunks of thick-crusted bread until they're soft and just a little chewy—but the line between lightly moistened and unpleasantly soggy is very thin. Toasting fresh bread in the oven, rather than using the traditional day-old bread, was a good start. The bread lost enough moisture in the oven to absorb the dressing without getting waterlogged. A 10-minute soak in the flavorful dressing yielded perfectly moistened, nutty-tasting bread ready to be tossed with the tomatoes, which we salted to intensify their flavor. A thinly sliced cucumber and shallot for crunch and bite plus a handful of chopped fresh basil perfected our salad. The success of this recipe depends on high-quality ingredients, including ripe, in-season tomatoes and fruity olive oil. Fresh basil is also a must. Your bread may vary in density, so you may not need the entire loaf. Be ready to serve the salad immediately after it is assembled.

1 (1-pound) loaf rustic Italian or French bread, cut or torn into 1-inch pieces (6 cups)

½ cup extra-virgin olive oil, divided

¾ teaspoon table salt, divided

1½ pounds ripe tomatoes, cored, seeded, and cut into 1-inch pieces

3 tablespoons red wine vinegar

¼ teaspoon pepper

1 cucumber, peeled, halved lengthwise, seeded, and sliced thin

1 shallot, sliced thin

¼ cup chopped fresh basil

1. Adjust oven rack to middle position and heat oven to 400 degrees. Toss bread pieces with 2 tablespoons oil and ¼ teaspoon salt in bowl and spread in single layer on rimmed baking sheet. Toast bread until just starting to turn light golden, 15 to 20 minutes, stirring halfway through baking. Let cool to room temperature.

2. Meanwhile, gently toss tomatoes with remaining ½ teaspoon salt in large bowl. Transfer to colander set over now-empty bowl and let drain for 15 minutes, tossing occasionally.

3. Whisk remaining 6 tablespoons oil, vinegar, and pepper into drained tomato juices. Add toasted bread, toss to coat, and let stand for 10 minutes, tossing occasionally. Add drained tomatoes, cucumber, shallot, and basil, and toss to coat. Season with salt and pepper to taste and serve immediately.

THE ITALIAN AMERICAN KITCHEN
Red Wine Vinegar

Americans might think balsamic vinegar is the most popular vinegar in Italy but red wine vinegar holds this honor. After tasters sampled 10 red wine vinegars plain, in vinaigrette, and in pickled onions, it was clear that they found highly acidic vinegars too harsh; products with moderate amounts of acidity scored higher. Tasters also preferred those vinegars that were blends—either blends of different grapes or blends of different vinegars—as they offered more complex flavor. Tasters ranked French import **Laurent du Clos Red Wine Vinegar** first; it won the day with its "good red wine flavor." However, this vinegar has become increasingly hard to find in stores or online, and its importer admits its distribution has become very limited. If you're unable to locate it, we recommend our second-place vinegar, **Pompeian Gourmet Red Wine Vinegar.**

WHITE BEAN SALAD WITH SAUTÉED SQUID AND PEPPERONCINI

Serves 4 to 6

Why This Recipe Works Recipes that pair savory white beans with lean, mild squid are common in Italian American restaurants, and it's easy to understand why: The delicate flavor of the beans complements but doesn't overpower the subtle seafood flavor of the squid. But recipes vary widely in both cooking method and ingredient additions, so we knew we had our work cut out for us. We started with the squid. Since we wanted to achieve some flavorful browning, we immediately ruled out steaming and boiling. We also decided that grilling was too fussy for just a pound of squid, so we settled on sautéing. In past recipes, we've used a baking soda brine to tenderize the squid and make it less likely to overcook, and we wondered if it was necessary here. A side-by-side test determined that it was: The unbrined squid turned rubbery by the time we achieved any browning, but the brined squid stayed beautifully tender even after spending several minutes in the skillet. Cooking the squid in two batches encouraged more even browning. Using canned beans kept the overall cooking time short, and simmering them in an aromatic liquid infused them with flavor. After a few tests, we determined that tasters preferred simpler salads that allowed the tender squid and beans to shine. Nutty sherry vinegar and tangy pepperoncini were winning additions, and to bring out more of the pepperoncini flavor, we also added some of the brine. Scallions and whole parsley leaves provided a finishing touch of freshness. Be sure to use small squid (with bodies 3 to 4 inches in length) because they cook more quickly and are more tender than larger squid.

1 tablespoon baking soda

1 tablespoon table salt, for brining

1 pound small squid, bodies sliced crosswise into ½-inch-thick rings, tentacles halved

6 tablespoons extra-virgin olive oil, divided

1 red onion, chopped fine

¼ teaspoon table salt

3 garlic cloves, minced

2 (15-ounce) cans cannellini beans, rinsed

⅓ cup pepperoncini, stemmed and sliced into ¼-inch-thick rings, plus 2 tablespoons brine

2 tablespoons sherry vinegar

½ cup fresh parsley leaves

3 scallions, green parts only, sliced thin

1. Dissolve baking soda and 1 tablespoon salt in 3 cups water in medium container. Add squid, cover, and refrigerate for 15 minutes. Dry squid thoroughly with paper towels and toss with 1 tablespoon oil.

2. Heat 1 tablespoon oil in medium saucepan over medium heat until shimmering. Add onion and ¼ teaspoon salt and cook, stirring occasionally, until softened and lightly browned, 5 to 7 minutes. Stir in garlic and cook until fragrant, about 30 seconds. Stir in beans and ¼ cup water and bring to simmer. Reduce heat to low, cover, and continue to simmer, stirring occasionally, for 2 to 3 minutes; set aside.

3. Heat 1 tablespoon oil in 12-inch nonstick skillet over high heat until just smoking. Add half of squid in single layer and cook, without moving, until well browned, about 3 minutes. Flip squid and continue to cook, without moving, until well browned on second side, about 2 minutes; transfer to bowl. Wipe skillet clean with paper towels and repeat with 1 tablespoon oil and remaining squid.

4. Whisk remaining 2 tablespoons oil, pepperoncini brine, and vinegar together in large bowl. Add pepperoncini, beans and any remaining cooking liquid, squid, parsley, and scallions and toss to combine. Season with salt and pepper to taste. Serve.

PIZZA AND MORE

NEW YORK THIN-CRUST PIZZA

Makes two 13-inch pizzas, serving 4 to 6

Why This Recipe Works Pizza in New York (as well as nearby New Haven) is typically described as "thin-crust," but actually has a puffy edge you can hold and tapers down to a thin layer in the center. This style of pizza usually relies on a very hot pizzeria oven to create the requisite chew, so making it at home requires some neat tricks. Kneading our pizza dough's ingredients in the food processor was quicker and just as efficient as using a stand mixer (using ice water prevented the dough from overheating). To keep our dough from puffing as it cooked and to give it more complex flavor, we let it proof slowly in the refrigerator for at least a day, which kept the bubbles tighter. Finally, positioning our pizza stone near the top of the oven crisped the pizza and quickly browned it in the heat radiating off the oven's ceiling (mimicking the shallow chamber of a commercial pizza oven). Shape the second dough ball while the first pizza bakes, but don't top the pizza until right before you bake it. Some baking stones can crack under the heat of the broiler; be sure to check the manufacturer's website. Our recommended stone is by Old Stone Oven. If you don't have a stone, bake the pizza on a preheated overturned rimmed baking sheet. If you don't have a pizza peel, you can use a rimless baking sheet. Semolina flour is ideal for dusting the peel; use it in place of bread flour if you have it. The sauce will yield more than needed; extra sauce can be refrigerated for up to 1 week or frozen for up to 1 month.

Dough

- 3 cups (16½ ounces) bread flour, plus more for work surface
- 2 tablespoons sugar
- ½ teaspoon instant or rapid-rise yeast
- 1⅓ cups (10½ ounces) ice water
- 1 tablespoon vegetable oil, plus more for work surface
- 1½ teaspoons table salt

Sauce

- 1 (28-ounce) can whole peeled tomatoes, drained
- 1 tablespoon extra-virgin olive oil
- 1 teaspoon red wine vinegar
- 2 garlic cloves, minced
- 1 teaspoon table salt
- 1 teaspoon dried oregano
- ¼ teaspoon pepper

Toppings

- 1 ounce finely grated Parmesan cheese (½ cup), divided
- 8 ounces whole-milk mozzarella cheese, shredded (2 cups), divided

1. For the dough Pulse flour, sugar, and yeast in food processor until combined, about 5 pulses. With processor running, slowly add ice water and process until dough is just combined and no dry flour remains, about 10 seconds. Let dough rest for 10 minutes.

2. Add oil and salt to dough and process until dough forms satiny, sticky ball that clears sides of bowl, 30 to 60 seconds. Transfer to lightly oiled counter and knead by hand to form smooth, round ball, about 30 seconds. Place dough seam side down in lightly greased bowl. Cover tightly with plastic wrap and refrigerate for at least 24 hours or up to 3 days.

3. For the sauce Process all ingredients in food processor until smooth, about 30 seconds. Transfer to medium bowl or container and refrigerate until ready to use.

4. For the pizza One hour before baking, adjust oven rack 4 inches from broiler element, set baking stone on rack, and heat oven to 500 degrees. Remove dough from refrigerator and divide in half. Shape each half into smooth, tight ball. Place on lightly greased baking sheet, spaced at least 3 inches apart; cover loosely with greased plastic wrap and let rest for 1 hour.

5. Heat broiler for 10 minutes. Meanwhile, coat 1 ball of dough generously with flour and place on well-floured counter. Using fingertips, gently flatten into 8-inch disk, leaving 1 inch of outer edge slightly thicker than center. Using hands, gently stretch disk into 12-inch round, working along edges and giving disk quarter turns as you stretch. Transfer dough to well-floured peel and stretch into 13-inch round. Using back of spoon or ladle, spread 1/2 cup tomato sauce evenly over surface of dough, leaving 1/4-inch border around edge. Sprinkle 1/4 cup Parmesan evenly over sauce, followed by 1 cup mozzarella.

6. Slide pizza carefully onto stone and return oven to 500 degrees. Bake until crust is well browned and cheese is bubbly and beginning to brown, 8 to 10 minutes, rotating pizza halfway through. Transfer pizza to wire rack for 5 minutes before slicing and serving. Heat broiler for 10 minutes. Repeat with remaining dough, sauce, and toppings, returning oven to 500 degrees when pizza is placed on stone.

CHICAGO DEEP-DISH PIZZA

Makes two 9-inch pizzas, serving 4 to 6

Why This Recipe Works Deep-dish pizza was born in Chicago, where it boasts a distinctly rich, flaky, and biscuit-like crust. To discover the secrets to achieving the perfect crust—an airy inside, a lightly crisp outside, and a rich taste that could hold its own under any topping—we visited several Chicago institutions, including Pizzeria Uno (the 1943 birthplace of this style of pizza) as well as Gino's East and Lou Malnati's. We ate more than a dozen pies in 36 hours. Back in the test kitchen, we learned that a combination of flour, cornmeal, and butter gave us the desired flavor. Rolling and folding the dough gave the crust delicious layers. Refrigerating the dough during the second rise allowed the butter to chill, resulting in a high and flaky rise. Following Chicago tradition, we covered the dough with shredded mozzarella before topping it with a thick tomato sauce. During kneading, place a damp dish towel under the stand mixer and watch the mixer at all times to prevent it from wobbling off the counter. Oil your hands before handling the dough, or it might stick. Grate the onion on the large holes of a box grater.

Dough

3¼ cups (16¼ ounces) all-purpose flour

½ cup (2½ ounces) yellow cornmeal

2¼ teaspoons instant or rapid-rise yeast

2 teaspoons sugar

1½ teaspoons table salt

1¼ cups water (10 ounces), room temperature

7 tablespoons unsalted butter, 3 tablespoons melted, 4 tablespoons softened, divided

1 teaspoon plus ¼ cup extra-virgin olive oil, divided

Sauce

2 tablespoons unsalted butter

¼ cup grated onion

½ teaspoon table salt

¼ teaspoon dried oregano

2 garlic cloves, minced

1 (28-ounce) can crushed tomatoes

¼ teaspoon sugar

2 tablespoons chopped fresh basil

1 tablespoon extra-virgin olive oil

Pepper

Toppings

1 pound mozzarella, shredded (4 cups), divided

¼ cup grated Parmesan cheese, divided

1. For the dough Using stand mixer fitted with dough hook, mix flour, cornmeal, yeast, sugar, and salt on low speed until incorporated, about 1 minute. Add room-temperature water and melted butter and mix on low speed until fully combined, 1 to 2 minutes, scraping down bowl as needed. Increase speed to medium and knead until dough is smooth and pulls away from sides of bowl, 4 to 5 minutes. (Dough will pull away from sides only while mixer is running.)

2. Coat large bowl with 1 teaspoon oil using your fingers, rubbing excess oil from your fingers onto blade of rubber spatula. Using oiled spatula, transfer dough to bowl, turning once to coat top; cover tightly with plastic wrap. Let rise at room temperature until nearly doubled in volume, 45 minutes to 1 hour.

3. For the sauce While dough rises, melt butter in medium saucepan over medium heat. Add onion, salt, and oregano; cook, stirring occasionally, until liquid has evaporated and onion is golden brown, about 5 minutes. Add garlic and cook until fragrant, about 30 seconds. Stir in tomatoes and sugar, increase heat to high, and bring to simmer. Reduce heat to medium-low and simmer until reduced to 2½ cups, 25 to 30 minutes. Off heat, stir in basil and oil, then season with salt and pepper to taste.

4. Adjust oven rack to lowest position and heat oven to 425 degrees. Using rubber spatula, turn out dough onto dry counter and roll into 15 by 12-inch rectangle with short side parallel to counter edge. Using offset spatula, spread softened butter over surface of dough, leaving ½-inch border along edges. Starting at short end closest to you, roll dough into tight cylinder. With seam side down, flatten cylinder into 18 by 4-inch rectangle.

Cut rectangle in half crosswise. Working with 1 half, fold into thirds like business letter; pinch seams together to form ball. Repeat with remaining half. Return balls to oiled bowl, cover tightly with plastic, and let rise in refrigerator until nearly doubled in volume, 40 to 50 minutes.

5. For the pizza Coat two 9-inch round cake pans with 2 tablespoons oil each. Transfer 1 dough ball to dry counter and roll into 13-inch disk about ¼ inch thick. Transfer dough to pan by rolling dough loosely around rolling pin and unrolling into pan. Lightly press dough into pan, working into corners and 1 inch up sides. If dough resists stretching, let it relax for 5 to 10 minutes before trying again. Repeat with remaining dough ball.

6. For each pizza, sprinkle 2 cups mozzarella evenly over surface of dough, spread 1¼ cups sauce over cheese, and sprinkle 2 tablespoons Parmesan over sauce. Bake until crust is golden brown, 20 to 30 minutes. Remove pizza from oven and let rest for 10 minutes before slicing and serving.

Pride of the South Side

Rose George is the third-generation owner of Vito & Nick's on Chicago's South Pulaski Road. She still adheres to the business philosophy instilled in her by her grandfather Vito Barraco: "You're working for the working-class person. Keep it affordable. And never vary the quality of the product, even when times are bad."

The dining room is a dizzying hodgepodge of colors and textures: teal chairs and booths, white-and-blue linoleum floors, avocado-green carpeting on the walls, and blue holiday lights dangling from the drop ceiling above the bar. But it all works. The pizza oven—a 1965 Blodgett—is a relic, complete with a cobbled together assortment of

tools for specific cleaning tasks. For example, "the Q-tip" is a sawed-off broomstick with a wad of towels wrapped at one end. It gets the job done.

The pizzas at Vito & Nick's are baked until they're dark—dark enough to have some customers send them back to the kitchen, complaining that they're burnt. It's the way Nick (Rose's father) insisted they be baked. According to Rose, Nick used to stand at the counter adjacent to the pizza oven, watching the pizzas come out of the oven. If they weren't well-done enough, he'd yell, "That's canary! Put it back in!"—implying that the cheese had gone only from white to golden (canary), not to the spotty brown he demanded.

CHICAGO THIN-CRUST PIZZA

Makes two 12-inch pizzas, serving 4

Why This Recipe Works When most people hear "Chicago-style pizza," they think doughy deep-dish. But deep-dish pizza is not the only pie in town. Head to the South Side, to restaurants such as Vito & Nick's, and you'll find locals devouring a different but equally local style of pie. The pizza is built on a thin, crisp crust similar to the cracker style made famous by St. Louis (page 82). It features a lightly sweet sauce and dark, spotty-brown cheese reaching all the way to the pie's charred edge, and is cut into easy-to-pick-up small squares. The trick for making this thin, crisp pizza at home is using the food processor, which brings the dough together quickly and prevents too much gluten from forming. Using ice water keeps the dough from overheating in the processor. A no-cook tomato sauce and shredded mozzarella sprinkled all the way to the outer edges cover the dough. A pizza peel is the best tool for moving the pizza in and out of the oven, but you can also use a rimless baking sheet.

Dough

- 2½ cups (12½ ounces) all-purpose flour
- 2 teaspoons sugar
- 1½ teaspoons instant or rapid-rise yeast
- 1 teaspoon table salt
- ¾ cup plus 2 tablespoons ice water
- 2 tablespoons extra-virgin olive oil
  Cornmeal

Sauce

- 1 (8-ounce) can tomato sauce
- 1 tablespoon tomato paste
- 2 teaspoons sugar
- ½ teaspoon Italian seasoning
- ½ teaspoon fennel seeds

Toppings

- 12 ounces sweet Italian sausage, casings removed, divided
- 12 ounces whole-milk mozzarella cheese, shredded (3 cups), divided
- ½ teaspoon dried oregano, divided

1. For the dough Process flour, sugar, yeast, and salt in food processor until combined, about 3 seconds. With processor running, slowly add ice water and oil and process until dough forms sticky ball that clears sides of bowl, 30 to 60 seconds.

2. Transfer dough to lightly oiled counter and knead until smooth, about 1 minute. Shape dough into tight ball and place in greased bowl. Cover bowl with plastic wrap and let dough rise at room temperature until almost doubled in size, 2 to 2½ hours. One hour before baking, adjust oven rack to lowest position, set baking stone (or inverted baking sheet) on rack, and heat oven to 500 degrees.

3. For the sauce Whisk all ingredients together in bowl. (Sauce can be refrigerated for up to 2 days.)

4. Transfer dough to lightly floured counter, divide in half, and gently shape each half into ball. Return 1 dough ball to bowl and cover with plastic. Coat remaining dough ball lightly with flour and gently flatten into 8-inch disk using your fingertips. Using rolling pin, roll dough into 12-inch circle, dusting dough lightly with flour as needed. (If dough springs back during rolling, let rest for 10 minutes before rolling again.)

5. For the pizza Sprinkle pizza peel with cornmeal. Transfer dough to prepared pizza peel and carefully stretch to return to 12-inch circle. Using back of spoon or ladle, spread scant ½ cup sauce in even layer over surface of dough, leaving ⅛-inch border around edge. Pinch half the sausage into approximate dime-size pieces and evenly distribute over sauce. Sprinkle 1½ cups mozzarella evenly over sausage to edge of pie. Sprinkle ¼ teaspoon oregano over top.

6. Carefully slide pizza onto baking stone and bake until cheese is well browned and edges of pizza are crisp and dark, 10 to 14 minutes. Transfer pizza to cutting board and let cool for 5 minutes. Repeat with remaining dough, sauce, sausage, mozzarella, and oregano. Cut pizzas into 2- to 3-inch squares and serve.

NEW ENGLAND BAR PIZZA

Makes two 9-inch pizzas, serving 4

Why This Recipe Works This New England favorite is baked in well-seasoned rimmed pans, with the dough forming a thin lip up the sides. The crust is tender yet crispy. Bar pizza is particularly popular on Massachusetts's South Shore, an area situated between Boston and Cape Cod. The Lynwood Cafe in Randolph serves a classic bar pizza with a potent tomato sauce, plenty of cheese, and the requisite tender, thin crust with a crisp underside. We created the distinctive edges by rolling the pizza dough thin and baking the pies in 9-inch cake pans, pressing the dough ¼ inch up the sides of the pan. Brushing the edges with tomato sauce and cheese also gave us the "laced" edges that bar pizza is known for. An uncooked tomato sauce delivered the desired fresh tomato punch. Finishing the pies with a mixture of cheddar and mozzarella best imitated the classic version's distinct tangy flavors. The sauce will yield more than needed in the recipe; extra sauce can be refrigerated for up to 1 week or frozen for up to 1 month.

Dough

1²/₃ cups (8⅓ ounces) all-purpose flour

  1 tablespoon sugar

  1 teaspoon instant or rapid-rise yeast

²/₃ cup ice water

1½ teaspoons extra-virgin olive oil

¾ teaspoon table salt

Sauce

  1 (14.5-ounce) can diced tomatoes

  1 teaspoon extra-virgin olive oil

½ teaspoon dried oregano

½ teaspoon sugar

¼ teaspoon table salt

⅛ teaspoon pepper

⅛ teaspoon red pepper flakes

Toppings

  4 ounces sharp cheddar cheese, shredded (1 cup)

  4 ounces whole-milk mozzarella, shredded (1 cup)

  1 tablespoon extra-virgin olive oil, divided

1. For the dough Process flour, sugar, and yeast in food processor until combined, about 3 seconds. With processor running, slowly add ice water; process dough until just combined and no dry flour remains, about 10 seconds. Let dough stand for 10 minutes. Add oil and salt to dough and process until dough forms satiny, sticky ball that clears sides of workbowl, 30 to 60 seconds.

2. Transfer dough to lightly oiled counter and knead until smooth, about 1 minute. Shape dough into tight ball and place in greased bowl. Cover with plastic wrap and let rise at room temperature until almost doubled in size, 2 to 2½ hours.

3. For the sauce Process all ingredients in clean, dry food processor until smooth, about 30 seconds; set sauce aside.

4. For the pizza Adjust oven rack to lowest position and heat oven to 500 degrees. Combine cheddar and mozzarella in bowl. Using pastry brush, grease bottom and sides of 2 dark-colored 9-inch round cake pans with 1½ teaspoons oil each.

5. Transfer dough to lightly floured counter, divide in half, and shape into balls. Gently flatten 1 dough ball into 6-inch disk using your fingertips. Using rolling pin, roll disk into 10-inch round. Transfer dough to prepared pan and press into corners, forcing ¼-inch lip of dough up sides of pan. Repeat with remaining dough ball.

6. Spread ⅓ cup sauce in even layer over entire surface of 1 dough. Using pastry brush, brush sauce over lip of dough. Sprinkle 1 cup cheese mixture evenly over pizza, including lip. Repeat with remaining dough, ⅓ cup sauce, and remaining 1 cup cheese mixture.

7. Bake until crust is browned and cheese is bubbly and beginning to brown, about 12 minutes, switching and rotating pans halfway through baking. To remove pizzas from pans, run offset spatula along top edge of crust. Once loosened, slide spatula underneath pizza and slide pizza onto wire rack. Let cool for 5 minutes. Slice and serve.

ST. LOUIS PIZZA

Makes two 12-inch pizzas, serving 4 to 6

Why This Recipe Works You can make terrific pizza without yeast. It may sound crazy to most bakers, but folks in St. Louis have been doing it for years. With its wafer-thin crust, thick and sweet tomato sauce, gooey Provel cheese (another local secret), and signature square slices, St. Louis–style pizza is unmistakable. Imo's, a popular local chain, is credited with creating it, and it's said that founder Ed Imo, a former tile layer, subconsciously cut the circular pizza into tile-shaped squares (the "square beyond compare," as the jingle goes). The chain and its pizza have since crossed into Illinois and Kansas. In the test kitchen, we found that adding cornstarch to the dough absorbed moisture and allowed the crust to crisp in a conventional oven. We doctored a simple pizza sauce by adding sugar, tomato paste, dried oregano, and fresh basil. The fresh herb wasn't typical, but it gave the pizza a flavorful lift. Smoky, melty Provel cheese was difficult to find outside the St. Louis area, so we crafted a respectable substitute with American cheese, Monterey Jack, and liquid smoke. If you can find Provel cheese, use 10 ounces in place of the American cheese, Monterey Jack cheese, and liquid smoke.

Sauce and Toppings

- 1 (8-ounce) can tomato sauce
- 3 tablespoons tomato paste
- 2 tablespoons chopped fresh basil
- 1 tablespoon sugar
- 2 teaspoons dried oregano
- 8 ounces white American cheese, shredded (2 cups)
- 2 ounces Monterey Jack cheese, shredded (½ cup)
- 3 drops liquid smoke

Dough

- 2 cups (10 ounces) all-purpose flour
- 2 tablespoons cornstarch
- 2 teaspoons sugar
- 1 teaspoon baking powder
- 1 teaspoon table salt
- ½ cup plus 2 tablespoons water
- 2 tablespoons extra-virgin olive oil

1. For the sauce and toppings Whisk together tomato sauce, tomato paste, basil, sugar, and oregano in small bowl; set aside. Toss cheeses with liquid smoke in medium bowl; set aside.

2. For the dough Combine flour, cornstarch, sugar, baking powder, and salt in large bowl. Combine water and oil in liquid measuring cup. Stir water mixture into flour mixture until dough starts to come together. Turn dough onto lightly floured surface and knead 3 or 4 times, until cohesive.

3. Adjust oven rack to lower-middle position, place baking stone (or inverted baking sheet) on rack, and heat oven to 475 degrees. Divide dough into 2 equal pieces. Working with 1 piece of dough, press into small circle and transfer to parchment paper dusted lightly with flour. Using rolling pin, roll and stretch dough to form 12-inch circle, rotating parchment as needed. Lift parchment and dough off work surface onto inverted baking sheet or pizza peel.

4. Top dough with half of sauce and half of cheese. Carefully pull parchment paper and pizza off baking sheet onto hot baking stone. Bake until underside is golden brown and cheese is completely melted, 9 to 12 minutes. Remove pizza and parchment from oven. Transfer pizza to wire rack and let cool briefly. Assemble and bake second pizza. Cut pizzas into 2-inch squares. Serve.

Old World Pie, New World Pan

We hit the streets of the Motor City to uncover the secrets to this topsy-turvy Michigan favorite, a deep-dish pizza like no other, originally made in the square blue steel pans used to collect errant nuts and bolts in the string of automobile-related factories along Detroit's Six Mile Road. The inspiration came from a waitress at Buddy's Pizzeria in the 1940s named Connie Piccinato, who grew up in Sicily and craved the squared-off wedges of focaccia of her youth. Since "square pizza" wasn't known in the States, she and owner August Guerra got creative using those discarded pans.

The rectangular pans, then made by a company named Dover Parkersburg, were "blued" at high temperatures to resist rust and came in two sizes, just right for small and large pizzas. After repeated use, the deeply seasoned pans gave the crusts an extra kick of flavor and a noticeably lacy, cheesy crunch, similar to the crusty edge of a baked lasagna. These pizzas were a huge hit and are still made to this day—though nowadays Buddy's pays five to six times the price it once did for the pans because they have to be specially made.

DETROIT PIZZA

Makes one 13 by 9-inch pizza, serving 4

Why This Recipe Works Detroit pizza, a deep-dish local favorite, is light and airy with a crunchy, buttery crust. It's topped with soft, stretchy cheese, and a slightly sweet tomato sauce full of herbs and spices. In the test kitchen, our big challenge was figuring out how to mimic the tender crumb and the mild and melty brick cheese (which can be found only in Michigan). The stand mixer did most of the kneading for us; the rich, hydrated dough required a 15-minute rest and a 2-hour rise to produce the tender, buttery crust we were after. We topped the pizza with handfuls of Monterey Jack cheese, which we found to be the only acceptable substitute for the brick cheese typically used on Detroit pizzas. A combination of dried herbs, sugar, and canned crushed tomatoes gave our sauce authentic flavor and texture. During kneading, place a damp dish towel under the stand mixer and watch the mixer at all times to prevent it from wobbling off the counter. To add more toppings, such as pepperoni or sausage, to your pizza, press them into the dough before adding the cheese. Note that we use a nonstick metal baking pan for this recipe.

Dough

- 1 tablespoon extra-virgin olive oil
- 2¼ cups (11¼ ounces) all-purpose flour
- 1½ teaspoons instant or rapid-rise yeast
- 1½ teaspoons sugar
- 1 cup water, room temperature
- ¾ teaspoon table salt

Sauce

- 1 cup canned crushed tomatoes
- 1 tablespoon extra-virgin olive oil
- 1 tablespoon chopped fresh basil
- 1 garlic clove, minced
- 1 teaspoon dried oregano
- 1 teaspoon dried basil
- ½ teaspoon sugar
- ½ teaspoon pepper
- ¼ teaspoon table salt

Topping

- 10 ounces Monterey Jack cheese, shredded (2½ cups)

1. For the dough Spray 13 by 9-inch nonstick baking pan with vegetable oil spray, then brush bottom and sides of pan with oil. Using stand mixer fitted with dough hook, mix flour, yeast, and sugar on low speed until combined, about 10 seconds. With mixer running, slowly add room-temperature water and mix until dough forms and no dry flour remains, about 2 minutes, scraping down bowl as needed. Cover with plastic wrap and let stand for 10 minutes.

2. Add salt to dough and knead on medium speed until it forms satiny, sticky ball that clears sides of bowl, 6 to 8 minutes. Turn dough onto lightly floured counter and knead until smooth, about 1 minute.

3. Transfer dough to prepared pan, cover with plastic, and let rest for 15 minutes. Using your well-oiled hands, press dough into corners of pan. (If dough resists stretching, let it rest for another 10 minutes before trying again to stretch.) Cover with plastic and let dough rise at room temperature until nearly tripled in volume and large bubbles form, 2 to 3 hours. Adjust oven rack to lowest position and heat oven to 500 degrees.

4. For the sauce Combine all ingredients in bowl. (Sauce can be refrigerated for up to 24 hours.)

5. For the pizza Sprinkle Monterey Jack evenly over dough to edges of pan. Spoon three 1-inch-wide strips of sauce, using ⅓ cup sauce for each, over cheese evenly down length of pan.

6. Bake until cheese is bubbly and browned, about 15 minutes. Let pizza cool in pan on wire rack for 5 minutes. Run knife around edge of pan to loosen pizza. Using spatula, slide pizza onto cutting board. Cut into 8 pieces and serve.

Beauty in the Basics

In 1953, Samuel Cacia purchased a turnkey bakery in South Philadelphia. At first, he offered tomato pie only on Fridays. Today, tomato pie is a permanent fixture. When the elder Cacia passed away in 1964, his grandson, Sam Cacia, and Sam's uncle, Raymond Cacia, took over the business. Although they've expanded to multiple locations, Sam says, "There's always a Cacia family member in each location."

In the kitchen of the South Philly branch, the true scale of Cacia's reveals itself. There's a light dusting of flour on every surface, emitted from a 50,000-pound-capacity flour silo. Sam grins at a large bubbling pot of tomato sauce. "I make the gravy every day myself. I'm the only one who knows how."

A massive brick oven anchors one wall, faced with subway tile and darkened grout lines, a weathered cast-iron door, and an antique dial thermometer. It's an "80-pan oven," Sam tells us, meaning it can hold 80 full-size sheet pans. (One pan yields two boxes of pizza.) The oven is heated for 90 minutes each morning until it hits 600 degrees. Then it's shut off; the bricks inside retain enough heat to keep cooking throughout the day. Sam slides pans of pizza deep into the oven with a pizza peel as long as a jousting lance.

But the massive oven isn't just for bread and pizza. Every Thanksgiving, Cacia offers it up to neighbors whose own kitchens are overburdened. Last year, they cooked 125 turkeys. Sam has a hard time pinning down the exact number of pies he makes on most days, but "the turkeys, we like to keep track of that."

PHILADELPHIA TOMATO PIE

Makes one 13 by 9-inch pizza, serving 4

Why This Recipe Works Created as a frugal way for local Italian American bakeries to use up leftover bread dough, this South Philadelphia specialty boasts a tender yet chewy crust topped with a bright, assertive tomato sauce—but no cheese. We achieved the signature chewy-soft crust by using less water by weight in proportion to the weight of the flour. This yielded fine holes and a pleasantly spongy chew. Delaying the addition of salt (a technique called autolyze) allows the flour to soak up liquid and become more thoroughly hydrated, which also promotes a chewier finished crust. Letting the dough rise twice—pressing it into the pan in between—gave it maximum yeasty flavor. For the invigorating, sweet-tart, herby sauce, we started with a savory base of onion and garlic and then added a hefty amount of dried oregano along with red pepper flakes for kick. One can of tomato sauce provided just the right tomato flavor and texture, and a tablespoon of sugar contributed the sauce's signature sweetness. When kneading the dough on medium speed, the mixer can wobble and move on the counter. Place a damp dish towel under the mixer to keep it in place and watch it closely. Note that we use a nonstick metal baking pan for this recipe.

Dough

2½ cups (12½ ounces) all-purpose flour

¾ teaspoon instant or rapid-rise yeast

1 cup water, room temperature

1½ tablespoons extra-virgin olive oil

1½ teaspoons table salt

Sauce

2 tablespoons extra-virgin olive oil

¼ cup finely chopped onion

2 garlic cloves, minced

2 teaspoons dried oregano

¼ teaspoon red pepper flakes

1 (15-ounce) can tomato sauce

1 tablespoon sugar

1. For the dough Spray 13 by 9-inch nonstick baking pan with vegetable oil spray. Using stand mixer fitted with dough hook, mix flour and yeast on medium speed until combined, about 10 seconds. With mixer running, slowly add room-temperature water and oil and mix until dough forms and no dry flour remains, about 30 seconds, scraping down bowl as needed. Turn off mixer, cover with plastic wrap, and let stand for 10 minutes.

2. Add salt to dough and knead on medium speed until dough is satiny, sticky, and clears sides of bowl but still sticks to bottom, 6 to 8 minutes. Transfer dough to prepared pan, cover tightly with plastic, and let rise at room temperature until doubled in volume, about 1½ hours.

3. For the sauce Meanwhile, heat oil in small saucepan over medium heat until shimmering. Add onion and cook, stirring occasionally, until softened and lightly browned, 3 to 5 minutes. Add garlic, oregano, and pepper flakes and cook until fragrant, about 30 seconds. Add tomato sauce and sugar and bring to boil. Reduce heat to medium-low and simmer until sauce is slightly thickened and measures about 1¼ cups, about 10 minutes. Set aside and let cool completely.

4. Using your well-oiled hands, press dough into corners of pan. (If dough resists stretching, let it rest for another 10 minutes before trying to stretch again.) Cover tightly with plastic and let dough rise again at room temperature until doubled in volume, about 1½ hours. Adjust oven rack to upper-middle position and heat oven to 450 degrees.

5. Spread sauce evenly over dough leaving ½- to ¼-inch border along sides. Bake until edges are light golden brown and sauce reduces in spots, about 20 minutes. Let tomato pie cool in pan on wire rack for 5 minutes. Run knife around edge of pan to loosen pie. Using spatula, slide pie onto cutting board. Cut into 8 pieces and serve.

SICILIAN-STYLE PIZZA

Makes one 18 by 13-inch pizza, serving 6 to 8

Why This Recipe Works Thick, rectangular slabs of Sicilian-style pizza are often a disappointment. At your typical American food court, Sicilian pizza is made with the same dough as thin-crust pizza and it bakes up dense and heavy. But at the best Sicilian-style pizza shops (many of which are found in New York), the crust is tight and cake-like and the bottom is crisp and delicate. To create a Sicilian pie with a creamy, golden interior and a delicate, crisp bottom, we use a mixture of semolina and all-purpose flours. For a fine-textured, almost cake-like crumb in the crust, we use a three-pronged approach: We use a generous amount of olive oil in the dough to tenderize it; we cold-ferment the dough overnight to let flavors develop without large bubbles forming; and then we roll it out and weigh it down with another baking sheet during the final proof to keep the crumb even and tight. Before baking, we top the dough with a concentrated and complex long-cooked tomato sauce and a mixture of cheeses, a combination that stands up to the thickness of the crust below. This recipe requires refrigerating the dough for 24 to 48 hours before shaping it. King Arthur all-purpose flour and Bob's Red Mill semolina flour work best in this recipe. It is important to use ice water in the dough to prevent overheating during mixing. Place a damp dish towel under the stand mixer and watch the mixer at all times during kneading to prevent it from wobbling off the counter. Anchovies give the sauce depth without a discernible fishy taste; if you decide not to use them, add an additional 1/4 teaspoon table salt.

Dough

2¼ cups (11¼ ounces) all-purpose flour

2 cups (12 ounces) semolina flour

1 teaspoon sugar

1 teaspoon instant or rapid-rise yeast

1⅔ cups (13⅓ ounces) ice water

3 tablespoons extra-virgin olive oil

2¼ teaspoons table salt

Sauce

1 (28-ounce) can whole peeled tomatoes, drained

2 teaspoons sugar

¼ teaspoon table salt

¼ cup extra-virgin olive oil

3 garlic cloves, minced

1 tablespoon tomato paste

3 anchovy fillets, rinsed, patted dry, and minced

1 teaspoon dried oregano

¼ teaspoon red pepper flakes

Toppings

¼ cup extra-virgin olive oil

2 ounces Parmesan cheese, grated (1 cup)

12 ounces whole-milk mozzarella, shredded (3 cups)

1. For the dough Using stand mixer fitted with dough hook, mix all-purpose flour, semolina flour, sugar, and yeast on low speed until combined, about 10 seconds. With machine running, slowly add ice water and oil until dough forms and no dry flour remains, 1 to 2 minutes. Cover with plastic wrap and let dough stand for 10 minutes.

2. Add salt to dough and mix on medium speed until dough forms satiny, sticky ball that clears sides of bowl, 6 to 8 minutes. Remove dough from bowl and knead briefly on lightly floured counter until smooth, about 1 minute. Shape dough into tight ball and place in large, lightly oiled bowl. Cover tightly with plastic and refrigerate for at least 24 hours or up to 2 days.

3. For the sauce Process tomatoes, sugar, and salt in food processor until smooth, about 30 seconds. Heat oil and garlic in medium saucepan over medium-low heat, stirring occasionally, until garlic is fragrant and just beginning to brown, about 2 minutes. Add tomato paste, anchovies, oregano, and pepper flakes and cook until fragrant, about 30 seconds. Add tomato mixture and cook, stirring occasionally, until sauce measures 2 cups, 25 to 30 minutes. Transfer to bowl, let cool, and refrigerate until needed.

4. For the pizza One hour before baking pizza, place baking stone on upper-middle rack and heat oven to 500 degrees. Spray rimmed baking sheet (including rim) with vegetable oil spray, then coat bottom of pan with oil. Remove dough from refrigerator and transfer to lightly floured counter. Lightly flour top of dough and gently press into 12 by 9-inch rectangle. Using rolling pin, roll dough into 18 by 13-inch rectangle. Transfer dough to prepared baking sheet, fitting dough into corners. Spray top of dough with vegetable oil spray and lay sheet of plastic wrap over dough. Place second baking sheet on dough and let stand for 1 hour.

5. Remove top baking sheet and plastic wrap. Gently stretch and lift dough to fill pan. Using back of spoon or ladle, spread sauce in even layer over surface of dough, leaving 1/2-inch border. Sprinkle Parmesan evenly over entire surface of dough to edges, followed by mozzarella.

6. Place pan with pizza on stone; reduce oven temperature to 450 degrees and bake until bottom crust is evenly browned and cheese is bubbly and browned, 20 to 25 minutes, rotating pizza halfway through baking. Remove pan from oven and let cool on wire rack for 5 minutes. Run knife around rim of pan to loosen pizza. Transfer pizza to cutting board, cut into squares, and serve.

THIN-CRUST WHOLE-WHEAT PIZZA WITH GARLIC OIL, THREE CHEESES, AND BASIL

Makes two 13-inch pizzas, serving 4 to 6

Why This Recipe Works The story of Italian America is one of continual re-interpretation of classic recipes. Whole-wheat pizza certainly falls into this category as American pizza masters put their own stamp on the recipe. In theory, this is good news, but in practice, we often find the marriage of whole wheat and pizza crust to be strained at best. Most recipes seem to fear commitment to the style, casually throwing a scant amount of whole-wheat flour into a white flour formula. The resulting pies may have decent texture, but if they have zilch when it comes to nuttiness or flavor complexity, what's the point? At the other end of the spectrum, we've tried following pizza dough recipes with a high ratio of whole-wheat flour (some with as much as 100 percent), and we've found that for the most part they produce dense pies devoid of satisfying chew or crisp crust. Not to mention that these crusts have an overly wheaty flavor that competes for attention with even the most potent toppings. We decided to rethink whole-wheat pizza, examining it through the lens of a bread baker in order to formulate a dough (and a baking technique) that would give us a crust with it all: good—but not overwhelming—wheat flavor; a crisp bottom; and a moist, chewy interior. Some baking stones can crack under the heat of the broiler; be sure to check the manufacturer's website. Our recommended stone is by Old Stone Oven. If you don't have a baking stone, use an overturned rimmed baking sheet. If you don't have a pizza peel, use a rimless baking sheet. If you have it, semolina flour is ideal for dusting the peel in place of bread flour.

Dough

1½ cups (8¼ ounces) whole-wheat flour

1 cup (5½ ounces) bread flour

2 teaspoons honey

¾ teaspoon instant or rapid-rise yeast

1¼ cups ice water

2 tablespoons extra-virgin olive oil

1¾ teaspoons table salt

Garlic Oil

¼ cup extra-virgin olive oil

2 garlic cloves, minced

2 anchovy fillets, rinsed, patted dry, and minced (optional)

½ teaspoon pepper

½ teaspoon dried oregano

⅛ teaspoon red pepper flakes

⅛ teaspoon table salt

Toppings

1 cup fresh basil leaves, divided

1 ounce Pecorino Romano cheese, grated (½ cup), divided

8 ounces whole-milk mozzarella cheese, shredded (2 cups), divided

6 ounces (¾ cup) whole-milk ricotta cheese, divided

1. For the dough Process whole-wheat flour, bread flour, honey, and yeast in food processor until combined, about 2 seconds. With processor running, add ice water and process until dough is just combined and no dry flour remains, about 10 seconds. Let dough stand for 10 minutes.

2. Add oil and salt to dough and process until it forms satiny, sticky ball that clears sides of workbowl, 45 to 60 seconds. Remove from bowl and knead on oiled countertop until smooth, about 1 minute. Shape dough into tight ball and place in large, lightly oiled bowl. Cover tightly with plastic wrap and refrigerate for at least 18 hours or up to 2 days.

3. For the garlic oil Heat oil in 8-inch skillet over medium-low heat until shimmering. Add garlic, anchovies if using, pepper, oregano, pepper flakes, and salt.

Cook, stirring constantly, until fragrant, about 30 seconds. Transfer to bowl and let cool completely before using.

4. For the pizza One hour before baking pizza, adjust oven rack 4½ inches from broiler element, set pizza stone on rack, and heat oven to 500 degrees. Remove dough from refrigerator and divide in half. Shape each half into smooth, tight ball. Place balls on lightly oiled baking sheet, spacing them at least 3 inches apart. Cover loosely with plastic coated with vegetable oil spray; let stand for 1 hour.

5. Heat broiler for 10 minutes. Meanwhile, coat 1 ball of dough generously with flour and place on well-floured countertop. Using your fingertips, gently flatten into 8-inch disk, leaving 1 inch of outer edge slightly thicker than center. Lift edge of dough and, using back of your hands and knuckles, gently stretch disk into 12-inch round, working along edges and giving disk quarter turns as you stretch. Transfer dough to well-floured peel and stretch into 13-inch round. Using back of spoon, spread half of garlic oil over surface of dough, leaving ¼-inch border. Layer ½ cup basil leaves over pizza. Sprinkle with ¼ cup Pecorino, followed by 1 cup mozzarella. Slide pizza carefully onto stone and return oven to 500 degrees. Bake until crust is well browned and cheese is bubbly and partially browned, 8 to 10 minutes, rotating pizza halfway through baking. Remove pizza and place on wire rack. Dollop half of ricotta over surface of pizza. Let pizza rest for 5 minutes, slice, and serve.

6. Heat broiler for 10 minutes. Repeat process of stretching, topping, and baking with remaining dough and toppings, returning oven to 500 degrees when pizza is placed on stone.

GRILLED PIZZA

Makes 3 oval pizzas, serving 4 to 6

Why This Recipe Works Many experts cite Al Forno, the legendary restaurant in Providence, Rhode Island, as the birthplace of grilled pizza. Since the 1980s, Al Forno has been cooking oblong pies on a custom-made wood-fired grill, which produces a gorgeously charred, crisp-tender crust. The grill at Al Forno features a brick enclosure that absorbs heat and then reflects it back onto the top of the pie, much like an oven would. To prevent a hot spot at the center that would burn the crust, we placed the coals only around the perimeter of the grill. Rather than spreading them in an even layer—this setup creates some reflective heat that cooks the pizza from the top. Grilled pizza cooks quickly, so it's critical to have all of your ingredients and tools ready. We recommend par-grilling the crusts, then topping and finishing grilling each in quick succession and serving the pizzas one at a time, rather than all at once.

Dough

- 3 cups (16½ ounces) bread flour
- 1 tablespoon sugar
- ¼ teaspoon instant or rapid-rise yeast
- 1¼ cups plus 2 tablespoons ice water (11 ounces)
- 1 tablespoon vegetable oil, plus extra for counter
- 1½ teaspoons table salt

Sauce

- 1 (14-ounce) can whole peeled tomatoes, drained with juice reserved
- 2 tablespoons extra-virgin olive oil
- 2 teaspoons minced fresh oregano
- ½ teaspoon sugar, plus extra for seasoning
- ½ teaspoon table salt
- ¼ teaspoon red pepper flakes

Toppings

- ½ cup plus 1 tablespoon extra-virgin olive oil, divided, plus extra for drizzling
- 3 ounces Parmesan cheese, grated (1½ cups), divided

- 8 ounces fresh whole-milk mozzarella cheese, torn into bite-size pieces (2 cups), divided
- 3 tablespoons shredded fresh basil, divided
  Coarse sea salt

1. For the dough Process flour, sugar, and yeast in food processor until combined, about 2 seconds. With processor running, slowly add ice water; process until dough is just combined and no dry flour remains, about 10 seconds. Let dough stand for 10 minutes.

2. Add oil and salt and process until dough forms satiny, sticky ball that clears sides of bowl, 30 to 60 seconds. Transfer dough to lightly oiled counter and knead until smooth, about 1 minute. Divide dough into 3 pieces (about 9⅓ ounces each). Shape each piece into tight ball, transfer to well-oiled baking sheet (alternatively, place dough balls in individual well-oiled bowls), and coat top of each ball lightly with oil. Cover tightly with plastic wrap (do not compress dough) and refrigerate for at least 24 hours or up to 3 days.

3. For the sauce Pulse tomatoes in food processor until finely chopped, 12 to 15 pulses. Transfer to medium bowl and stir in reserved juice, oil, oregano, sugar, salt, and pepper flakes. Season with extra sugar and salt to taste, cover, and refrigerate until ready to use.

4. One hour before cooking pizza, remove dough from refrigerator and let stand at room temperature.

5A. For a charcoal grill Open bottom vent halfway. Light large chimney starter three-quarters filled with charcoal briquettes (4½ quarts). When top coals are partially covered with ash, pour into ring around perimeter of grill, leaving 8-inch clearing in center. Set cooking grate in place, cover, and open lid vent halfway. Heat grill until hot, about 5 minutes.

5B. For a gas grill Turn all burners to high, cover, and heat grill until hot, about 15 minutes. Leave all burners on high.

6. While grill is heating, transfer sauce to small saucepan and bring to simmer over medium heat. Cover and keep warm.

7. For the pizza Clean and oil cooking grate. Pour ¼ cup oil onto center of rimmed baking sheet. Transfer 1 dough round to sheet and coat both sides of dough with oil. Using your fingertips and palms, gently press and stretch dough toward edges of sheet to form rough 16 by 12-inch oval of even thickness. Using both your hands, lift dough and carefully transfer to grill. (When transferring dough from sheet to grill, it will droop slightly to form half-moon or snowshoe shape.) Cook (over clearing if using charcoal; covered if using gas) until grill marks form, 2 to 3 minutes. Using tongs and spatula, carefully peel dough from grate, then rotate dough 90 degrees and continue to cook (covered if using gas) until second set of grill marks appears, 2 to 3 minutes. Flip dough and cook (covered if using gas) until second side of dough is lightly charred in spots, 2 to 3 minutes. Using tongs or pizza peel, transfer crust to cutting board, inverting so side that

was grilled first is facing down. Repeat with remaining 2 dough rounds, adding 1 tablespoon oil to sheet for each round and keeping grill cover closed when not in use to retain heat.

8. Drizzle top of 1 crust with 1 tablespoon oil. Sprinkle one-third of Parmesan evenly over surface. Arrange one-third of mozzarella pieces, evenly spaced, on surface of pizza. Dollop one-third of sauce in evenly spaced 1-tablespoon mounds over surface of pizza. Using pizza peel or overturned baking sheet, transfer pizza to grill; cover and cook until bottom is well browned and mozzarella is melted, 3 to 5 minutes, checking bottom and rotating frequently to prevent burning. Transfer pizza to cutting board, sprinkle with 1 tablespoon basil, drizzle lightly with extra oil, and season with salt to taste. Cut into wedges and serve. Repeat with remaining 2 crusts and ingredients.

SPINACH RICOTTA CALZONES

Makes 2 calzones, serving 4

Why This Recipe Works What's not to love about calzones, with their cheesy filling encased in a crisp and chewy crust? Nothing, if this were always the reality. Unfortunately, bad calzones, with wet fillings and bready crusts, are all too common. To develop our version, we started with the dough. Pizzerias use their pizza dough for the crust, but when we tried using the dough for our New York Thin-Crust Pizza (page 74), we got bloated, misshapen calzones with unacceptable air bubbles. A dough with less water proved more sturdy, and we skipped the overnight fermentation in the refrigerator—with so much filling the crust doesn't have to supply as much flavor to the finished dish. For the flavorful filling, we used a base of spinach and creamy ricotta to which we added an egg yolk to thicken the mixture, a bit of oil for richness, and two more cheeses, easy-melting mozzarella and nutty-tasting Parmesan. We spread the filling on half of each of two rolled-out pizza dough rounds and then brushed egg wash over the edges before folding the bare halves over and sealing the dough so the calzones would stay closed as they baked. Cutting vents in the tops allowed excess moisture in the filling to escape during baking so the crust didn't become soggy. After the calzones baked for just 15 minutes, we let them cool briefly on a wire rack to keep the bottoms crisp. Serve the calzones with your favorite marinara sauce or see recipe on page 102.

- 10 ounces frozen chopped spinach, thawed and squeezed dry
- 8 ounces (1 cup) whole-milk ricotta cheese
- 4 ounces mozzarella cheese, shredded (1 cup)
- 1 ounce Parmesan cheese, grated (½ cup)
- 1 tablespoon extra-virgin olive oil
- 1 large egg yolk
- 2 garlic cloves, minced
- 1½ teaspoons minced fresh oregano
- ¼ teaspoon table salt
- ⅛ teaspoon red pepper flakes
- 1 recipe Simple Pizza Dough (page 97)
- 1 large egg, lightly beaten with 1 tablespoon water and pinch salt

1. Adjust oven rack to lower-middle position and heat oven to 500 degrees. Cut two 9-inch square pieces of parchment paper. Combine spinach, ricotta, mozzarella, Parmesan, oil, egg yolk, garlic, oregano, salt, and pepper flakes in bowl.

2. Press down on dough to deflate. Transfer dough to lightly floured counter, divide in half, and cover loosely with greased plastic wrap. Press and roll 1 piece of dough (keep remaining piece covered) into 9-inch round of even thickness. Transfer to parchment square and reshape as needed. Repeat with remaining piece of dough.

3. Spread half of spinach filling evenly over half of each dough round, leaving 1-inch border at edge. Brush edges with egg mixture. Fold bare half of dough over filling, leaving ½-inch border of bottom half uncovered. Press edges of dough together, pressing out any air pockets in calzones. Starting at 1 end of calzone, place your index finger diagonally across edge and pull bottom layer of dough over tip of your finger and press to seal.

4. Using sharp knife or single-edge razor blade, cut 5 steam vents, about 1½ inches long, in top of calzones. Brush tops with remaining egg mixture. Transfer calzones (still on parchment) to rimmed baking sheet, trimming parchment as needed to fit. Bake until golden brown, about 15 minutes, rotating sheet halfway through baking. Transfer calzones to wire rack and discard parchment. Let cool for 10 minutes before serving.

VARIATION
Three-Meat Calzones

Toss 4 ounces sliced salami, 4 ounces sliced capicola, and 2 ounces sliced pepperoni, all quartered, together in bowl. Working in 3 batches, microwave meats between triple layers of paper towels on plate for 30 seconds to render some fat; use fresh paper towels for each batch. Let meats cool. Omit spinach, oregano, salt, and pepper flakes from filling and add meats instead.

BROCCOLI RABE AND SALAMI STROMBOLI

Serves 4

Why This Recipe Works Imagine an Italian cold-cut sandwich rolled up in pizza dough and baked into something akin to a savory jelly roll, and you've pictured a stromboli. This recipe is named after the Italian island and 1950 Roberto Rossellini film with Ingrid Bergman. Most sources suggest Philadelphia as its birthplace and cite Romano's Pizzeria and Italian Restaurant, located in Essington, Pennsylvania. Our Simple Pizza Dough worked perfectly in this recipe, although you can certainly use store-bought pizza dough. After rolling the dough into a rectangle, we arranged provolone, salami, mozzarella, and slightly bitter sautéed broccoli rabe evenly over the dough. Then we brushed the borders of the dough with egg (to seal the seams) and folded the stromboli like a letter to seal in all the filling ingredients. We then brushed the stromboli with egg, sprinkled it with sesame seeds, and baked it in a 375-degree oven—hot enough to promote browning but moderate enough to allow the dough in the center of the stromboli to cook through. Stromboli is delicious eaten as is, but even better when served with tomato sauce. Serve with your favorite marinara sauce or see the recipe on page 102.

- 1 teaspoon extra-virgin olive oil
- 2 garlic cloves, minced
- ¼ teaspoon red pepper flakes
- 6 ounces broccoli rabe, trimmed and cut into ¼-inch pieces
- 2 tablespoons water
- 1 recipe Simple Pizza Dough (recipe follows)
- 4 ounces thinly sliced aged provolone cheese
- 2 ounces thinly sliced Genoa salami
- 4 ounces mozzarella cheese, shredded (1 cup)
- 1 large egg, lightly beaten
- 1 teaspoon sesame seeds

1. Adjust oven rack to middle position and heat oven to 375 degrees. Line rimmed baking sheet with aluminum foil and grease foil. Heat oil in 12-inch non-stick skillet over medium heat until shimmering. Add garlic and pepper flakes and cook until fragrant, about 30 seconds. Add broccoli rabe and water, cover, and cook until just tender, about 1 minute. Uncover and cook until liquid has evaporated, about 1 minute. Transfer broccoli rabe to dish towel; gather corners of towel and squeeze out excess moisture.

2. Roll dough into 12 by 10-inch rectangle on lightly floured counter with long side parallel to counter edge. Shingle provolone evenly over dough, leaving ½-inch border along top and sides. Layer salami over provolone. Sprinkle mozzarella and broccoli rabe evenly over salami.

3. Brush borders with egg (reserve remaining egg for brushing top of stromboli). Fold bottom third of stromboli in toward middle. Fold top third of stromboli down to cover first fold, creating log. Pinch seam firmly to seal. Transfer stromboli to prepared sheet, seam side down. Pinch ends firmly to seal and tuck underneath.

4. Brush top of stromboli with remaining egg. Using sharp knife, make 5 evenly spaced ½-inch-deep slashes, 2 inches long, on top of stromboli. Sprinkle with sesame seeds. Bake until crust is golden and center registers 200 degrees, 30 to 35 minutes, rotating sheet halfway through baking. Transfer stromboli to wire rack and let cool for 10 minutes. Transfer to cutting board and cut into 2-inch-thick slices. Serve.

SIMPLE PIZZA DOUGH
Makes 1 pound

- 2 cups (11 ounces) plus 2 tablespoons bread flour
- 1⅛ teaspoons instant or rapid-rise yeast
- ¾ teaspoon table salt
- 1 tablespoon extra-virgin olive oil
- ¾ cup (6 ounces) ice water

1. Pulse flour, yeast, and salt in food processor until combined, about 5 pulses. With processor running, add oil, then ice water, and process until rough ball forms, 30 to 40 seconds. Let dough rest for 2 minutes, then process for 30 seconds.

2. Transfer dough to lightly floured counter and knead by hand to form smooth, round ball, about 30 seconds. Place dough seam side down in lightly greased large bowl or container, cover tightly with plastic wrap, and let rise until doubled in size, 1½ to 2 hours. (Unrisen dough can be refrigerated for at least 8 hours or up to 16 hours; let sit at room temperature for 30 minutes before shaping.)

PASTA NIGHT

SPAGHETTI WITH FRESH TOMATO SAUCE

Serves 4

Why This Recipe Works The backyard garden has been a tradition in many Italian American families for generations. For some families, the garden was a way to economize and grow things not easily purchased. Peppers, eggplant, and zucchini were (and still are) commonly grown, but tomatoes were no doubt the star crop, and what better way to highlight them than with a fresh sauce for pasta. The best recipes for this summer classic are simple, consisting of nothing more than garlic, olive oil, tomatoes, herbs (also from the garden), salt, a bit of sugar, and pepper. We found that cooking the garlic and oil over medium heat for no more than a minute or two prevented it from burning. The tomatoes, which we cooked for just 10 minutes, broke down readily and thickened slightly, just enough to ably coat the pasta. Be sure to choose the ripest tomatoes you can find—if not from your garden, then from a farmers' market. While this sauce is best when eaten right away, it can be frozen for up to one month. If you plan to freeze it, hold off on adding the basil until right before serving. If you're using exceptionally sweet in-season tomatoes, omit the sugar.

- 3 tablespoons extra-virgin olive oil
- 2 garlic cloves, minced
- 2 pounds plum tomatoes, cored and cut into ½-inch pieces
- ¾ teaspoon table salt, plus salt for cooking pasta
- ½ teaspoon pepper
- ½ teaspoon sugar
- 2 tablespoons chopped fresh basil
- 1 pound spaghetti

1. Heat oil and garlic in large saucepan over medium heat until garlic is fragrant but not browned, 1 to 2 minutes. Stir in tomatoes, ¾ teaspoon salt, pepper, and sugar. Increase heat to medium-high and cook until tomatoes are broken down and sauce is slightly thickened, about 10 minutes. Stir in basil and season with salt and pepper to taste.

2. Meanwhile, bring 4 quarts water to boil in large pot. Add pasta and 1 tablespoon salt and cook, stirring often, until al dente. Reserve ½ cup cooking water, then drain pasta and return it to pot. Add sauce to pasta and toss to combine. Adjust consistency with reserved cooking water as needed. Serve.

VARIATIONS
Spaghetti with Amatriciana Sauce
Reduce oil to 1 tablespoon. Cook oil and 4 ounces finely chopped pancetta in saucepan over medium heat until pancetta is rendered and crispy, 5 to 7 minutes, before adding garlic.

Spaghetti with Arrabbiata Sauce
Add 3 rinsed, minced anchovy fillets and ¾ teaspoon red pepper flakes with garlic.

Spaghetti with Puttanesca Sauce
Add ¼ cup coarsely chopped pitted kalamata olives and ¼ cup rinsed capers to saucepan with tomatoes.

THE ITALIAN AMERICAN KITCHEN
Extra-Virgin Olive Oil

Extra-virgin oils range wildly in price, color, and quality, so it's hard to know which to buy. While many things can affect the quality and flavor of olive oil, the type of olive, the time of harvest (earlier means greener, more bitter, and pungent; later, more mild and buttery), and the processing are the most important factors. The best-quality olive oil comes from olives pressed as quickly as possible without heat (which coaxes more oil from the olives at the expense of flavor). Our favorite supermarket extra-virgin olive oil, **California Olive Ranch Everyday Extra Virgin Olive Oil** ($9.99 for 500 ml), is a standout for its "fruity," "fragrant" flavor. In fact, it rivaled our favorite high-end extra-virgin oil.

PASTA WITH CLASSIC MARINARA

Serves 4 to 6

Why This Recipe Works This smooth, tomato-forward sauce (made with canned rather than fresh tomatoes) is truly an Italian American invention. In Italy, this sauce typically has anchovies (the name does refer to the sea) as well as capers. But in the New World, the sauce emphasizes the onions and herbs. For the best, most robustly flavored marinara sauce, we started by picking the right tomatoes. Canned whole tomatoes provide great flavor and texture year-round; using our hands to remove the hard core and seeds was easy. For a sauce with intense tomato flavor, we sautéed the drained tomatoes until they glazed the bottom of the pan, then added the reserved juice. Using a skillet provided more surface area and encouraged faster evaporation and flavor concentration, while red wine added depth. Adding a portion of uncooked tomatoes, along with chopped basil and a drizzle of olive oil, just before serving gave our sauce a bright, fresh finish. If you prefer a chunkier sauce, give it just 3 or 4 pulses in the food processor in step 4.

2 (28-ounce) cans whole peeled tomatoes
3 tablespoons extra-virgin olive oil, divided
1 onion, chopped fine
2 garlic cloves, minced
2 teaspoons minced fresh oregano or ½ teaspoon dried
⅓ cup dry red wine
3 tablespoons chopped fresh basil
Sugar
1 pound spaghetti
Table salt for cooking pasta
Grated Parmesan cheese

1. Drain tomatoes in fine-mesh strainer set over large bowl. Open tomatoes with hands and remove and discard seeds and fibrous cores; let tomatoes drain, about 5 minutes. Measure out and reserve ¾ cup tomatoes separately. Reserve 2½ cups drained tomato juice; discard extra juice.

2. Heat 2 tablespoons oil in 12-inch skillet over medium heat until shimmering. Add onion and cook until softened and lightly browned, 5 to 7 minutes. Stir in garlic and oregano and cook until fragrant, about 30 seconds. Stir in drained tomatoes from strainer and increase heat to medium-high. Cook, stirring often, until liquid has evaporated and tomatoes begin to brown and stick to pan, 10 to 12 minutes.

3. Stir in wine and cook until thick and syrupy, about 1 minute. Stir in reserved tomato juice, scraping up any browned bits. Bring to simmer and cook, stirring occasionally, until sauce is thickened, 8 to 10 minutes.

4. Transfer sauce to food processor, add reserved ¾ cup tomatoes, and pulse until slightly chunky, about 8 pulses. Return sauce to now-empty skillet, stir in basil and remaining 1 tablespoon oil, and season with salt, pepper, and sugar to taste. (Sauce can be refrigerated for up to 3 days or frozen for up to 1 month.)

5. Meanwhile, bring 4 quarts water to boil in large pot. Add pasta and 1 tablespoon salt and cook, stirring often, until al dente. Reserve ½ cup cooking water, then drain pasta and return it to pot. Add sauce and toss to combine. Season with salt and pepper to taste and add reserved cooking water as needed to adjust consistency. Serve with Parmesan.

Canned Whole Tomatoes

If you believe the hype, San Marzano tomatoes are the best tomatoes in the world. Promoters of the prized crop loudly claim that the climate and soil in the eponymous southern region of Italy where they grow are behind the fruit's meaty texture, juiciness, and exceptional flavor. Since San Marzanos are more expensive than domestic canned tomatoes, we decided to test 10 brands (domestic and imported) straight out of the can as well as simmered in both quick- and long-cooked sauces. Good balance was the key to both optimal flavor and satisfying texture. Overly firm specimens lost points, while tomatoes that broke

down completely were docked for "mushiness." Our top-ranking product was all-American **Muir Glen Organic Whole Peeled Tomatoes.** These tomatoes' strong acidity and high level of sweetness made for flavor that was "vibrant." The addition of calcium chloride gave the tomatoes a "nice firm texture" that held up even after hours of simmering. Another American brand, **Hunt's Whole Plum Tomatoes,** finished a close second.

PASTA ALLA NORMA

Serves 4

Why This Recipe Works This pasta with its intriguing name and history can be found on myriad Italian restaurant menus and no wonder. With its lively combination of tender eggplant, robust tomato sauce, al dente pasta, and salty, milky ricotta salata, *pasta alla norma* sings with each bite—appropriate, given that it was named for the title character of an opera. For our version, we microwaved salted eggplant pieces on coffee filters to draw out their moisture. A secret ingredient, anchovies, gave our tomato sauce a deep, savory flavor without any fishiness. Finally, shards of ricotta salata, a slightly aged ricotta, added a salty tang. If you can't find ricotta salata you can substitute French feta, Pecorino Romano, or cotija (a firm, crumbly Mexican cheese). We prefer to use kosher salt in this recipe because it clings best to the eggplant in step 1; if using table salt, reduce salt amounts by half. To prevent the eggplant from breaking up into small pieces, be sure not to peel away the skin, and do not stir it frequently when sautéing in step 2. To give this dish a little extra kick, add additional pepper flakes.

1½	pounds eggplant, cut into ½-inch pieces
1	teaspoon kosher salt, plus salt for cooking pasta
¼	cup extra-virgin olive oil, divided
4	garlic cloves, minced
2	anchovy fillets, rinsed, patted dry, and minced
¼–½	teaspoon red pepper flakes
1	(28-ounce) can crushed tomatoes
6	tablespoons chopped fresh basil
1	pound ziti, rigatoni, or penne
3	ounces ricotta salata, shredded (1 cup)

1. Toss eggplant with 1 teaspoon salt in large bowl. Line large plate with double layer of coffee filters and lightly spray with vegetable oil spray. Spread eggplant in even layer over coffee filters; wipe out bowl with paper towels and set aside. Microwave eggplant until dry to touch and slightly shriveled, about 10 minutes, tossing halfway through cooking. Let cool slightly.

2. Transfer eggplant to now-empty bowl, drizzle with 1 tablespoon oil, and toss gently to coat; discard coffee filters and reserve plate. Heat 1 tablespoon oil in 12-inch nonstick skillet over medium-high heat until shimmering. Add eggplant and cook, stirring every 1½ to 2 minutes (more frequent stirring may cause eggplant pieces to break apart), until well browned and fully tender, about 10 minutes. Transfer eggplant to now-empty plate and set aside. Let skillet cool slightly, about 3 minutes.

3. Heat 1 tablespoon oil, garlic, anchovies, and pepper flakes in now-empty skillet over medium heat. Cook, stirring often, until garlic turns golden but not brown, about 3 minutes. Stir in tomatoes, bring to simmer, and cook, stirring occasionally, until slightly thickened, 8 to 10 minutes. Add eggplant and continue to cook, stirring occasionally, until eggplant is heated through and flavors meld, 3 to 5 minutes. Stir in basil and remaining 1 tablespoon oil and season with salt to taste.

4. Meanwhile, bring 4 quarts water to boil in large pot. Add pasta and 2 tablespoons salt and cook, stirring often, until al dente. Reserve ½ cup cooking water, then drain pasta and return it to pot. Add sauce to pasta and toss to combine. Adjust consistency with reserved cooking water as needed. Serve immediately with ricotta salata.

THE ITALIAN AMERICAN KITCHEN
Ricotta Salata

Ricotta salata is a firm, tangy Italian sheep's-milk cheese that bears little resemblance to the moist ricotta cheese sold in tubs and used in dishes like lasagna and baked ziti. We love using this cheese, with its salty, milky flavor, in numerous pasta dishes—its gamy flavor certainly stands up to all the bold flavors in pasta alla Norma. Since ricotta salata is a semihard cheese, we typically shave it or shred it on the large holes of a box grater. While ricotta salata is available at most well-stocked cheese shops, feta is a reasonable alternative.

PENNE ALLA VODKA

Serves 4

Why This Recipe Works This American creation was the winner of a 1970s recipe contest promoting vodka. An instant classic, penne alla vodka became a featured item on the menus of Italian restaurants across the country and has even made it back to Italy. We think the simple yet well-thought-out blend of power ingredients accounts for its popularity. Cream provides luxurious richness. Red pepper flakes ratchet up the heat. Splashes of vodka heighten the taste of the tomatoes without adding competing flavors. Some classic vodka sauces simmer away for hours to build flavor. Discovering a faster approach, we used assertive sun-dried tomatoes and convenient crushed ones, yielding a full-flavored homemade sauce in roughly the time it takes to cook the pasta. Use decent-quality vodka; the cheap stuff will make the sauce harsh. To avoid flare-ups, add the vodka off the heat.

- 1 tablespoon extra-virgin olive oil
- 3 garlic cloves, minced
- ¼ teaspoon red pepper flakes
- 1 (28-ounce) can crushed tomatoes
- ½ cup oil-packed sun-dried tomatoes, rinsed and chopped fine
- ½ cup vodka
- ¾ cup heavy cream
  Pepper
  Table salt for cooking pasta
- 1 pound penne
- ⅓ cup chopped fresh basil
  Grated Parmesan cheese

1. Bring 4 quarts water to boil in large pot. Meanwhile, heat oil in 12-inch skillet over medium heat until shimmering. Add garlic and pepper flakes and cook until fragrant, about 30 seconds. Add crushed tomatoes and sun-dried tomatoes and cook until slightly thickened, about 5 minutes. Off heat, add vodka. Bring sauce to boil, reduce heat to medium, and simmer until thickened, 12 to 15 minutes. Off heat, stir in cream. Season with salt and pepper to taste; cover and keep warm.

2. Add pasta and 1 tablespoon salt to boiling water and cook, stirring often, until al dente. Reserve ¼ cup cooking water, then drain pasta and return it to pot. Toss sauce and basil with pasta, adding reserved pasta water as needed. Serve with Parmesan.

THE ITALIAN AMERICAN KITCHEN
Crushed Tomatoes

Crushed tomatoes are a convenience product. Rather than haul out the food processor to break down canned whole tomatoes for a quick sauce, you should be able to just pop the can lid and pour the tomatoes into a pot. As for texture, they should walk that line between a smooth puree and chunkier diced tomatoes and be topped off by puree or juice, offering both body and fluidity. We tested eight nationally available products served plain and in a simple pasta sauce tossed with spaghetti. Our favorite, **SMT Crushed Tomatoes,** tasted "very bright and sweet" with "full tomato flavor." Added diced tomatoes, though nontraditional in crushed tomato products, contributed a firm, tender texture. Although the letters SMT bring to mind the famed San Marzano tomatoes of Italy, the tomatoes are grown domestically, and the manufacturer declined to disclose the exact variety.

TAGLIATELLE WITH WEEKNIGHT BOLOGNESE

Serves 4 to 6

Why This Recipe Works Bolognese is the slow-simmered meat sauce typically served with fresh pasta and a dusting of grated Parmesan. Its preparation is an all-day affair and often requires four or more types of meat. Quick versions, designed to appeal to busy Americans, are a staple in cookbooks, newspapers, and magazines, but most of them disappoint. To create a quick Bolognese sauce that would rival the depth and richness of a long-cooked version, we started by browning the aromatic vegetables (but not the ground beef, which would dry out and toughen if seared) to develop a flavorful fond; we also treated the ground beef with a baking soda solution to ensure that it stayed tender. Adding pancetta, which we ground and browned deeply with the aromatic vegetables, boosted the sauce's meaty flavor, and a healthy dose of tomato paste added depth and brightness without much acid or overwhelming tomato flavor. We also added Parmesan cheese, usually reserved for serving, directly to the sauce as it cooked for its umami richness. To develop concentrated flavor and a consistency that nicely coated the pasta, we boiled beef broth until it was reduced by half (mixing up a concentrated beef broth also works) and added it to the sauce, which then needed to simmer only 30 minutes longer. Finally, we intentionally made the sauce thin because the eggy noodles (traditionally tagliatelle or pappardelle) absorb a lot of liquid; once they have soaked up some of the sauce, it will coat the noodles beautifully. If you use our recommended beef broth, Better Than Bouillon Roasted Beef Base, make a concentrated broth by adding 4 teaspoons paste to 2 cups water and skip step 2. To ensure the best flavor, be sure to brown the pancetta-vegetable mixture in step 4 until the fond on the bottom of the pot is quite dark. Tagliatelle is a long, flat, dry egg pasta that is about 1/4 inch wide; if you can't find it, substitute pappardelle. Substituting other pasta may result in a too-wet sauce.

- 1 pound 93 percent lean ground beef
- 2 tablespoons water
- 1/4 teaspoon baking soda
- 1/2 teaspoon pepper, divided

- 4 cups beef broth
- 6 ounces pancetta, chopped coarse
- 1 onion, chopped coarse
- 1 large carrot, peeled and chopped coarse
- 1 celery rib, chopped coarse
- 1 tablespoon unsalted butter
- 1 tablespoon extra-virgin olive oil
- 3 tablespoons tomato paste
- 1 cup dry red wine
- 1 ounce Parmesan cheese, grated (1/2 cup), plus extra for serving
- 1 pound tagliatelle
  Table salt for cooking pasta

1. Toss beef with water, baking soda, and 1/4 teaspoon pepper in bowl until thoroughly combined. Set aside.

2. While beef sits, bring broth to boil over high heat in large pot (this pot will be used to cook pasta in step 6) and cook until reduced to 2 cups, about 15 minutes; set aside.

3. Pulse pancetta in food processor until finely chopped, 15 to 20 pulses. Add onion, carrot, and celery and pulse until vegetables are finely chopped and mixture has paste-like consistency, 12 to 15 pulses, scraping down sides of bowl as needed.

4. Heat butter and oil in large Dutch oven over medium-high heat until shimmering. When foaming subsides, add pancetta-vegetable mixture and remaining 1/4 teaspoon pepper and cook, stirring occasionally, until liquid has evaporated, about 8 minutes. Spread mixture in even layer in bottom of pot and continue to cook, stirring every couple of minutes, until very dark browned bits form on bottom of pot, 7 to 12 minutes. Stir in tomato paste and cook until paste is rust-colored and bottom of pot is dark brown, 1 to 2 minutes.

5. Reduce heat to medium, add beef, and cook, using wooden spoon to break meat into pieces no larger than ¼ inch, until beef has just lost its raw pink color, 4 to 7 minutes. Stir in wine, scraping up any browned bits, and bring to simmer. Cook until wine has evaporated and sauce has thickened, about 5 minutes. Stir in broth and Parmesan. Return sauce to simmer; cover, reduce heat to low, and simmer for 30 minutes (sauce will look thin). Remove from heat and season with salt and pepper to taste. .

6. Rinse pot that held broth. While sauce simmers, bring 4 quarts water to boil in now-empty pot. Add pasta and 1 tablespoon salt and cook, stirring occasionally, until al dente. Reserve ¼ cup cooking water, then drain pasta. Add pasta to pot with sauce and toss to combine. Adjust sauce consistency with reserved cooking water as needed. Transfer to platter or individual bowls and serve, passing extra Parmesan separately.

PASTA WITH SAUSAGE RAGU

Serves 4 to 6

Why This Recipe Works Replacing ground beef with flavorful Italian sausage is another American shortcut for creating a meat sauce with slow-simmered flavor. To build flavor fast, we turned to the food processor to handle the chopping of the aromatic vegetables (also known as the *soffritto*). Whirring fennel, onion, and fennel seeds together created a savory flavor base. (We found the usual carrot and celery didn't add much, so left them out.) Pulsing canned whole tomatoes created a silky tomato sauce, and processing sweet Italian sausage delivered bites of well-seasoned meat in every forkful. We cooked the components in stages, browning the sausage before softening the soffritto in the rendered fat. Minced garlic and dried oregano, bloomed in tomato paste, further defined the Italian flavors, and red wine offered brightness. A 45-minute simmer produced a rich ragu with the perfect consistency. For a spicier sauce, substitute hot Italian sausage for sweet. You will have 3 cups of extra sauce, which can be refrigerated (for 3 days) or frozen (for 1 month) and used to sauce another pound of pasta—now, that's convenient.

½ fennel bulb, stalks discarded, bulb cored and chopped coarse

½ onion, chopped coarse

1 tablespoon fennel seeds

1 (28-ounce) can whole peeled tomatoes

2 pounds sweet Italian sausage, casings removed

1 tablespoon extra-virgin olive oil, plus extra for drizzling

½ teaspoon table salt, plus salt for cooking pasta

2 tablespoons tomato paste

4 garlic cloves, minced

1½ teaspoons dried oregano

¾ cup red wine

1 cup water

Pepper

1 pound pappardelle or tagliatelle

Grated Parmesan cheese

1. Pulse fennel, onion, and fennel seeds in food processor until finely chopped, about 10 pulses, scraping down sides of bowl as needed; transfer to separate bowl. Process tomatoes in now-empty processor until smooth, about 10 seconds; transfer to second bowl. Pulse sausage in now-empty processor until finely chopped, about 10 pulses, scraping down sides of bowl as needed.

2. Heat oil in Dutch oven over medium-high heat until shimmering. Add sausage and cook, breaking up meat with spoon, until all liquid has evaporated and meat begins to sizzle, 10 to 15 minutes.

3. Add fennel mixture and ½ teaspoon salt and cook, stirring occasionally, until softened, about 5 minutes. (Fond on bottom of pot will be deeply browned.) Add tomato paste, garlic, and oregano and cook, stirring constantly, until fragrant, about 30 seconds.

4. Stir in wine, scraping up any browned bits, and cook until nearly evaporated, about 1 minute. Add water and pureed tomatoes and bring to simmer. Reduce heat to low and simmer gently, uncovered, until thickened, about 45 minutes. (Wooden spoon should leave trail when dragged through sauce.) Season with salt and pepper to taste; cover and keep warm.

5. Bring 4 quarts water to boil in large pot. Add pasta and 1 tablespoon salt and cook, stirring often, until al dente. Reserve 1 cup cooking water, then drain pasta and return it to pot. Add 3 cups sauce and ½ cup reserved cooking water to pasta and toss to combine. Adjust consistency with remaining reserved cooking water as needed. Transfer to serving dish. Drizzle with extra oil, sprinkle with Parmesan, and serve.

A Million Meatballs in Rocky's Shadow

When we stepped out the front door of Villa di Roma, we couldn't help but notice the faded black and white photo of Sylvester Stallone hanging above the bar, a sure sign we were solidly in South Philly. In the restaurant's prep kitchen just down the street from the bar, we watch Basil DeLuca, a member of the family behind the restaurant, and his daughter, Carmella Garofoli, making meatballs, while two massive pots of "gravy" simmer on the stovetop.

In his thick Philly accent DeLuca tells us, without taking his eyes off the meatballs, that he makes 145 a day, 6 days a week, and he's been at it for 25 years. That's more than a million meatballs, and he claims he's no less enthusiastic or passionate about the process than he was the day he started making them. When asked for the recipe, he denies one exists. "We don't measure. We eye everything up." DeLuca forms each meatball with careful hands, adding or removing a bit until it feels "just right," which is about 3 ounces.

DROP MEATBALLS

Serves 6 to 8

Why This Recipe Works Every nonna worth her salt can make meatballs in her sleep, and certainly most have their own "secret" recipe whether the meatballs are small or large, roasted in batches in the oven or laboriously pan-fried. And while we've made our share of meatballs here in the test kitchen, we were after a streamlined route to tender meatballs in a brightly flavored sauce—enter drop meatballs. In our first few batches of meatballs, using 85 percent lean ground beef, two eggs, a hefty dose of Parmesan, and a panade, we found that our unbrowned meatballs fell apart in the sauce. Clearly, we needed a different binder than the traditional milk-soaked bread we'd been using. Plus, we needed to ditch any wet ingredients we could. So we first lost the eggs, though now our meatballs were a bit gummy. Turning to the panade, we tested fresh bread crumbs, store-bought crumbs, panko, and crushed saltines, each soaked with milk. The saltines proved to be the hands-down winner: They broke down easily and didn't add any moisture to the meatballs (as opposed to fresh bread crumbs, which are surprisingly full of moisture). Turning to our sauce, we knew that since we weren't browning our meatballs, we'd be losing all that flavor from building a sauce on top of the flavorful browned bits normally left behind. So we amped up the flavor by cooking smashed garlic cloves in olive oil as the first step, then added red pepper flakes and crushed tomatoes. And to ensure our meatballs simmered gently and evenly in the sauce, we transferred our pot to the oven after bringing the meatballs and sauce to a simmer. Now we had an easy route to tender meatballs that would make Nonna proud. The recipe yields enough sauce and meatballs for 2 pounds of pasta. To serve, toss the pasta with some sauce and top it with the meatballs.

Meatballs
- 22 square saltines
- 1 cup milk
- 2 pounds 85 percent lean ground beef
- 2 ounces Parmesan cheese, grated (1 cup)
- 1 teaspoon garlic powder
- 1 teaspoon dried oregano
- 1 teaspoon table salt
- 1/2 teaspoon pepper

Sauce
- 1/4 cup extra-virgin olive oil
- 10 garlic cloves, peeled and smashed
- 1/2 teaspoon red pepper flakes
- 2 (28-ounce) cans crushed tomatoes
- 1 teaspoon table salt
- 3 tablespoons chopped fresh basil
- Pepper

1. **For the meatballs** Adjust oven rack to lower-middle position and heat oven to 400 degrees. Place saltines in large zipper-lock bag, seal bag, and crush saltines fine with rolling pin (you should have 1 cup). Combine saltines and milk in large bowl and let sit for 5 minutes for saltines to soften. Mash with fork until smooth paste forms.

2. Add beef, Parmesan, garlic powder, oregano, salt, and pepper to saltine mixture and mix with your hands until thoroughly combined. Divide meat mixture into 24 scant 1/4-cup portions. Roll portions between your wet hands to form balls. Transfer to plate, cover with plastic wrap, and refrigerate until ready to use. (Meatballs can be refrigerated for up to 24 hours.)

3. **For the sauce** Combine oil and garlic in large Dutch oven. Cook over low heat until garlic is soft and golden on all sides, 10 to 12 minutes, stirring occasionally. Add pepper flakes and cook until fragrant, about 30 seconds. Stir in tomatoes and salt. Nestle meatballs into sauce. Bring to simmer over medium-high heat.

4. Cover and bake in oven until meatballs are cooked through and tender, about 40 minutes. Let cool, uncovered, for 20 minutes. Gently stir in basil and season with salt and pepper to taste. Serve.

AGLIO E OLIO

Serves 4 to 6

Why This Recipe Works The ingredient list for *spaghetti aglio e olio* (spaghetti with garlic and olive oil) is very simple, which is one reason this pasta is standard fare on restaurant menus. But in many Italian American restaurants the dish has strayed from its humble roots and includes heavy cream and/or cheese. According to the traditional method, the starches from the pasta should thicken the sauce. We started by lightly cooking sliced garlic in olive oil in a small saucepan to soften the harshness of the garlic and to infuse the oil, waiting until the end to add red pepper flakes to prevent burning. The big secret here is to parcook the pasta, reserve a lot of the starchy cooking water, and then finish cooking the pasta with the garlic oil and the starchy water. We combined everything in the pasta cooking pot, set the pot over medium-high heat, and stirred for about 5 minutes to create a full-bodied sauce while the pasta finished cooking through. As a final touch, we added parsley for color and vibrancy. Be sure to use only the 3 quarts of water specified for cooking the pasta. The starch that leaches from the pasta is essential for the consistency of the sauce and using less water than usual ensures that the water is quite starchy.

1/3 cup extra-virgin olive oil

8 garlic cloves, sliced thin

1/2 teaspoon red pepper flakes

1 pound spaghetti

1/2 teaspoon table salt, plus salt for cooking pasta

3 tablespoons chopped fresh parsley

1. Heat oil and garlic in small saucepan over medium-low heat until pale golden and fragrant, about 6 minutes. Remove from heat and stir in pepper flakes; set aside.

2. Meanwhile, bring 3 quarts water to boil in large Dutch oven. Add pasta and 1 tablespoon salt and cook, stirring frequently, until noodles are flexible but still very firm in center, about 5 minutes. Using ladle, reserve 3 cups of pasta cooking water, then drain pasta.

3. Combine pasta, oil mixture, 2 cups cooking water, and 1/2 teaspoon salt in now-empty Dutch oven and bring to boil over medium-high heat. Cook, stirring frequently with tongs and folding pasta over itself, until water is mostly absorbed but still pools slightly in bottom of pot, about 5 minutes.

4. Remove pot from heat and let pasta sit for 2 minutes. Stir in parsley and additional cooking water as needed (approximately 1/4 cup) to adjust consistency (noodles should be slightly wet, not oily). Serve.

THE ITALIAN AMERICAN KITCHEN
Spaghetti

Besides convenience, the other draw of dried spaghetti is that it's inexpensive—or at least it used to be. When we recently browsed the options at the supermarket, we discovered that while you can still pick up a 1-pound package for as little as a dollar and change, you can also spend more than three times that amount. How much better could a pound of pasta costing more than $4 really be? To answer that question, we tasted several products ranging in price from $1.39 to $4.17 per pound. So when it comes to spaghetti, do you get what you pay for? Not necessarily: Our winner, **De Cecco Spaghetti No. 12,** stood out for its particularly good texture and flavor—and it was one of the two least expensive spaghettis we tasted.

FETTUCCINE ALFREDO

Serves 4 to 6

Why This Recipe Works The pedigree of this Italian recipe has an interesting, and important, American twist. Its glory days began in 1914, when Roman restaurateur Alfredo di Lelio needed a high-calorie meal to serve his wife, who was pregnant and having trouble keeping her food down. He created the first version of this cheesy dish, hoping that it would hold her over for a while. Bonus: It was also delicious enough to add to his restaurant's menu. Cue American silent film stars Mary Pickford and Douglas Fairbanks, who visited Rome and made several meals of di Lelio's dish. They brought the recipe home and in 1928 it was printed in *The Rector Cook Book*. It soon became standard fare in Italian American restaurants, but because real Parmigiano-Reggiano wasn't always available many chefs added cream to mask the use of blander domestic cheeses. This version returns to the roots of the dish and calls for imported Parmigiano-Reggiano and no cream. Stir the pasta frequently while cooking so that it doesn't stick together. And make sure to reserve some of the starchy pasta cooking liquid to help make the sauce. (Note that cooking the pasta in less water than usual helps increases the starchy content in the liquid.) It's important to move quickly after draining the pasta. When the grated cheese, butter, and pasta cooking water are stirred into the still-hot fettuccine, the sauce will appear very watery. Cover the pot for 1 minute to let the pasta cool slightly, and then stir vigorously to fully combine the dish and create a creamy emulsion. For best results, heat ovensafe bowls in a 200-degree oven for 10 minutes prior to serving and serve the pasta hot. If you are using fresh pasta, increase the amount to 1¼ pounds.

- 1 pound fettuccine
- ½ teaspoon table salt, plus salt for cooking pasta
- 4 ounces Parmigiano-Reggiano cheese, grated (2 cups), plus extra for serving
- 5 tablespoons unsalted butter, cut into 5 pieces

1. Bring 3 quarts water to boil in large Dutch oven. Add pasta and 1 tablespoon salt and cook, stirring frequently, until al dente. Reserve 1 cup cooking water, then drain pasta and return it to pot.

2. Add Parmigiano-Reggiano, butter, reserved cooking water, and ½ teaspoon salt to pot. Set pot over low heat and, using tongs, toss and stir pasta vigorously to thoroughly combine, about 1 minute. Remove pot from heat, cover, and let pasta sit for 1 minute.

3. Toss pasta vigorously once more so sauce thoroughly coats pasta and any cheese clumps are emulsified into sauce, about 30 seconds. (Mixture may look wet at this point, but pasta will continue to absorb excess moisture as it cools slightly.) Season with salt to taste.

4. Transfer pasta to individual bowls. (Use rubber spatula as needed to remove any clumps of cheese stuck to tongs and bottom of pot.) Serve pasta immediately, passing extra Parmigiano-Reggiano separately.

THE ITALIAN AMERICAN KITCHEN
Parmesan

Buttery, nutty, slightly fruity Parmigiano-Reggiano cheese has been produced using traditional methods for the past 800 years in one government-designated area of northern Italy. This hard cow's-milk cheese has a distinctive flavor that is touted as coming as much from the production process as from the region's geography. We strongly recommend authentic Italian Parmigiano-Reggiano. Most of the other Parmesan-type cheeses are too salty and one-dimensional. When shopping, make sure some portion of the words "Parmigiano-Reggiano" is stenciled on the golden rind. To ensure that you're buying a properly aged cheese, examine the condition of the rind. It should be a few shades darker than the straw-colored interior and penetrate about ½ inch deep. And closely scrutinize the center of the cheese. Those small white spots found on many samples are actually good things—they signify the presence of calcium phosphate crystals, which are formed only after the cheese has been properly aged.

SPAGHETTI CARBONARA

Serves 4

Why This Recipe Works This quintessential Roman pasta dish is made with basic ingredients (eggs, grated cheese, garlic, and black pepper) readily available to Italian Americans, except one: *guanciale*, or cured pork jowl. American bacon, while delicious, isn't quite as chewy as guanciale. But this problem was easily solved with some test kitchen ingenuity: To approximate the meaty chew of guanciale, we cooked the bacon with a little water, which produced tender-chewy pieces. We also used just a touch of the rendered fat in our sauce for consistent bacon flavor in every bite. To make a rich eggy sauce that wouldn't become dry and clumpy when mixed with the pasta, we used three eggs and an extra yolk for richness. But the real secret here was adding starch in the form of pasta water. Boiling the pasta in half the usual amount of water gave us extra-starchy water to coat the proteins and fats in the cheese, preventing them from separating or clumping, making for a perfectly velvety sauce. Tossing the spaghetti with the sauce in a warm serving bowl allowed the warm pasta to gently "cook" the carbonara sauce without overcooking the eggs. It's important to work quickly in steps 2 and 3. The heat from the cooking water and the hot spaghetti will "cook" the sauce only if used immediately. Warming the mixing and serving bowls helps the sauce stay creamy.

- 8 slices bacon, cut into ½-inch pieces
- ½ cup water
- 3 garlic cloves, minced
- 2½ ounces Pecorino Romano, grated (1¼ cups)
- 3 large eggs plus 1 large yolk
- 1 teaspoon pepper
- 1 pound spaghetti
- Table salt for cooking pasta

1. Bring bacon and water to simmer in 10-inch nonstick skillet over medium heat and cook until water evaporates and bacon begins to sizzle, about 8 minutes. Reduce heat to medium-low and continue to cook until fat renders and bacon browns, 5 to 8 minutes. Add garlic and cook, stirring constantly, until fragrant, about 30 seconds. Strain bacon mixture through fine-mesh strainer set in bowl. Set aside bacon mixture. Measure out 1 tablespoon fat from bowl and transfer to medium bowl. Whisk Pecorino, eggs and yolk, and pepper into fat until combined.

2. Meanwhile, bring 2 quarts water to boil in Dutch oven. Set colander in large bowl. Add spaghetti and 1 teaspoon salt to pot and cook, stirring frequently, until al dente. Drain spaghetti in colander set in bowl, reserving cooking water. Pour 1 cup cooking water into liquid measuring cup and discard remainder. Return spaghetti to now-empty warmed bowl.

3. Slowly whisk ½ cup reserved cooking water into Pecorino mixture. Gradually pour Pecorino mixture over spaghetti, tossing to coat. Add bacon mixture and toss to combine. Let spaghetti rest, tossing frequently, until sauce has thickened slightly and coats spaghetti, 2 to 4 minutes, adjusting consistency with remaining reserved cooking water if needed. Serve immediately in warmed serving bowls.

PASTA PRIMAVERA

Serves 4 to 6

Why This Recipe Works Don't be fooled by the Italian name. What we now call pasta primavera was actually born in New York City, although nonnas had likely been making something similar in Italy for centuries. The credit goes to Sirio Maccioni of Le Cirque, who put the dish—a toss of pasta, vegetables, cream, butter, and cheese—on his menu in 1975. It soon became, according to the *New York Times*, "by far the most talked about dish in Manhattan." But the recipe required a brigade of cooks and a stack of pots and pans to execute. We streamlined this Italian American favorite by using fewer dishes and paring down the number of vegetables. By overcooking zucchini, we were able to create a silky sauce that nicely coated our favorite spring vegetables (asparagus and peas) without cream or butter. Spaghetti proved the best choice, and cherry tomatoes that we marinated briefly in garlic (a tip we picked up from an old-school Little Italy chef) finished off our dish with a lively lilt. The zucchini slices will break down as they cook and create a base for the sauce; do not be alarmed when the slices turn soft and creamy and lose their shape.

- 6 ounces cherry tomatoes, halved
- 6 tablespoons extra-virgin olive oil, divided, plus extra for drizzling
- 5 garlic cloves, 1 clove minced, 4 cloves sliced thin, divided
- 3/4 teaspoon table salt, divided, plus salt for cooking pasta
- 1/4 teaspoon pepper
- 1 pound spaghetti
- 1 zucchini, halved lengthwise and sliced 1/4 inch thick
- 1/8 teaspoon red pepper flakes
- 1 pound asparagus, trimmed and cut on bias into 1-inch lengths
- 1 cup frozen peas, thawed
- 3/4 cup water
- 1/4 cup minced fresh chives
- 1 tablespoon lemon juice
- 1/4 cup grated Pecorino Romano cheese, plus extra for serving
- 2 tablespoons torn fresh mint leaves

1. Toss tomatoes, 1 tablespoon oil, minced garlic, 1/4 teaspoon salt, and pepper together in bowl; set aside.

2. Bring 4 quarts water to boil in large Dutch oven. Add pasta and 1 tablespoon salt and cook, stirring often, until al dente. Drain pasta and return it to pot.

3. Meanwhile, heat 3 tablespoons oil in 12-inch nonstick skillet over medium-low heat until shimmering. Add zucchini, pepper flakes, sliced garlic, and remaining 1/2 teaspoon salt and cook, covered, until zucchini softens and breaks down, 10 to 15 minutes, stirring occasionally. Add asparagus, peas, and water and bring to simmer over medium-high heat. Cover and cook until asparagus is crisp-tender, about 2 minutes.

4. Add vegetable mixture, chives, lemon juice, and remaining 2 tablespoons oil to pasta and toss to combine. Transfer to serving bowl, sprinkle with Pecorino, and drizzle with extra oil. Spoon tomatoes and their juices over top and sprinkle with mint. Serve, passing extra Pecorino separately.

THE ITALIAN AMERICAN KITCHEN
Pecorino Romano

Imported Pecorino Romano starts with sheep's milk while its American cousin, labeled "Romano," is made with cow's milk. No wonder these cheeses bear little resemblance to each other. Imported Pecorino Romano has a distinctively pungent, salty flavor. Domestic Romano is milder, less aromatic, and more like Swiss cheese than sharper, funkier, and crystalline Pecorino Romano. The imported cheeses are aged longer so they are drier and more crumbly, making them perfect for punching up flavors when grated over a bowl of hot pasta. Our favorite brand is **Boar's Head Pecorino Romano** from Sardinia.

CHICKEN RIGGIES

Serves 6

Why This Recipe Works In Utica, New York, this spicy chicken and pasta dish is so popular it has its own food festival. But "riggies" aren't well known beyond Utica, so we set out to make it a new favorite on dinner tables coast to coast. Starting with the sauce, we developed rustic Italian flavor with crushed tomatoes, onion, garlic, oregano, bell pepper, and mushrooms. To inject riggies' signature spice, we stirred in chopped hot pickled cherry peppers and their brine before balancing out the sauce's acidity with cream. To infuse the meat with a little heat, we brined the chicken in cherry pepper brine and olive oil for just 30 minutes. With this much flavor in place, we could afford to simply poach the chicken in the sauce at the end. The sauce is stirred into al dente rigatoni (where "riggies" get their name) with a generous helping of Pecorino Romano. If you can find only sweet cherry peppers, add ¼ to ½ teaspoon red pepper flakes with the garlic in step 2. Parmesan cheese can be substituted for the Pecorino Romano. The dish is often served with Utica Greens (page 207).

- 4 (6-ounce) boneless, skinless chicken breasts, trimmed and cut into 1-inch pieces
- ¼ cup finely chopped jarred sliced hot cherry peppers, plus 3 tablespoons cherry pepper brine, divided
- 3 tablespoons extra-virgin olive oil, divided
- 1½ teaspoons table salt, divided, plus salt for cooking pasta
- 10 ounces white mushrooms, trimmed and quartered
- 2 red bell peppers, stemmed, seeded, and cut into 1-inch pieces
- 1 onion, cut into 1-inch pieces
- 5 garlic cloves, minced
- 1½ teaspoons dried oregano
- 1 (28-ounce) can crushed tomatoes
- ¾ cup heavy cream
- ½ teaspoon pepper
- ¾ cup pitted kalamata olives, halved lengthwise
- 1 pound rigatoni
- 2½ ounces Pecorino Romano cheese, grated (1¼ cups), plus more for serving

1. Combine chicken, 2 tablespoons cherry pepper brine, 1 tablespoon oil, and 1 teaspoon salt in zipper-lock bag and refrigerate for at least 30 minutes or up to 1 hour.

2. Heat 1 tablespoon oil in Dutch oven over medium-high heat until shimmering. Stir in mushrooms, bell peppers, and remaining ½ teaspoon salt and cook until browned, about 8 minutes. Transfer vegetables to bowl; set aside. Add remaining 1 tablespoon oil and onion to now-empty pot and cook over medium heat until softened, about 5 minutes. Stir in cherry peppers, garlic, and oregano and cook until fragrant, about 30 seconds. Add tomatoes, cream, and pepper and bring to boil. Reduce heat to medium and simmer, stirring occasionally, until sauce is very thick, 10 to 15 minutes. Stir in chicken and reserved vegetables and simmer, covered, until chicken is cooked through, 6 to 8 minutes. Add olives and remaining 1 tablespoon cherry pepper brine. Cover to keep warm.

3. Meanwhile, bring 4 quarts water to boil in large pot. Add rigatoni and 1 tablespoon salt and cook, stirring often, until al dente. Reserve ½ cup cooking water, then drain rigatoni and return it to pot. Add sauce and Pecorino and toss to combine, adding reserved cooking water as needed to adjust consistency. Season with salt and pepper to taste and serve with additional Pecorino Romano.

THE ITALIAN AMERICAN KITCHEN
Jarred Cherry Peppers

Pickled peppers, both hot and sweet, come in all shapes and colors. Riggies just wouldn't be riggies without jarred cherry peppers, which come in both green and red varieties (either is fine in this recipe). Normally, these peppers add heat to the sauce. To flavor the chicken with their spicy tang, we marinate it in oil plus brine from the pepper jar. Cherry peppers can also be used in sandwiches or on an antipasto plate with cheeses and cured meats.

SPAGHETTI WITH FRESH CLAMS

Serves 4

Why This Recipe Works Most Italian American restaurants in the New York metro area offer two versions of this dish—white and red. The white version is lighter and puts more emphasis on the juice exuded by the clams and white wine. In contrast, red versions are often made with a thick tomato sauce and canned clams. This version adds a touch of fresh tomato for acidity but otherwise follows the script for a typical white clam sauce. To ensure the clams don't overcook, we steam them until they give up their juice, which we use to build the flavorful sauce, then recombine the clams with the sauce at the last minute, which allows just enough time for the clams to finish cooking. Any small clams, such as littlenecks, cherrystones, or cockles, will work in this recipe. To save money, you can also use a combination of 24 littlenecks and 6 quahogs. Simply add the quahogs along with the littlenecks and leave them in the pot for 5 minutes longer than the smaller clams. Discard the quahogs along with any unopened clams; though the quahogs are too tough to be enjoyed with the pasta, they help provide a richly flavored broth.

- 4 pounds littleneck clams, scrubbed
- ½ cup dry white wine
  Pinch cayenne pepper
- ¼ cup extra-virgin olive oil
- 2 garlic cloves, minced
- 2 plum tomatoes, peeled, seeded, and chopped fine
- 1 pound spaghetti or linguine
  Table salt for cooking pasta
- ¾ cup chopped fresh parsley

1. Bring clams, wine, and cayenne to boil in 12-inch straight-sided sauté pan, cover, and cook, shaking pan occasionally, for 5 minutes. Stir clams thoroughly, cover, and continue to cook until they just begin to open, 2 to 5 minutes longer. Using slotted spoon, transfer partially opened clams to large bowl. Discard any unopened clams.

2. Strain clam steaming liquid through fine-mesh strainer lined with coffee filter, avoiding any gritty sediment that has settled on bottom of pan. Set aside 1 cup liquid. (Add water as needed to equal 1 cup.) Wipe out pan with paper towels.

3. Heat oil and garlic in now-empty pan over medium heat. Cook, stirring often, until garlic turns golden but not brown, about 3 minutes. Stir in tomatoes, increase heat to medium-high, and cook until tomatoes soften, about 2 minutes. Stir in clams, cover, and cook until all clams are completely opened, about 2 minutes.

4. Meanwhile, bring 4 quarts water to boil in large pot. Add pasta and 1 tablespoon salt and cook, stirring often, until al dente. Drain pasta and return it to pot. Add clam sauce and reserved steaming liquid to pasta and cook over medium heat, tossing to combine, until flavors meld, about 30 seconds. Stir in parsley and season with salt and pepper to taste. Serve immediately.

SHRIMP PICCATA PASTA

Serves 4 to 6

Why This Recipe Works Though piccata dishes traditionally center around veal or chicken, Italian Americans have applied classic piccata flavors of lemon juice, capers, and garlic to other proteins, including shrimp. For this dish, we liked how quickly shrimp cooks and how well it pairs with pasta. So we seared shrimp over high heat until just barely cooked through, then set them aside until the sauce was ready. To maximize the flavor of the red pepper flakes, we first cooked them briefly with the garlic before adding wine, clam juice, and lemon juice. A few minutes of simmering reduced the sauce to a desirable, syrupy consistency. Using just one pan for both the shrimp and the sauce allowed the sauce to pick up the flavors left behind by the shrimp and made for an easy cleanup. Be sure to toss the shrimp and sauce with the pasta immediately after draining. The hot pasta will heat the shrimp and melt the butter.

  1 pound linguine

    Table salt for cooking pasta

  2 tablespoons extra-virgin olive oil, divided

  1 pound large shrimp (26 to 30 per pound), peeled, deveined, and halved lengthwise

  4 garlic cloves, minced

  1/8 teaspoon red pepper flakes

  1/2 cup dry white wine

  1 (8-ounce) bottle clam juice

  3 tablespoons lemon juice

  3 tablespoons capers, rinsed

  1/3 cup chopped fresh parsley

  4 tablespoons unsalted butter, softened

1. Bring 4 quarts water to boil in large pot for pasta. Add pasta and 1 tablespoon salt and cook, stirring often, until al dente. Reserve 1/2 cup cooking water, then drain pasta and return it to pot.

2. Meanwhile, heat 1 tablespoon oil in large skillet over high heat. Add shrimp and cook, stirring, until just opaque, about 1 minute. Transfer to large plate. Heat remaining 1 tablespoon oil in now-empty skillet over medium heat. Add garlic and pepper flakes and cook until fragrant but not browned, about 30 seconds. Add wine, increase heat to high, and simmer until liquid is reduced and syrupy, about 2 minutes. Add clam juice and lemon juice, bring to boil, and cook until mixture is reduced to 1/3 cup, about 8 minutes.

3. Add capers, parsley, butter, and shrimp and its sauce to pasta and toss to combine until butter melts and shrimp are warmed through. Season with salt and pepper to taste, adding reserved cooking water as needed to adjust consistency. Serve.

THE ITALIAN AMERICAN KITCHEN
Capers

These tiny green spheres are actually flower buds harvested from a spiny shrub (*Capparis spinosa*) that thrives in the hot, dry climate of countries such as Italy, Turkey, and Spain. Capers packed in salt are especially tender and often have a wider range of delicate flavors, but they must be repeatedly rinsed before use, and their nuanced flavors are easily over-shadowed in recipes. For everyday cooking, we like the convenience of brined capers. We prefer the small size known as nonpareils and our favorite brand is **Reese Non Pareil Capers.** They have a pleasantly firm texture and are perfectly "salty" and "tangy" without overwhelming other flavors, even the delicate shrimp in this recipe.

EASY WEEKDAY MEALS

CHICKEN MARSALA

Serves 4 to 6

Why This Recipe Works Beloved for its boozy, savory sauce, chicken Marsala is a restaurant favorite that we wanted to make more approachable for the home cook. First, we cut each chicken breast in half crosswise. Then, we cut the thicker half in half horizontally to make three identically sized pieces that could easily be pounded into cutlets. We salted the cutlets briefly and then dredged them in flour, which helped accelerate browning and prevented the meat from overcooking. We seared the cutlets quickly on both sides and set them aside while making the sauce. Our sauce uses reduced dry Marsala and chicken broth, along with cremini and dried porcini mushrooms for rich flavor and gelatin for a silky texture. It is worth spending a little extra for a moderately priced dry Marsala ($10 to $12 per bottle).

2¼ cups dry Marsala, divided

4 teaspoons unflavored gelatin

1 ounce dried porcini mushrooms, rinsed

4 (6- to 8-ounce) boneless, skinless chicken breasts, trimmed

2 teaspoons kosher salt

½ teaspoon pepper

2 cups chicken broth

¾ cup all-purpose flour

¼ cup plus 1 teaspoon vegetable oil, divided

3 ounces pancetta, cut into ½-inch pieces

1 pound cremini mushrooms, trimmed and sliced thin

1 shallot, minced

1 tablespoon tomato paste

1 garlic clove, minced

2 teaspoons lemon juice

1 teaspoon minced fresh oregano

3 tablespoons unsalted butter, cut into 6 pieces

2 teaspoons chopped fresh parsley

1. Bring 2 cups Marsala, gelatin, and porcini mushrooms to boil in medium saucepan over high heat. Reduce heat to medium-high and cook at vigorous simmer until reduced by half, 6 to 8 minutes.

2. Meanwhile, cut each chicken breast in half crosswise, then cut thick half in half again horizontally, creating 3 cutlets of similar thickness. Using meat pounder, gently pound each cutlet between 2 pieces of plastic wrap to even ½-inch thickness. Place cutlets in bowl and toss with salt and pepper. Set aside for 15 minutes.

3. Strain Marsala reduction through fine-mesh strainer, pressing on solids to extract as much liquid as possible; discard solids. Return Marsala reduction to saucepan, add broth, and return to boil over high heat. Lower heat to medium-high and simmer until reduced to 1½ cups, 10 to 12 minutes. Set aside.

4. Spread flour in shallow dish. Working with 1 cutlet at a time, dredge cutlets in flour, shaking gently to remove excess. Place on wire rack set in rimmed baking sheet. Heat 2 tablespoons oil in 12-inch skillet over medium-high heat until smoking. Place 6 cutlets in skillet and lower heat to medium. Cook until golden brown on 1 side, 2 to 3 minutes. Flip and cook until golden brown on second side, 2 to 3 minutes. Return cutlets to wire rack. Repeat with 2 tablespoons oil and remaining 6 cutlets.

5. Return now-empty skillet to medium-low heat and add pancetta. Cook, stirring occasionally, scraping pan bottom to loosen browned bits, until pancetta is brown and crisp, about 4 minutes. Add cremini mushrooms and increase heat to medium-high. Cook, stirring occasionally and scraping pan bottom, until liquid released by mushrooms evaporates and mushrooms begin to brown, about 8 minutes. Using slotted spoon, transfer cremini mushrooms and pancetta to bowl. Add remaining 1 teaspoon oil and shallot to pan and cook until softened, 1 minute. Add tomato paste and garlic and cook until fragrant, 30 seconds. Add lemon juice, oregano, reduced Marsala mixture, and remaining ¼ cup Marsala and bring to simmer.

6. Add cutlets to sauce and simmer for 3 minutes, flipping halfway through simmering. Transfer cutlets to platter. Off heat, whisk butter into sauce. Stir in parsley and cremini mushroom mixture. Season with salt and pepper to taste. Spoon sauce over chicken and serve.

Marsala

Marsala, which originally hails from the Sicilian port city of the same name, is a fortified wine. This means that brandy or a neutral spirit has been added to it. It can be found in both sweet and dry styles, a classification based primarily on the residual sugar content of the wine. In addition to imports from Italy, the supermarket shopper will find domestic options made in California. Aside from the obvious—sweet Marsala tasted sweeter than dry—the dry type features raisin and prune flavors balanced by sharp acidity and savory, nutty notes. Sweet Marsalas possess those same dried-fruit flavors but also offer hints of molasses and caramel. Most tasters found sweet Marsala more palatable when sampled straight. However, when we tried both styles in recipes for chicken Marsala, mushroom stuffing, and zabaglione, tasters preferred the dry style in all instances. Dry Marsala offered more depth of flavor, while sweet Marsala wasn't as complex. The takeaway? For both savory and sweet applications, we suggest using dry Marsala if a recipe doesn't specify a style.

CHICKEN FRANCESE

Serves 4

Why This Recipe Works This simple but refined dish consists of pan-fried chicken cutlets with a light but substantial eggy coating and a bright lemony sauce. Although its name hints at a rich pedigree—one account claims that Italians once made this dish for Napoleon Bonaparte—there is no classic French or Italian version. Instead, chicken Francese is most strongly identified with Italian American cooking in and around New York City. It's a humble dish with a fancy name. Its hazy background aside, we found that chicken Francese was related to the familiar but loosely defined group of thin-cut chicken (and sometimes veal) dishes that includes scaloppini, piccata, parmigiana, Milanese, and Marsala. But Francese also has much in common with a well-known egg-coated breakfast dish: French toast. While many of the other thin-cut chicken dishes are dusted with flour or shrouded in crisp bread crumbs, chicken Francese has a soft, rich, eggy coating. The silky lemon sauce nestles into the nooks in the soft coating so that each bite reveals just the right balance of chicken, coating, and sauce. We discovered that the key to success when making this egg-coated, pan-fried Italian American favorite was to cut and pound our own chicken cutlets so that they were perfectly even and thin. Dredging the cutlets in cornstarch before dipping them in the egg mixture ensured optimal adherence. We made sure that the quick-cooking cutlets spent as little time as possible in the pan so that the coating didn't burn or scramble. The coating adhered tightly to the cutlets, soaking up the tangy, buttery sauce without sloughing off. Freezing the chicken breasts for just 15 minutes makes them easier to slice into cutlets. To help keep the fragile egg coating in place, use a fork instead of tongs to flip the cutlets.

½ cup plus 1 teaspoon cornstarch, divided
2 large eggs
2 tablespoons milk
1 cup chicken broth
½ cup dry white wine
1¼ teaspoons table salt, divided
4 (6- to 8-ounce) boneless, skinless chicken breasts, trimmed
½ teaspoon pepper
6 tablespoons unsalted butter, cut into 6 pieces, divided
2 tablespoons capers, rinsed
1 garlic clove, minced
2 tablespoons lemon juice
1 tablespoon chopped fresh parsley

1. Adjust oven rack to middle position and heat oven to 200 degrees. Set wire rack in rimmed baking sheet.

2. Place ½ cup cornstarch in shallow dish. Whisk eggs and milk together in second shallow dish. Whisk broth, wine, ¼ teaspoon salt, and remaining 1 teaspoon cornstarch together in bowl.

3. Working with 1 breast at a time, starting at thick end, cut breasts in half horizontally. Using meat pounder, gently pound each cutlet between 2 pieces of plastic wrap to even ½-inch thickness. Pat cutlets dry with paper towels and season with remaining 1 teaspoon salt and pepper. Working with 1 cutlet at a time, dredge cutlets in cornstarch, shaking off excess; dip in egg mixture to coat, letting excess drip off; then place on large plate in single layer.

4. Melt 2 tablespoons butter in 12-inch nonstick skillet over medium-high heat. Transfer 4 cutlets to skillet and cook until golden brown and cooked through, 2 to 3 minutes per side, using fork to flip. Transfer to prepared rack and place in oven to keep warm. Repeat with 2 tablespoons butter and remaining 4 cutlets.

5. Add capers and garlic to now-empty skillet and cook until fragrant, about 30 seconds. Add broth mixture to skillet and bring to boil. Cook until reduced by half, about 5 minutes. Off heat, stir in lemon juice and remaining 2 tablespoons butter.

6. Transfer chicken to serving platter. Spoon sauce over chicken and sprinkle with parsley. Serve.

CHICKEN SCALOPPINI WITH MUSHROOMS AND PEPPERS

Serves 4

Why This Recipe Works Scaloppini with mushrooms and peppers is an Italian American restaurant classic. The term "scaloppini" refers to thinly sliced cuts of meat, traditionally veal but also chicken and turkey. The classic recipe calls for dredging the "scallops" (aka cutlets) in flour, cooking them in a hot pan, and serving them in a vibrant pan sauce enlivened with vegetables. The quick dish is an ideal weeknight meal and, with a few tweaks, we perfected the recipe. Most call for browning the chicken before building the sauce, but we found that the thin cutlets overcooked and became dry as they sat while the sauce simmered. Bucking tradition, we first make the sauce and then dredge and brown the chicken. Mushrooms, peppers, shallots, garlic, and capers make for a flavorful sauce, finished with butter for silky texture and parsley for freshness. The chicken breasts will be easier to slice in half if you freeze them for 15 minutes.

- 4 (6- to 8-ounce) boneless, skinless chicken breasts, trimmed
- ¾ teaspoon table salt, divided
- ¼ teaspoon pepper
- 6 tablespoons vegetable oil, divided
- 8 ounces white mushrooms, trimmed and quartered
- 1 red bell pepper, stemmed, seeded, and cut into thin matchsticks
- 1 shallot, sliced thin
- ¼ cup capers, rinsed
- 2 garlic cloves, minced
- 1¼ cups chicken broth
- ¾ cup white wine
- ⅓ cup all-purpose flour
- 3 tablespoons unsalted butter, cut into 3 pieces
- 1 tablespoon chopped fresh parsley

1. Working with 1 breast at a time, starting on thick side, cut breasts in half horizontally. Using meat pounder, gently pound each cutlet into even ½-inch thickness between 2 pieces of plastic wrap. Pat cutlets dry with paper towels and season with ½ teaspoon salt and pepper; set aside.

2. Heat 2 tablespoons oil in 12-inch nonstick skillet over medium-high heat until just smoking. Add mushrooms, bell pepper, shallot, and remaining ¼ teaspoon salt and cook until liquid has evaporated and vegetables begin to brown, 8 to 10 minutes. Add capers and garlic and cook until fragrant, about 1 minute. Add broth and wine and bring to boil, scraping up any browned bits. Cook until slightly thickened and mixture is reduced to 2 cups (measured with vegetables), about 8 minutes. Set aside in measuring cup. Wipe out skillet with paper towels.

3. Spread flour in shallow dish. Working with 1 cutlet at a time, dredge cutlets in flour, shaking off excess, and transfer to plate. Heat 2 tablespoons oil in now-empty skillet over medium-high heat until just smoking. Add 4 cutlets and cook until golden and cooked through, about 2 minutes per side. Transfer to platter and tent loosely with aluminum foil. Repeat with remaining 4 cutlets and remaining 2 tablespoons oil.

4. Discard any oil remaining in skillet. Return sauce to now-empty skillet and bring to boil. Once boiling, remove skillet from heat and whisk in butter. Stir in any accumulated juices from platter. Season sauce with salt and pepper to taste. Spoon sauce and vegetables over chicken. Sprinkle with parsley. Serve.

SCAMPI-STYLE CHICKEN

Serves 4 to 6

Why This Recipe Works Millions of Americans enjoy Italian American fare at the Olive Garden. While the menu is a long way from Italy, or even Little Italy, it certainly influences how we perceive "Italian" food. The chain's chicken scampi recipe is a perfect example. *Scampi* means "langoustine" in Italian, and there are no langoustines anywhere near this dish. Rather, this rendition features fried chicken tenders served in the style of shrimp scampi, the classic lemony, garlicky, saucy dish often found on Italian American menus. The restaurant's cream-based sauce felt a little heavy and unusual for something in the "scampi" style. And the red onions in the dish looked odd and tasted unpleasantly strong. But we liked the breaded chicken tenders and garlicky sauce studded with strips of colorful bell pepper. We decided to tweak this dish—a remake of a remake, if you will. To emulate the golden, crisp coating of the restaurant dish, we seasoned chicken tenderloins (you can use cut-up strips of chicken breast, too) and dredged them first in beaten egg and then in flour. Then we shallow-fried the chicken in just 2 tablespoons of oil until browned on both sides and removed the golden tenders (tenting them with aluminum foil to keep them warm) so we could build the sauce in the skillet. We added a little more oil to the hot skillet and tossed in some sliced red bell pepper. When it was soft and browned, we added eight cloves of sliced garlic. After about a minute, the garlic smelled amazing and was just starting to color, so we stirred in some flour (for thickening) and then a combination of chicken broth and white wine. We let the sauce bubble away until it was slightly reduced, and then finished it with lemon for brightness and butter for richness and a glossy sheen. Finally, we returned the fried chicken tenders to the pan to warm through and meld with the flavorful sauce. If you can't find chicken tenderloins, slice boneless, skinless chicken breasts lengthwise into 3/4-inch-thick strips. You can use torn basil in place of the parsley, if desired. If you like, serve with crusty bread and lemon wedges.

2 large eggs

2 teaspoons table salt, divided

3/4 cup plus 1 tablespoon all-purpose flour, divided

2 pounds chicken tenderloins, trimmed

1/2 teaspoon pepper

6 tablespoons extra-virgin olive oil, divided

1 red bell pepper, stemmed, seeded, and sliced thin

8 garlic cloves, sliced thin

1 1/4 cups chicken broth

3/4 cup dry white wine

4 tablespoons unsalted butter, cut into 4 pieces

2 tablespoons chopped fresh parsley

1. Lightly beat eggs and 1/2 teaspoon salt together in shallow dish. Place 3/4 cup flour in second shallow dish. Pat chicken dry with paper towels and season with 1 teaspoon salt and pepper. Working with 1 piece of chicken at a time, dip in eggs, allowing excess to drip off, then dredge in flour, shaking off any excess. Transfer to large plate.

2. Heat 2 tablespoons oil in 12-inch nonstick skillet over medium-high heat until just smoking. Add half of chicken and cook until golden brown and registering 160 degrees, about 3 minutes per side. Transfer chicken to clean plate and tent with aluminum foil. Wipe skillet clean with paper towels and repeat with 2 tablespoons oil and remaining chicken.

3. Wipe skillet clean with paper towels. Heat remaining 2 tablespoons oil in now-empty skillet over medium-high heat until just smoking. Add bell pepper and remaining 1/2 teaspoon salt and cook until softened and well browned, 5 to 7 minutes. Add garlic and cook until fragrant and golden brown, about 1 minute. Stir in remaining 1 tablespoon flour and cook for 1 minute.

4. Stir in broth and wine and bring to boil, scraping up any browned bits. Cook until mixture is reduced to about 1 1/2 cups, 5 to 7 minutes. Reduce heat to low and stir in butter until melted. Return chicken to skillet and cook, turning to coat with sauce, until heated through, about 2 minutes. Season with salt and pepper to taste. Transfer to shallow serving platter and sprinkle with parsley. Serve.

CHICKEN PARMESAN

Serves 4

Why This Recipe Works Traditional chicken Parmesan (a purely American invention you won't find in Italy) is a minefield of potential problems: dry meat, soggy crust, and a chewy blanket of mozzarella. To keep the meat moist, we salted the cutlets first, and to keep the exterior crunchy, we replaced more than half of the bread crumbs with grated Parmesan cheese. Mixing the usual shredded mozzarella with creamy fontina ensured that the cheese stayed smooth and melty, not congealed, and we placed it directly on the fried cutlets to form a waterproof layer between crust and sauce. A simple tomato sauce made with plenty of aromatics and fresh basil was the perfect finishing touch to this improved classic. This recipe makes enough sauce to top the cutlets as well as four servings of pasta. The chicken breasts will be easier to slice in half if you freeze them for 15 minutes.

Sauce

- 2 tablespoons extra-virgin olive oil, divided
- 2 garlic cloves, minced
- ¾ teaspoon kosher salt
- ¼ teaspoon dried oregano
  Pinch red pepper flakes
- 1 (28-ounce) can crushed tomatoes
- ¼ teaspoon sugar
- 2 tablespoons chopped fresh basil

Chicken

- 2 (6- to 8-ounce) boneless, skinless chicken breasts, trimmed
- 1 teaspoon kosher salt
- 2 ounces whole-milk mozzarella cheese, shredded (½ cup)
- 2 ounces fontina cheese, shredded (½ cup)
- 1 large egg
- 1 tablespoon all-purpose flour
- 1½ ounces Parmesan cheese, grated (¾ cup)
- ½ cup panko bread crumbs
- ½ teaspoon garlic powder
- ¼ teaspoon dried oregano

- ¼ teaspoon pepper
- ⅓ cup vegetable oil
- ¼ cup torn fresh basil

1. For the sauce Heat 1 tablespoon oil in medium saucepan over medium heat until shimmering. Stir in garlic, salt, oregano, and pepper flakes and cook until fragrant, about 30 seconds. Stir in tomatoes and sugar, increase heat to high, and bring to simmer. Reduce heat to medium-low and simmer until thickened, about 20 minutes. Off heat, stir in basil and remaining 1 tablespoon oil. Season with salt and pepper to taste and cover to keep warm.

2. For the chicken Working with 1 breast at a time, starting at thick end, cut breasts in half horizontally. Using meat pounder, gently pound each cutlet between 2 pieces of plastic wrap to even ½-inch thickness. Sprinkle each side of each cutlet with ⅛ teaspoon salt and let stand at room temperature for 20 minutes. Combine mozzarella and fontina in bowl and set aside.

3. Adjust oven rack 4 inches from broiler element and heat broiler. Whisk egg and flour together in shallow dish until smooth. Combine Parmesan, panko, garlic powder, oregano, and pepper in second shallow dish. Pat chicken dry with paper towels. Working with 1 cutlet at a time, dredge in egg mixture, allowing excess to drip off, then coat with Parmesan mixture, pressing gently to adhere; transfer to large plate.

4. Heat oil in 10-inch nonstick skillet over medium-high heat until shimmering. Carefully place 2 cutlets in skillet and cook until crispy and deep golden, 1½ to 2 minutes per side. Transfer to paper towel–lined plate and repeat with remaining 2 cutlets.

5. Place cutlets on rimmed baking sheet and sprinkle cheese mixture evenly over top. Broil until cheese is melted and beginning to brown, 2 to 4 minutes.

6. Transfer chicken to serving platter and top each cutlet with 2 tablespoons sauce. Sprinkle with basil and serve immediately, passing remaining sauce separately.

Fontina

The "true" fontina—Fontina Val d'Aosta—has been made in the northwest corner of Italy since at least the 13th century. This cheese has Denominazione di Origine Protetta (DOP) status, meaning it must be made according to exacting specifications. If you can find it at your local supermarket, it probably costs upwards of $20 per pound. You're more likely to spot more affordable cheeses labeled fontina or similar-sounding names like fontal or fontinella.

Some, puzzlingly, are described as "Swedish-style." Though a few are made in Europe, most of these cheeses are made in America. The Italian original is our top choice for a cheese board or antipasto plate. But when it comes to cooking, any of the cheaper supermarket options will provide the requisite buttery flavor and will melt better than the real deal from Italy.

BAKED RICOTTA CHICKEN

Serves 4

Why This Recipe Works Baked ricotta chicken is another American invention, a relative of chicken Parmesan but with the cheese stuffed inside breaded chicken breasts. We knew that ricotta has a tendency to break and dry out when baked, so we processed it with some oil to both add richness and smooth out its texture. We jump-started the chicken by browning it in a skillet before shingling the pieces in a pasta sauce–lined baking dish. We avoided the complicated step of stuffing the chicken by instead layering the chicken with the sauce, ricotta mixture, and bread crumbs. Skipping the stuffing step made this recipe easy enough to execute in 30 minutes. Instead of toasting the bread crumbs on a baking sheet in the oven, we simply microwaved them with some olive oil, salt, and pepper for about 2 minutes until they were light golden brown—another nod to streamlining this recipe. The partially toasted crumbs finished browning and crisping up in the oven on top of the chicken. A good-quality ricotta that is creamy and dense, not watery, is recommended so it stays in place when the chicken is baked (see our favorite below). Rao's Homemade Marinara Sauce is our favorite jarred pasta sauce and will work well in this recipe. Serve the chicken with pasta or bread.

Bread Crumbs

- ½ cup panko bread crumbs
- 1 tablespoon extra-virgin olive oil
- ⅛ teaspoon table salt
- ⅛ teaspoon pepper

Chicken

- 8 ounces (1 cup) whole-milk ricotta cheese
- 1½ ounces Parmesan cheese, grated (¾ cup)
- 1 teaspoon dried oregano
- 1¼ teaspoons table salt, divided
- ¾ teaspoon pepper, divided
- ¼ cup extra-virgin olive oil, divided
- 4 (6- to 8-ounce) boneless, skinless chicken breasts, trimmed
- 1½ cups Classic Marinara (page 102) or jarred pasta sauce
- 2 tablespoons chopped fresh basil

1. For the bread crumbs Combine all ingredients in bowl. Microwave until panko is light golden brown, 1 to 2 minutes, stirring occasionally; set aside.

2. For the chicken Adjust oven rack to upper-middle position and heat oven to 425 degrees. Process ricotta, Parmesan, oregano, ¼ teaspoon salt, and ¼ teaspoon pepper in food processor until smooth, about 10 seconds. With processor running, slowly add 3 tablespoons oil until incorporated; transfer ricotta mixture to bowl and set aside.

3. Using meat pounder, gently pound each chicken breast between 2 pieces of plastic wrap to even ½-inch thickness. Pat chicken dry with paper towels and season with remaining 1 teaspoon salt and remaining ½ teaspoon pepper. Heat remaining 1 tablespoon oil in 12-inch skillet over medium heat until shimmering. Add chicken and cook until browned on both sides, about 6 minutes.

4. Evenly spread ¾ cup sauce in bottom of 13 by 9-inch baking dish. Transfer chicken to dish, shingling breasts in center of dish on top of sauce. Pour remaining ¾ cup sauce over chicken, then top each piece with ⅓ cup ricotta mixture. Sprinkle chicken evenly with panko mixture. Bake until chicken registers 160 degrees, about 15 minutes. Sprinkle with basil and serve.

THE ITALIAN AMERICAN KITCHEN
Ricotta

Ricotta is the key ingredient in dishes such as lasagna, stuffed pastas, cannoli, and cheesecake, as well as simple antipasti. Good ricotta should be both creamy and dense, not wet, with a fresh dairy flavor. Our favorite, **BelGioioso Ricotta con Latte Whole Milk Ricotta Cheese**, is made with sweet whey that is the byproduct of the company's mozzarella-making process, as well as a small amount of milk. This ricotta has a rich, dense consistency that tasters described as "luscious."

CHICKEN CACCIATORE

Serves 8

Why This Recipe Works Cacciatore, which means "hunter-style" in Italian, originally referred to a simple method of cooking fresh-killed game. Game hen or rabbit would be sautéed along with wild mushrooms, onions, and other foraged vegetables and then braised with wine or stock. Unfortunately, when applied to chicken and translated by American cooks, cacciatore turned into a generic "red sauce" dish, often featuring sauces that were greasy and overly sweet along with dry chicken. Instead of using a cut-up whole chicken, we made our cacciatore with chicken thighs exclusively: Not only is it easier to buy a package of thighs than it is to butcher a chicken, the thighs gave the braising liquid a more intense flavor. But the skin on the chicken turned flabby after braising and the sauce was greasy. To avoid this problem, we browned the thighs to render the flavorful fat and then removed the skin before braising them. Cooking the chicken in a combination of red wine, diced tomatoes, and chicken broth; adding earthy portobello mushrooms and a Parmesan cheese rind; and finishing with sage gave our cacciatore the rich flavor we desired. However, the sauce was more like a broth. Adding a little flour directly to the sautéing vegetables gave the finished sauce the perfect silky consistency. The Parmesan cheese rind is optional, but we highly recommend it for the savory flavor it adds to the dish.

8 (5- to 7-ounce) bone-in chicken thighs, trimmed

2¼ teaspoons table salt, divided

¾ teaspoon pepper

1 tablespoon extra-virgin olive oil

1 onion, chopped

6 ounces portobello mushroom caps, cut into ¾-inch pieces

4 garlic cloves, minced

2 teaspoons minced fresh thyme

1½ tablespoons all-purpose flour

1½ cups dry red wine

½ cup chicken broth

1 (14.5-ounce) can diced tomatoes, drained

1 Parmesan cheese rind (optional)

2 teaspoons chopped fresh sage

1. Adjust oven rack to middle position and heat oven to 300 degrees. Pat chicken dry with paper towels and season with 1¾ teaspoons salt and pepper. Heat oil in Dutch oven over medium-high heat until just smoking. Brown thighs, 5 to 6 minutes per side. Transfer thighs to plate; discard skin. Pour off all but 1 tablespoon fat from pot.

2. Add onion, mushrooms, and remaining ½ teaspoon salt to fat left in pot and cook, stirring occasionally, until softened and beginning to brown, 6 to 8 minutes. Stir in garlic and thyme and cook until fragrant, about 30 seconds. Stir in flour and cook for 1 minute. Slowly whisk in wine, scraping up any browned bits and smoothing out any lumps.

3. Stir in broth, tomatoes, and cheese rind, if using, and bring to simmer. Nestle thighs into pot, cover, and transfer to oven. Cook until chicken registers 195 degrees, 35 to 40 minutes.

4. Remove pot from oven and transfer chicken to serving platter. Discard cheese rind, if using. Stir sage into sauce and season with salt and pepper to taste. Spoon sauce over chicken and serve.

THE ITALIAN AMERICAN KITCHEN
Portobello Mushrooms

Portobellos are the giants of the mushroom family, ranging from 4 to 6 inches in diameter. They are the mature form of cremini mushrooms and, as a result of the extra growing time, they have a particularly intense, meaty flavor and a steaklike texture. They are ideal for being sautéed, stir-fried, roasted, grilled, or stuffed. Look for mushrooms with fully intact caps and dry gills. Wet, damaged gills are a sign of spoilage. The stems are woody and are often discarded, so buy mushrooms with stems only if you plan to use them (such as in soup, stock, or stuffing). To clean portobellos, simply wipe them with a damp towel.

CHICKEN VESUVIO

Serves 4 to 6

Why This Recipe Works Ask a Chicago native where to find the best version of chicken Vesuvio, and you'll be provided with a long list. But of all the restaurants in the city, Harry Caray's Italian Steakhouse is probably the most well-known for this regional favorite: crisp-skinned chicken and deeply browned potatoes in a potent garlic and white wine sauce. To transfer chicken Vesuvio to the home kitchen, we traded the customary skillet for a large, heavy roasting pan, which gave us plenty of room for four servings. We heated oil in the roasting pan on the stovetop, browned the chicken thighs and halved Yukon Gold potatoes, and added the traditional dried herbs and plenty of garlic cloves. We poured wine into the pan and moved it to the oven so the chicken, potatoes, and garlic could finish cooking unattended. After transferring the cooked chicken and potatoes to a platter, we returned the pan to the stovetop to reduce the sauce further. Mashing the cooked garlic cloves brought the oil and wine together in a rich emulsion, and some fresh minced garlic, tempered with lemon juice, delivered robust flavor. For this recipe you'll need a roasting pan that measures at least 16 by 12 inches. Trim all the skin from the under-side of the chicken thighs, but leave the skin on top intact. To ensure that all the potatoes fit in the pan, halve them crosswise to minimize their surface area. For efficient browning, heat the roasting pan over two burners. Combining the garlic with lemon juice in step 1 makes the garlic taste less harsh, but only if the lemon juice is added immediately after the garlic is minced.

- 8 (5- to 7-ounce) bone-in chicken thighs, trimmed
- 2½ teaspoons kosher salt, divided
- 1 teaspoon pepper, divided
- 1½ pounds Yukon Gold potatoes, 2 to 3 inches in diameter, halved crosswise
- 2 tablespoons vegetable oil, divided
- 14 garlic cloves, peeled (2 whole, 12 halved lengthwise)
- 1 tablespoon lemon juice
- 1½ teaspoons dried oregano
- ½ teaspoon dried thyme
- 1½ cups dry white wine
- 2 tablespoons minced fresh parsley, divided

1. Adjust oven rack to upper-middle position and heat oven to 450 degrees. Pat chicken dry with paper towels and sprinkle on both sides with 1½ teaspoons salt and ½ teaspoon pepper. Toss potatoes with 1 tablespoon oil and remaining 1 teaspoon salt. Mince 2 whole garlic cloves and immediately combine with lemon juice in small bowl; set aside.

2. Heat remaining 1 tablespoon oil in large roasting pan over medium-high heat until shimmering. Place chicken, skin side down, in single layer in pan and cook, without moving it, until chicken has rendered about 2 tablespoons of fat, 2 to 3 minutes. Place potatoes cut side down in chicken fat, arranging so that cut sides are in complete contact with surface of pan. Sprinkle chicken and potatoes with oregano and thyme. Continue to cook until chicken and potatoes are deeply browned and crisp, 8 to 12 minutes, moving chicken and potatoes to ensure even browning and flipping pieces when fully browned. When all pieces have been flipped, tuck halved garlic cloves among chicken and potatoes. Remove pan from heat and pour wine into pan (do not pour over chicken or potatoes). Transfer pan to oven and roast until potatoes are tender when pierced with tip of paring knife and chicken registers 185 to 190 degrees, 15 to 20 minutes.

3. Transfer chicken and potatoes to deep platter, browned sides up. Place pan over medium heat (handles will be hot) and stir to incorporate any browned bits. Using slotted spoon, transfer garlic cloves to cutting board. Chop coarse, then mash to smooth paste with side of knife. Whisk garlic paste into sauce in pan. Continue to cook until sauce coats back of spoon, 3 to 5 minutes. Remove from heat and whisk in reserved lemon juice mixture and 1 tablespoon parsley. Pour sauce around chicken and potatoes. Sprinkle with remaining 1 tablespoon parsley and serve.

CHICKEN SCARPARIELLO

Serves 4 to 6

Why This Recipe Works Chicken scarpariello is an Italian American dish of browned chicken and sausage bathed in a spicy, garlicky sauce chock-full of onions, bell peppers, and pickled hot cherry peppers. When done right, it's a hearty weeknight supper, especially well-suited to folks who love strong flavors. Its exact origins are murky, but it first became popular stateside in the early 1900s among New York City's burgeoning Italian population, particularly those immigrants from Naples. Some say that the name *scarpariello,* which loosely translates to "shoemaker-style," was bestowed upon this dish because it features ingredients inexpensive enough for a poor cobbler to afford. Others say the name came about because, much like a shoe, the dish is something you "cobble" together. Whatever the story, we wanted our version to be bright and flavorful, not too briny and certainly not too spicy. We started by tempering the heat of the cherry peppers by removing their seeds. We wanted some extra flavor, so we added just a couple of tablespoons of the vinegary cherry pepper brine. After browning the sausage and chicken, we sautéed the vegetables and then nestled in the chicken and sausage to finish cooking in the oven, which kept the chicken skin crispy. A tablespoon of flour and ¾ cup of chicken broth resulted in a sauce with the perfect consistency—thick enough to coat the chicken and sausage without being gloppy. We used sweet Italian sausage to balance the spiciness of the cherry peppers. Feel free to substitute hot Italian sausage if you prefer a spicier dish.

- 3 pounds bone-in chicken pieces
  (2 split breasts cut in half crosswise,
  2 drumsticks, and 2 thighs), trimmed
- 1 teaspoon table salt
- ½ teaspoon pepper
- 1 tablespoon vegetable oil
- 8 ounces sweet Italian sausage,
  casings removed
- 1 onion, halved and sliced thin
- 1 red bell pepper, stemmed, seeded,
  and sliced thin
- 5 jarred hot cherry peppers, seeded,
  rinsed, and sliced thin (½ cup),
  plus 2 tablespoons brine
- 5 garlic cloves, minced
- 1 teaspoon dried oregano
- 1 tablespoon all-purpose flour
- ¾ cup chicken broth
- 2 tablespoons chopped fresh parsley

1. Adjust oven rack to middle position and heat oven to 350 degrees. Pat chicken dry with paper towels and season with salt and pepper. Heat oil in ovensafe 12-inch skillet over medium-high heat until just smoking. Add chicken to skillet, skin side down, and cook without moving until well browned, about 5 minutes. Flip chicken and continue to cook until browned on second side, about 3 minutes. Transfer chicken to plate.

2. Add sausage to fat left in skillet and cook, breaking up with spoon, until browned, about 3 minutes. Transfer sausage to paper towel–lined plate.

3. Pour off all but 1 tablespoon fat from skillet and return to medium-high heat. Add onion and bell pepper and cook until vegetables are softened and lightly browned, about 5 minutes. Add cherry peppers, garlic, and oregano and cook until fragrant, about 1 minute. Stir in flour and cook for 30 seconds. Add broth and cherry pepper brine and bring to simmer, scraping up any browned bits.

4. Remove skillet from heat and stir in sausage. Arrange chicken pieces, skin side up, in single layer in skillet and add any accumulated juices. Transfer skillet to oven and bake until breasts register 160 degrees and drumsticks/thighs register 175 degrees, 20 to 25 minutes.

5. Being careful of hot skillet handle, carefully remove skillet from oven. Transfer chicken to serving platter. Season onion mixture with salt and pepper to taste, then spoon over chicken. Sprinkle with parsley. Serve.

RAO'S LEMON CHICKEN

Serves 4

Why This Recipe Works Unless you're a New York City A-lister, you probably haven't dined at Rao's. The tiny East Harlem institution is like a club for long-time regulars and celebrities, including Al Pacino and Robert De Niro. This recipe is our take on the restaurant's *pollo al limone,* in which two small chickens are cut in half and cooked under the restaurant's powerful broiler (called a salamander). The deeply bronzed birds are then cut into pieces and bathed in a simple, pungent sauce of lemon juice (a full cup per bird), olive oil, red wine vinegar, garlic, and dried oregano before being briefly broiled again and served with crusty bread for dipping. Our version translates the dish from the restaurant kitchen to the home kitchen—and makes a few improvements at the same time. We substituted easy-to-find chicken parts that don't require butchering. Because home broilers are not as powerful as restaurant broilers, we browned the skin in a skillet and then braised the chicken pieces in the pan with a lemon-juice-and-chicken-broth-based sauce; the skin was above the liquid, so it continued to brown and crisp while in the oven. We browned the dark-meat pieces on both sides so that they would finish cooking at the same time as the breasts, eliminating the need to remove the chicken from the pan in batches. A mere ¼ cup of lemon juice in the sauce gave it just the right degree of brightness, and adding lemon zest gave us more lemon flavor without adding acidity. We serve our version of Rao's chicken with crusty bread, but it can also be served with rice, potatoes, or egg noodles. To ensure crisp skin, dry the chicken well after brining and pour the sauce around, not on, the chicken right before serving.

½ cup table salt, for brining

3 pounds bone-in chicken pieces (2 split breasts cut in half crosswise, 2 drumsticks, and 2 thighs), trimmed

1 teaspoon vegetable oil

2 tablespoons unsalted butter

1 large shallot, minced

1 garlic clove, minced

4 teaspoons all-purpose flour

1 cup chicken broth

4 teaspoons grated lemon zest, divided, plus ¼ cup juice (2 lemons)

1 tablespoon fresh parsley leaves

1 teaspoon fresh oregano leaves

1. Dissolve salt in 2 quarts cold water in large container. Submerge chicken in brine, cover, and refrigerate for 30 minutes to 1 hour. Remove chicken from brine and pat dry with paper towels.

2. Adjust oven rack to lower-middle position and heat oven to 475 degrees. Heat oil in ovensafe 12-inch skillet over medium-high heat until just smoking. Place chicken skin side down in skillet and cook until skin is well browned and crisp, 8 to 10 minutes. Transfer breasts to large plate. Flip thighs and legs and continue to cook until browned on second side, 3 to 5 minutes. Transfer thighs and legs to plate with breasts.

3. Pour off and discard fat in skillet. Return skillet to medium heat; add butter, shallot, and garlic and cook until fragrant, 30 seconds. Sprinkle flour evenly over shallot-garlic mixture and cook, stirring constantly, until flour is lightly browned, about 1 minute. Slowly stir in broth and lemon juice, scraping up any browned bits, and bring to simmer. Cook until sauce is slightly reduced and thickened, 2 to 3 minutes. Stir in 1 tablespoon zest and remove skillet from heat. Return chicken, skin side up (skin should be above surface of liquid), and any accumulated juices to skillet. Transfer to oven and bake, uncovered, until breasts register 160 degrees and thighs and legs register 175 degrees, 10 to 12 minutes.

4. While chicken cooks, chop parsley, oregano, and remaining 1 teaspoon zest together until finely minced and well combined. Remove skillet from oven and let chicken sit for 5 minutes.

5. Transfer chicken to serving platter. Whisk sauce, incorporating any browned bits from sides of pan, until smooth and homogeneous, about 30 seconds. Whisk half of herb-zest mixture into sauce and sprinkle remaining half over chicken. Pour some sauce around chicken. Serve, passing remaining sauce separately.

GRILLED CHICKEN ALLA DIAVOLA

Serves 4

Why This Recipe Works In Italian, *alla diavola* means "in the style of the devil," or in this case with heat from a good amount of red pepper flakes and black pepper. Butterflying a chicken is a win-win when it comes to grilling. It allows the chicken to cook through more quickly and evenly and also exposes more skin to the grill so it can brown and become ultracrisp. But crisp skin and tender meat are only half the battle—the chicken has to be flavorful, too. To that end, we set out to infuse our bird with bold heat and garlicky flavor. Adding two heads of garlic to a brine was our first move. Next, we created a potent garlic-pepper oil and rubbed some under the skin of the chicken before grilling. For one last punch of flavor, we reserved some of the garlicky oil to serve with the chicken. If using a kosher chicken, do not brine in step 1. This dish is very spicy; for milder heat, reduce the amount of red pepper flakes.

- 2 garlic heads, plus 4 cloves, minced
- 3 bay leaves
- ½ cup table salt, for brining
- 1 (3½- to 4-pound) whole chicken, giblets discarded
- ¼ cup extra-virgin olive oil
- 2 teaspoons red pepper flakes
- 2 teaspoons pepper
- 1 (13 by 9-inch) disposable aluminum roasting pan (if using charcoal)
- Lemon wedges

1. Combine garlic heads, bay leaves, and salt in 1-gallon zipper-lock bag, crush gently with meat pounder, and transfer to large container. Stir in 2 quarts water to dissolve salt. With chicken breast side down, use kitchen shears to cut through bones on either side of backbone. Discard backbone and trim away excess fat and skin around neck. Flip chicken, press firmly on breastbone to flatten, then pound breast to be same thickness as legs and thighs. Submerge chicken in brine, cover, and refrigerate for 1 hour.

2. Meanwhile, cook oil, minced garlic, pepper flakes, and pepper in small saucepan over medium heat until fragrant, about 3 minutes. Let oil cool, then reserve 2 tablespoons for serving.

3. Remove chicken from brine and pat dry with paper towels. Gently loosen skin covering breast and thighs and rub remaining garlic-pepper oil underneath skin. Tuck wingtips behind back.

4A. For a charcoal grill Open bottom vent completely and place disposable pan in center of grill. Light large chimney starter filled with charcoal briquettes (6 quarts). When top coals are partially covered with ash, pour into 2 even piles on either side of disposable pan. Set cooking grate in place, cover, and open lid vent completely. Heat grill until hot, about 5 minutes.

4B. For a gas grill Turn all burners to high, cover, and heat grill until hot, about 15 minutes. Turn all burners to medium-low. (Adjust burners as needed to maintain grill temperature of 350 degrees.)

5. Clean and oil cooking grate. Place chicken skin side down in center of grill (over pan if using charcoal). Cover and cook until skin is crisp, breast registers 160 degrees, and thighs register 175 degrees, 30 to 45 minutes.

6. Transfer chicken to carving board and let rest for 5 to 10 minutes. Carve chicken and serve with reserved garlic-pepper oil and lemon wedges.

STEAK PIZZAIOLA

Serves 4

Why This Recipe Works Tender steak bathed in a garlicky tomato sauce sounds pretty good, right? The dish is called steak pizzaiola ("pizza maker's steak"), and it's a staple of old-school Italian American restaurants. We tried many recipes, and the results were all over the place. For our version, we were after steak that tasted like it had been cooked in the sauce to marry the flavors—good steak pizzaiola is more than just the sum of its parts. Draining canned whole peeled tomatoes of their liquid before using them helped mitigate the watery flavor canned tomatoes can sometimes have. Quickly dredging the steaks in flour before searing gave the exterior of the meat a velvety layer that helped the steaks hold on to the sauce. Adding the steaks back to a quick-simmered sauce to finish cooking tenderized them without turning them tough. Though we prefer less-expensive blade steaks, strip steaks of the same size also work here.

1 (28-ounce) can whole peeled tomatoes

½ teaspoon red pepper flakes

1½ teaspoons table salt, divided

¾ teaspoon pepper, divided

4 (6- to 8-ounce) beef blade steaks, 1 inch thick, trimmed

½ cup all-purpose flour

¼ cup extra-virgin olive oil, divided

4 garlic cloves, sliced thin

2 anchovy fillets, rinsed, patted dry, and minced

¼ cup fresh basil leaves, torn

1. Drain tomatoes in colander set over bowl; reserve ½ cup liquid and discard remaining liquid. Pulse tomatoes, reserved liquid, pepper flakes, ½ teaspoon salt, and ¼ teaspoon pepper in food processor until chopped, about 7 pulses. Set aside.

2. Using meat pounder, gently pound each steak between 2 pieces of plastic wrap to even ¼-inch thickness. Pat steaks dry with paper towels and season with remaining 1 teaspoon salt and remaining ½ teaspoon pepper. Place flour in shallow dish. Lightly dredge each steak in flour, shaking off excess, and transfer to plate.

3. Heat 2 tablespoons oil in 12-inch nonstick skillet over medium-high heat until just smoking. Add 2 steaks and cook until lightly browned, about 2 minutes per side. Return steaks to plate. Add 1 tablespoon oil to now-empty skillet and repeat with remaining 2 steaks.

4. Reduce heat to medium-low and add garlic, anchovies, and remaining 1 tablespoon oil to now-empty skillet. Cook until fragrant and lightly browned, about 30 seconds. Stir in tomato mixture and bring to simmer. Cook, stirring often, until sauce has thickened slightly, about 5 minutes.

5. Add steaks to sauce and cook until tender and just cooked through, about 3 minutes. Transfer steaks to platter. Stir basil into sauce and season with salt and pepper to taste. Spoon sauce over steaks. Serve.

THE ITALIAN AMERICAN KITCHEN
Anchovies

Anchovies are a test kitchen favorite, capable of building meaty, savory flavors in countless stews, soups, and sauces. They don't make dishes like steak pizzaiola taste fishy. Rather, all the umami-producing compounds in the little fish make things taste beefier. Trust us. All preserved anchovies have been cured in salt, but they come to the market in two forms: packed in olive oil or in salt. The salt-packed variety is less processed, having only the heads and some entrails removed, leaving the filleting and rinsing to the home cook. Oil-packed anchovies have been filleted at the factory and are ready to use. Our favorite anchovies are **King Oscar Anchovies Flat Fillets in Olive Oil,** which have a firm, meaty texture and pleasantly briny, savory flavor.

FLANK STEAK PEPERONATA

Serves 4 to 6

Why This Recipe Works *Peperonata* is an Italian condiment of sweet peppers stewed in olive oil with onion, tomato, wine or vinegar, and garlic until the peppers are soft and the flavors have melded—think roasted red peppers without the char. Its sweet, earthy flavor and smooth texture make it good hot, cold, or at room temperature. You'll find it on Italian American tables alongside meats, fish, and eggs; on salads and sandwiches; or as part of antipasti platters. It's also an easy way to dress up a simple steak. For our recipe, we started by cutting flank steak with the grain into three equal pieces, seasoning all sides with salt and oregano, and wrapping the pieces in plastic and refrigerating them so the salt can work its magic. Meanwhile, we cooked bell peppers (sliced thin for easy eating), onion, and garlic in a hefty amount of extra-virgin olive oil until softened; added diced tomatoes, capers, and red pepper flakes; and cooked the mixture until the vegetables were softened. After wiping out the skillet, we seared the seasoned steak pieces on all sides to a perfect medium-rare. While the meat rested, we stirred fresh basil into the peperonata mixture. To serve, we sliced the meat into smaller pieces against the grain, seasoned the slices with salt and pepper and the accumulated meat juices, and arranged the meat with the peperonata. A final drizzle of olive oil balanced the tangy, meaty flavors. You must salt the meat for at least 30 minutes or up to 24 hours before making this dish.

- 2 teaspoons dried oregano
- 1½ teaspoons table salt, divided
- 1 (1½-pound) flank steak, trimmed
- ⅓ cup plus 1 tablespoon extra-virgin olive oil, divided, plus extra for serving
- 4 red or yellow bell peppers (or a mix), quartered, stemmed, seeded, and cut crosswise into ¼-inch-wide strips
- 1 onion, quartered through root end and sliced crosswise into ¼-inch-wide strips
- 6 garlic cloves, lightly crushed and peeled
- 1 (14.5-ounce) can diced tomatoes
- 2 tablespoons capers, plus 4 teaspoons caper brine
- ⅛ teaspoon red pepper flakes
- ½ cup chopped fresh basil

1. Combine oregano and 1 teaspoon salt in bowl. Cut steak with grain into 3 equal pieces. Sprinkle steak with oregano mixture, wrap tightly in plastic wrap, and refrigerate for at least 30 minutes or up to 24 hours.

2. Heat ⅓ cup oil in 12-inch nonstick skillet over medium-high heat until just smoking. Add bell peppers, onion, garlic, and remaining ½ teaspoon salt. Cover and cook, stirring occasionally, until vegetables are soft, about 10 minutes.

3. Stir in tomatoes and their juice, capers and brine, and pepper flakes and cook, uncovered, until slightly thickened, about 5 minutes. Season with salt and pepper to taste. Transfer peperonata to bowl, cover, and keep warm.

4. Wipe skillet clean with paper towels. Pat steaks dry with paper towels and season with pepper. Heat remaining 1 tablespoon oil in now-empty skillet over medium-high heat until just smoking. Cook steaks until well browned and meat registers 120 to 125 degrees (for medium-rare), 5 to 7 minutes per side. Transfer steaks to carving board, tent loosely with aluminum foil, and let rest for 10 minutes.

5. Stir basil into peperonata. Slice steaks thin against grain on bias. Season steak slices with salt and pepper to taste and drizzle with extra oil. Serve steak with peperonata.

Diced Tomatoes

Supermarket shelves are teeming with different diced tomato products, and in recent years most manufacturers have come out with "petite diced" versions as well. To make sense of the growing selection, we gathered 16 widely available samples and 21 staff members. There was only one way to begin identifying the best: Open the cans, pass around some spoons, and hold a blind tasting of plain, unheated tomatoes. When the products were sampled this way, their potential flaws had no place to hide. To our surprise, nearly half of the products fell short. The lowest-rated tomatoes were flat-out awful, eliciting slams like "mushy, gruel-like texture" and "tastes like wet socks." Although we asked our tasters to consider a range of factors (natural sweetness and texture, for example), their primary criterion for loving—or loathing— a tomato was freshness of flavor. "Nothing tinny here," wrote a taster about their favorite tomato in this round. Our winner, **Hunt's Diced Tomatoes,** boasted a balance of sweet and tart, along with a "beautiful" firm-ripe texture.

STEAK MODIGA

Serves 4

Why This Recipe Works Visit the Italian neighborhood known as The Hill in St. Louis, and you'll find steak modiga on many restaurant menus. What is it? A steak (usually strip or filet mignon) that's piled with seasoned bread crumbs and grilled or broiled until juicy inside and crunchy on top. It's served with a buttery white wine and mushroom sauce enriched with a local specialty: salty, smoky Provel cheese. We had trouble getting the crumbs to stay put when we tried recipes that employed the grill, the broiler, or a grill pan. Instead, we brushed the steaks with olive oil and then pressed the seasoned crumbs onto one side. We then seared the steaks on both sides, starting with the breaded side, in a nonstick skillet. Since the searing didn't fully cook the steaks, we transferred them (breaded side up) to a wire rack set in a rimmed baking sheet and finished them in a 400-degree oven, which took about 5 minutes. After a few tests, we learned that letting the raw, breaded steaks rest for just 5 minutes before searing gave the crumb coating a chance to set up and stick better. Since Provel cheese is not widely available outside of St. Louis, we tested American, cheddar, Swiss, and provolone, with the latter winning out for its mild tang and smooth melting. Note that only one side of each steak is coated with bread crumbs; the other sides remain bare.

- 4 (10- to 12-ounce) boneless strip steaks, about 1 inch thick, trimmed
- 2¾ teaspoons table salt, divided
- 2 teaspoons pepper, divided
- 1 tablespoon unsalted butter
- 8 ounces white mushrooms, trimmed and sliced thin
- ¼ cup dry white wine
- 1 tablespoon all-purpose flour
- 4 garlic cloves, minced, divided
- 1 cup chicken broth
- ¼ cup heavy cream
- ¼ cup plus 1 teaspoon extra-virgin olive oil, divided
- 1 cup panko bread crumbs
- ¼ cup chopped fresh parsley, divided
- 2 slices deli provolone cheese (2 ounces), torn into 1-inch pieces

1. Adjust oven rack to middle position and heat oven to 400 degrees. Set wire rack in rimmed baking sheet. Pat steaks dry with paper towels and season with 1½ teaspoons salt and ¾ teaspoon pepper; set aside.

2. Melt butter in large saucepan over medium-high heat. Add mushrooms, ½ teaspoon salt, and ½ teaspoon pepper and cook until liquid has evaporated and mushrooms begin to brown, 5 to 7 minutes. Add wine and cook until evaporated, about 3 minutes.

3. Stir in flour and half of garlic and cook until mushrooms are well coated and garlic is fragrant, about 1 minute. Stir in broth and cream, scraping up any browned bits. Bring to boil and cook until slightly thickened, about 3 minutes. Remove from heat, cover, and keep warm.

4. Pour ¼ cup oil into shallow dish. Process panko in food processor until finely ground, about 10 seconds. Combine ground panko, 3 tablespoons parsley, remaining garlic, remaining ¾ teaspoon salt, and remaining ¾ teaspoon pepper in second shallow dish.

5. Working with 1 steak at a time, add to oil and turn to coat on all sides. Transfer oiled steak to panko mixture and press firmly to coat only 1 side of steak with mixture. Transfer steak, breaded side up, to prepared wire rack. Let stand for 5 minutes.

6. Heat remaining 1 teaspoon oil in 12-inch nonstick skillet over medium-high heat until shimmering. Place steaks in skillet, breaded side down, and cook until well browned, about 3 minutes. Flip steaks and continue to cook until well browned on second side, about 3 minutes. Return steaks to wire rack, breaded side up.

7. Transfer to the oven and roast until meat registers 120 to 125 degrees (for medium-rare), 4 to 7 minutes. Let steaks cool on wire rack for 5 minutes while finishing sauce.

8. Return sauce to simmer over medium heat. Whisk in provolone until melted, about 1 minute. Serve steaks with sauce, sprinkled with remaining 1 tablespoon parsley.

GRILLED STUFFED FLANK STEAK

Serves 4 to 6

Why This Recipe Works While spirals of flank steak stuffed with Italian ingredients may look nice in the butcher case, the meat buckles when cooked, forcing the filling to escape. To avoid this problem, we butterflied and pounded the steak for the flattest and widest surface possible. As for the filling, the combo of prosciutto and provolone won raves for its salty savor and the way the dry cheese melted inside the pinwheel yet turned crisp where exposed to the grill. To prevent the meat from shrinking on the grill and squeezing the centers of the pinwheels, we rolled up our flank steak, tied it with kitchen twine, and skewered it at 1-inch intervals before slicing and grilling it. The twine kept the steak from unraveling, while the skewers prevented the meat from shrinking. Look for a flank steak measuring approximately 8 by 6 inches, with the grain running the long way. Freezing the steak for 30 minutes will make butterflying easier. Depending on the steak's size, you may have more or less than 8 slices of meat at the end of step 2.

- 2 garlic cloves, minced
- 1 small shallot, minced
- 2 tablespoons minced fresh parsley
- 1 teaspoon minced fresh sage
- 2 tablespoons extra-virgin olive oil
- 1 (2- to 2½-pound) flank steak
- 4 ounces thinly sliced prosciutto
- 4 ounces thinly sliced provolone
- 1 teaspoon table salt
- ½ teaspoon pepper
- 8–12 wooden skewers soaked in water for 30 minutes

1. Combine garlic, shallot, parsley, sage, and oil in small bowl. Lay steak on cutting board with grain running parallel to counter edge. Cut horizontally through meat, leaving ½-inch "hinge" along far edge. Open up steak, cover with plastic wrap, and pound into rough rectangle, trimming any ragged edges.

With steak still positioned so that grain runs parallel to edge of counter, spread herb mixture evenly over surface. Lay prosciutto evenly over steak, leaving 2-inch border along top edge. Cover prosciutto with even layer of cheese, leaving 2-inch border along top edge. Starting from bottom edge and rolling away from you, roll beef into tight log and place on cutting board seam-side down.

2. Starting ½ inch from end of rolled steak, evenly space eight to twelve 14-inch pieces of kitchen twine at 1-inch intervals underneath steak. Tie middle string first; then working from outermost strings toward center, tightly tie roll. Roll tied steak 90 degrees so seam is facing you. Skewer beef directly through outermost flap of steak near seam through each piece of string, allowing skewer to extend ½ inch on opposite side. Using chef's knife, slice roll between pieces of twine into 1-inch-thick pinwheels. Season pinwheels with salt and pepper.

3A. **For a charcoal grill** Light large chimney starter nearly full with charcoal (5 quarts); allow to burn until coals are fully ignited and partially covered with thin layer of ash, about 20 minutes. Build modified two-level fire by arranging all coals over half of grill, leaving other half empty. Position cooking grate over coals, cover grill, and heat grill until hot, about 5 minutes.

3B. **For a gas grill** Turn all burners to high and heat with lid down until very hot, about 15 minutes. Leave primary burner on high and turn off other burner(s).

4. Clean and oil cooking grate. Grill pinwheels directly over hot side of grill until well browned, 3 to 6 minutes. Using tongs, flip pinwheels; grill until second side is well browned, 3 to 5 minutes. Transfer pinwheels to cooler side of grill, cover, and continue to cook until center of pinwheels registers 125 degrees, 1 to 4 minutes (slightly thinner pinwheels may not need time on cooler side of grill). Transfer pinwheels to plate, tent loosely with foil, and let rest 5 minutes. Discard skewers and twine and serve immediately.

Provolone

Provolone, a cow's-milk cheese originally from Italy, is made in two styles. The semifirm mild version is widely available and is usually sold sliced. These sliced cheeses are typically made domestically. There is also a firm, aged style that is salty, nutty, and spicy, with a light caramel sweetness. The latter, imported from Italy and sold in wedges, makes a nice addition to any cheese platter. We tasted five leading brands of sliced provolone and found minimal differences among them. All were fairly consistent in their mild flavor and soft texture regardless of brand. Any of them will work fine in this recipe or sandwiches.

PORK MILANESE

Serves 4

Why This Recipe Works In Italian American restaurants, chicken, pork, or veal cutlets that are served Milanese-style are generally floured, coated with bread crumbs, and then fried until the crumbs are crispy and golden brown. The test kitchen's tried-and-true method for breading cutlets begins with a dredge in flour and a dunk in lightly beaten eggs before coating with bread crumbs that have been seasoned with salt and pepper. We then shallow-fry the cutlets in a bit of oil until they're golden brown. For our pork Milanese recipe, we added parsley, lemon zest, and Parmesan cheese to the bread-crumb mixture to give our cutlets freshness, brightness, and a bit of that unmistakable Parmesan savoriness. We wanted pork that was easy to cut through, not the tough and leathery cutlets we have encountered so often in restaurants. After trying pounded pork chops and pork loin, we found a winner: pork tenderloin, cut into four pieces and pounded thin. The cutlets were easy to work with, handled the breading and pan-frying well, and cooked up tender. Since we couldn't fit all four pieces of tenderloin in a 12-inch skillet at once, we worked in batches and relied on a low 200-degree oven to keep the cooked pork warm. Traditionally, pork Milanese is served with a dressed arugula salad topped with a handful of shaved Parmesan. We followed suit, tossing a bowlful of baby arugula with a vibrant lemon vinaigrette and sprinkling the salad with some shaved Parmesan. You can serve the cutlets with pasta or potatoes if you prefer.

- 1 tablespoon plus 1 cup extra-virgin olive oil, divided
- ½ teaspoon grated lemon zest plus 2 teaspoons juice, plus lemon wedges for serving
- ¾ teaspoon table salt, divided
- 1 teaspoon pepper, divided
- 1 (12- to 16-ounce) pork tenderloin, trimmed
- ½ cup all-purpose flour
- 2 large eggs
- 1 cup panko bread crumbs
- ¼ cup grated Parmesan cheese, plus 1 ounce shaved with vegetable peeler
- 2 tablespoons chopped fresh parsley
- 4 ounces (4 cups) baby arugula

1. Adjust oven rack to lower-middle position and heat oven to 200 degrees. Whisk 1 tablespoon oil, lemon juice, ¼ teaspoon salt, and ¼ teaspoon pepper together in bowl; set dressing aside.

2. Cut tenderloin crosswise into 4 equal pieces. Stand pieces cut side up on cutting board, cover with plastic wrap, and pound with meat pounder to even ¼-inch thickness. Pat cutlets dry with paper towels and season with ¼ teaspoon pepper.

3. Place flour in shallow dish. Lightly beat eggs in second shallow dish. Combine panko, grated Parmesan, parsley, lemon zest, remaining ½ teaspoon salt, and remaining ½ teaspoon pepper in third shallow dish.

4. Working with 1 cutlet at a time, dredge cutlets in flour, shaking off excess; dip in eggs, allowing excess to drip off; and coat with panko mixture, pressing gently to adhere. Transfer to large plate. (Cutlets can be wrapped in plastic and refrigerated for up to 2 hours before frying.)

5. Set wire rack in rimmed baking sheet. Line large plate with triple layer of paper towels. Heat remaining 1 cup oil in 12-inch nonstick skillet over medium-high heat until shimmering. Place 2 cutlets in skillet and cook until deep golden brown and cooked through, 2 to 3 minutes per side, gently pressing on cutlets with spatula to ensure even browning.

6. Transfer cutlets to prepared plate and let drain on each side for 15 seconds, then transfer to prepared rack and place rack in oven to keep cutlets warm. Repeat with remaining 2 cutlets.

7. Just before serving, gently toss arugula with shaved Parmesan and dressing. Serve pork with salad, passing lemon wedges separately.

PORK CHOPS WITH VINEGAR PEPPERS

Serves 4

Why This Recipe Works Thick, meaty chops braised with vinegar peppers have been an Italian American restaurant favorite for decades. Slow braising creates lots of flavor, but it also dries out lean pork chops. For the flavor of a long-cooked dish in less time, we fortify our tangy vinegar sauce with anchovies, rosemary, onions, garlic, and chicken broth. We opt for thick rib chops instead of leaner center-cut chops. We brine them for seasoning and juiciness and then coat them with flour to promote flavorful browning. We browned the chops on just one side and then were careful to keep the nicely browned side above the braising liquid. Once the chops were cooked, we set them aside on a plate and reduced the sauce. A few extra minutes of simmering thickened the sauce, and a pat of butter swirled in at the end made it rich and silky.

- 3 tablespoons sugar
- 3 tablespoons table salt, for brining
- 4 (8- to 10-ounce) bone-in pork rib chops, 1 inch thick, trimmed
- 1/3 cup all-purpose flour
- 3/4 teaspoon pepper
- 2 tablespoons extra-virgin olive oil, divided
- 1 onion, halved and sliced thin
- 8 garlic cloves, lightly crushed and peeled
- 2 anchovy fillets, rinsed, patted dry, and minced
- 2 cups thinly sliced sweet green vinegar peppers
- 1 sprig fresh rosemary
- 1 cup chicken broth
- 1/2 cup red wine vinegar
- 1 tablespoon unsalted butter

1. Dissolve sugar and salt in 1½ quarts cold water in large container. Add chops, cover, and refrigerate for 30 minutes or up to 1 hour.

2. Place flour in shallow dish. Remove chops from brine. Pat chops dry with paper towels and season with pepper. Working with 1 chop at a time, dredge both sides in flour, shaking off excess. Heat 1 tablespoon oil in 12-inch skillet over medium-high heat until just smoking. Add chops and cook until well browned on first side, 5 to 7 minutes. Flip chops and cook on second side for 1 minute; transfer to plate, browned side up.

3. Reduce heat to medium and add remaining 1 tablespoon oil, onion, garlic, and anchovies to now-empty skillet. Cook, stirring frequently, until onion is softened and golden brown, 6 to 8 minutes. Add peppers and rosemary and cook until peppers begin to caramelize, about 5 minutes. Add broth and vinegar and bring to boil.

4. Arrange chops, browned side up, in skillet and add any accumulated juices from plate. Reduce heat to low, cover, and simmer until chops register 145 degrees, 6 to 10 minutes. Transfer chops to serving platter and tent loosely with aluminum foil.

5. Increase heat to high and boil sauce until slightly thickened, about 3 minutes. Off heat, stir in butter and season with salt and pepper to taste. Stir any accumulated juices from platter into sauce. Discard rosemary and spoon sauce over chops. Serve.

ONE-PAN SWEET ITALIAN SAUSAGE WITH POLENTA

Serves 4

Why This Recipe Works It's hard to imagine a more comforting wintertime supper than flavorful sausages and peppers resting atop a scoop of soft, creamy cornmeal polenta. But this Italian American classic often ends with a sink full of pots and pans. We set out to rewrite that ending with a simple one-pan recipe designed for the skillet. Our first decision: We turned to instant polenta—already cooked and dried—because it needed only to be whisked into hot liquid to turn into a savory porridge. We typically don't recommend this product, but in the name of speed it can't be beat; plus, all the big flavors in this dish will compensate for the mild flavor of the instant polenta. First we lightly browned sliced onion, red bell pepper, and fennel and transferred them to a plate. After adding milk (for extra flavor) and water to the now-empty skillet and bringing it to a boil, we whisked in the polenta along with butter and Parmesan cheese to add richness. We then topped the mixture with the partially cooked vegetables and raw sausages and slid the skillet into the oven to finish cooking and brown the sausages. Since the vegetables left flavorful browning on the bottom of the skillet, which then released into the polenta cooking liquid and turned it grayish-brown, we switched to a nonstick skillet so that the bits stayed on the vegetables rather than in the pan. But while the hot 450-degree oven browned the raw sausages nicely, it was too much heat for the skillet's silicone handle. The solution? A tried-and-true test kitchen trick: Wrapped in a double layer of wet paper towels and a double layer of aluminum foil, the handle is protected from the oven's intense heat. Good-quality Parmesan cheese makes a difference here.

2 tablespoons extra-virgin olive oil

1 red bell pepper, stemmed, seeded, and sliced thin

1 onion, halved and sliced thin

1 fennel bulb, stalks discarded, bulb halved, cored, and sliced thin

3 garlic cloves, minced

1¾ teaspoons table salt, divided

½ teaspoon pepper, divided

¼ teaspoon red pepper flakes

1½ cups whole milk

1½ cups water

¾ cup instant polenta

2 ounces Parmesan cheese, grated (1 cup)

4 tablespoons unsalted butter

1 pound sweet Italian sausage

1 tablespoon minced fresh parsley

1. Adjust oven rack to upper-middle position and heat oven to 450 degrees. Heat oil in 12-inch nonstick skillet over medium-high heat until shimmering. Add bell pepper, onion, fennel, garlic, ¾ teaspoon salt, ¼ teaspoon pepper, and pepper flakes and cook until vegetables are softened and browned, about 10 minutes, stirring occasionally. Transfer to bowl.

2. Add milk, water, remaining 1 teaspoon salt, and remaining ¼ teaspoon pepper to now-empty skillet and bring to boil over high heat. Whisking constantly, slowly add polenta. Reduce heat to low and cook, whisking constantly, until polenta thickens and whisk leaves distinct trail, about 2 minutes.

3. Off heat, whisk in Parmesan and butter until incorporated. Distribute vegetable mixture over polenta, then evenly space sausages on top of vegetables. Transfer to oven and bake until sausages are browned and register at least 160 degrees, about 25 minutes. Let rest for 10 minutes. Sprinkle with parsley and serve.

SHRIMP SCAMPI

Serves 4

Why This Recipe Works In many Italian American restaurants, this shrimp dish is the most popular item on the menu. And with good reason—it boasts briny shrimp, tangy lemon, sweet butter, and rich garlic flavor. But often the sauce breaks (and seems greasy) and most renditions are light on shrimp flavor. Our shrimp scampi recipe uses a few test kitchen tricks to ensure flavorful and well-cooked shrimp along with a cohesive, garlicky wine-and-butter sauce. First, we quickly brine the shrimp in salt and sugar to season them throughout and keep them moist and juicy. Then we poach rather than sauté them, so they cook evenly and gently. To get good seafood flavor into the sauce, we make a stock from the shrimp shells and wine (this also served as our poaching liquid). And for potent garlic flavor, we use a generous amount of sliced garlic—too much minced garlic made the sauce grainy. Finally, to keep the sauce silky and emulsified, we add a teaspoon of cornstarch. Emulsifying with cornstarch meant that we could use a little less butter, so the sauce wasn't overly rich. Extra-large shrimp (21 to 25 per pound) can be substituted for jumbo shrimp. If you use them, reduce the cooking time in step 3 by 1 to 2 minutes. Many manufacturers add salt or sodium tripolyphosphate to shrimp to prevent darkening or water loss, but we found that these treatments made the shellfish watery and bland; the latter also produced a chemical taste. When buying frozen shrimp, look for a brand with "shrimp" as the only ingredient listed on the bag. If you can only find shrimp that have been treated with sodium or preservatives, skip the brining in step 1 and add ¼ teaspoon table salt to the sauce in step 4. We think scampi is best served with crusty bread rather than pasta.

3 tablespoons table salt, for brining

2 tablespoons sugar

1½ pounds shell-on jumbo shrimp (16 to 20 per pound), peeled, deveined, and tails removed, shells reserved

2 tablespoons extra-virgin olive oil, divided

1 cup dry white wine

4 sprigs fresh thyme

3 tablespoons lemon juice, plus lemon wedges for serving

1 teaspoon cornstarch

8 garlic cloves, sliced thin

½ teaspoon red pepper flakes

¼ teaspoon pepper

4 tablespoons unsalted butter, cut into ½-inch pieces

1 tablespoon chopped fresh parsley

1. Dissolve salt and sugar in 1 quart cold water in large container. Submerge shrimp in brine, cover, and refrigerate for 15 minutes. Remove shrimp from brine and pat dry with paper towels.

2. Heat 1 tablespoon oil in 12-inch skillet over high heat until shimmering. Add shrimp shells and cook, stirring frequently, until they begin to turn spotty brown and skillet starts to brown, 2 to 4 minutes. Off heat, carefully add wine and thyme sprigs. When bubbling subsides, return skillet to medium heat and simmer gently, stirring occasionally, for 5 minutes. Strain mixture through colander set over large bowl. Discard shells and reserve liquid (you should have about ⅔ cup). Wipe skillet clean with paper towels.

3. Combine lemon juice and cornstarch in small bowl and set aside. Heat remaining 1 tablespoon oil, garlic, pepper flakes, and pepper in now-empty skillet over medium-low heat, stirring occasionally, until garlic is fragrant and just beginning to brown at edges, 3 to 5 minutes. Add reserved wine mixture, increase heat to high, and bring to simmer. Reduce heat to medium, add shrimp, cover, and cook, stirring occasionally, until shrimp are just opaque, 5 to 7 minutes. Remove skillet from heat and, using slotted spoon, transfer shrimp to bowl.

4. Return skillet to medium heat, add lemon juice–cornstarch mixture, and cook until slightly thickened, 1 minute. Off heat, whisk in butter and parsley until combined. Return shrimp and any accumulated juices to skillet and toss to combine. Serve, passing lemon wedges separately.

SHRIMP FRA DIAVOLO

Serves 4

Why This Recipe Works Shrimp fra diavolo is a classic 20th-century Italian American combo of shrimp, tomatoes, garlic, and hot pepper, often served over spaghetti or with crusty bread. At its best, it's lively and piquant, the tangy tomatoes countering the sweet and briny shrimp, and the pepper and garlic providing a spirited kick. Unfortunately, the spice is often used so heavy-handedly that it completely overwhelms the other flavors, and the fragile shrimp are often over-cooked and flavorless, identifiable only by their shape. We wanted to preserve the fiery character of fra diavolo but also heighten the other flavors—particularly the brininess of the shrimp—so that they could stand up to the heat. To build a rich, briny seafood base, we borrowed a technique from shrimp bisque: sautéing the shrimp shells in a little oil until they and the surface of the pan were spotty brown, then deglazing the pan with wine to pick up the flavorful fond. Some canned tomato liquid rounded out our shrimp stock. To bloom the flavors of our aromatics, we sautéed some garlic, red pepper flakes, oregano, and a couple of anchovy fillets for extra savory (but not fishy) seafood flavor. We added our stock back to the aromatics and used this flavorful sauce to gently poach the shrimp. At the end of cooking, we stirred in some minced pepperoncini and their brine for a boost of tangy heat. Handfuls of chopped basil and parsley lent freshness, and a drizzle of fruity extra-virgin olive oil made for a rich finish. If the shrimp you are using have been treated with salt (check the bag's ingredient list), skip the salting in step 1 and add ¼ teaspoon table salt to the sauce in step 3. Adjust the amount of pepper flakes depending on how spicy you want the dish. Serve the shrimp with a salad and crusty bread or over spaghetti. If serving with spaghetti, adjust the consistency of the sauce with some reserved pasta cooking water.

- 1½ pounds shell-on large shrimp (26 to 30 per pound), peeled, deveined, and tails removed, shells reserved
- ½ teaspoon table salt
- 1 (28-ounce) can whole peeled tomatoes
- 3 tablespoons vegetable oil, divided
- 1 cup dry white wine
- 4 garlic cloves, minced
- ½–1 teaspoon red pepper flakes
- ½ teaspoon dried oregano
- 2 anchovy fillets, rinsed, patted dry, and minced
- ¼ cup chopped fresh basil
- ¼ cup chopped fresh parsley
- 1½ teaspoons minced pepperoncini, plus 1 teaspoon brine
- 2 tablespoons extra-virgin olive oil

1. Toss shrimp with salt and set aside. Pour tomatoes into colander set over large bowl. Pierce tomatoes with edge of rubber spatula and stir briefly to release juice. Transfer drained tomatoes to small bowl and reserve juice. Do not wash colander.

2. Heat 1 tablespoon vegetable oil in 12-inch skillet over high heat until shimmering. Add shrimp shells and cook, stirring frequently, until they begin to turn spotty brown and skillet starts to brown, 2 to 4 minutes. Remove skillet from heat and carefully add wine. When bubbling subsides, return skillet to heat and simmer until wine is reduced to about 2 tablespoons, 2 to 4 minutes. Add reserved tomato juice and simmer to meld flavors, 5 minutes. Pour contents of skillet into colander set over bowl. Discard shells and reserve liquid. Wipe out skillet with paper towels.

3. Heat remaining 2 tablespoons vegetable oil, garlic, pepper flakes, and oregano in now-empty skillet over medium heat, stirring occasionally, until garlic is straw-colored and fragrant, 1 to 2 minutes. Add anchovies and stir until fragrant, about 30 seconds. Remove from heat. Add drained tomatoes and mash with potato masher until coarsely pureed. Return to heat and stir in reserved tomato juice mixture. Increase heat to medium-high and simmer until mixture has thickened, about 5 minutes.

4. Add shrimp to skillet and simmer gently, stirring and turning shrimp frequently, until they are just cooked through, 4 to 5 minutes. Remove pan from heat. Stir in basil, parsley, and pepperoncini and brine and season with salt to taste. Drizzle with olive oil and serve.

SUNDAY SUPPERS AND CELEBRATIONS

CHICAGO-STYLE ITALIAN ROAST BEEF

Serves 8

Why This Recipe Works Ask a Chicago native living elsewhere in the country what they miss most about their home city and it's a good bet the list will include spicy Italian beef. Unlike deep-dish pizza, this local favorite is almost impossible to find outside the Chicago city limits. The bold roast beef relies on strong herb flavors, usually achieved with a marinade. In Chicago, meat prepared this way is served with a spicy jus. To build flavor in our version without inhibiting browning, we turned to a spicy rub rather than a marinade. Before cooking, we salted the meat and let it sit for at least an hour, which helped season it through and through and keep it moist. We seared the salted roast in a skillet to jump-start browning and build a flavorful crust; we then made a rich base for the jus by cooking onion, garlic, flour, and some of our spice rub in the roast's rendered fat. With our roast elevated in a V-rack, we poured the jus into the roasting pan below. Next, we rubbed the meat with a flavorful blend of garlic powder, dried basil and oregano, black pepper, red pepper flakes, and oil. As the meat roasted in the oven, its drippings landed right in the jus, reinforcing its meaty flavor, and the jus was done at exactly the same time as the roast, with no need for last-minute fuss. This recipe requires refrigerating the salted beef for at least 1 hour or up to 24 hours before cooking (a longer time is preferable). Save leftover meat and jus for sandwiches (page 42) the next day. In fact, many Chicago natives will tell you the reason to make this roast is to have leftovers for sandwiches.

4 teaspoons kosher salt

1 (4-pound) center-cut boneless top sirloin roast, fat trimmed to ¼ inch and tied at 1½-inch intervals

4 teaspoons garlic powder

4 teaspoons dried basil

4 teaspoons dried oregano

1 tablespoon pepper

2 tablespoons vegetable oil, divided

1 onion, chopped fine

3 garlic cloves, minced

1 tablespoon all-purpose flour

2 cups beef broth

2 cups chicken broth

1½ cups water

1 teaspoon red pepper flakes

1. Rub salt on roast and refrigerate, uncovered, for at least 1 hour or up to 24 hours.

2. Adjust oven rack to lower-middle position and heat oven to 300 degrees. Set V-rack in large roasting pan and spray with vegetable oil spray. Combine garlic powder, basil, oregano, and pepper in small bowl; set aside.

3. Pat roast dry with paper towels. Heat 1 tablespoon oil in 12-inch skillet over medium-high heat until just smoking. Brown roast on all sides, 8 to 12 minutes; transfer to prepared V-rack.

4. Add onion to fat left in skillet and cook over medium heat until softened, about 5 minutes. Stir in garlic, flour, and 1 teaspoon spice mixture and cook until fragrant, about 1 minute. Whisk in beef broth, chicken broth, and water, scraping up any browned bits and smoothing out any lumps. Bring mixture to boil, then pour into roasting pan.

5. Stir pepper flakes and remaining 1 tablespoon oil into remaining spice mixture. Rub mixture all over roast and set in rack, fat side up, Transfer pan to oven and roast until beef registers 120 to 125 degrees (for medium-rare), 1¼ to 1½ hours. Transfer roast to carving board and let rest for 20 minutes.

6. Strain jus from roasting pan through fine-mesh strainer into bowl and keep warm. Remove twine and slice roast into ¼-inch-thick slices. Serve with jus.

BRACIOLE

Serves 4 to 6

Why This Recipe Works If you grew up in an Italian American household—especially if your relatives came from southern Italy—you know braciole (pronounced "brah-ZHUL"). You most likely ate it for supper as part of "Sunday gravy," a long-simmered tomato sauce that's also packed with meatballs and sausage. If you're not familiar with this dish, you're in for a real treat. The basic description—rolled, stuffed beef that is browned and simmered in tomato sauce—doesn't do justice to its savory deliciousness. But what cut of beef to use? What to stuff it with? How to develop the flavor yet minimize the work? These were just a few of the questions we explored. For our take on this Italian American Sunday supper, we found flank steak had the beefiest flavor. Bread-based fillings were stodgy, so we went with a simple mixture of sweet raisins, fresh parsley and basil, and savory Parmesan cheese. Brushing the meat with oil before applying the filling helped it stay put while we rolled up the braciole. First infusing the oil with garlic in the microwave added another layer of flavor. A quick sear prevented the meat from toughening, and a long braise in an easy-to-prepare sauce kept it flavorful and tender. Some supermarkets sell meat labeled specifically for braciole, but we recommend buying flank steak and trimming it yourself. Look for flank steak of even thickness, without tapered ends. Braciole is usually served with pasta, sometimes together and sometimes separately, as when a pasta course with the sauce is followed by the meat. Our recipe makes enough sauce for at least 1 pound of pasta. We like to serve our braciole with spaghetti or penne.

1 (2-pound) flank steak, trimmed

¼ cup extra-virgin olive oil

10 garlic cloves, sliced thin

½ cup golden raisins, chopped coarse

1 ounce Parmesan cheese, grated (½ cup), plus extra for serving

½ cup chopped fresh basil, divided

¼ cup chopped fresh parsley

1 teaspoon dried oregano, divided

½ teaspoon red pepper flakes, divided

¾ teaspoon pepper

½ teaspoon table salt

1 onion, chopped

3 tablespoons tomato paste

2 (28-ounce) cans crushed tomatoes

1. Adjust oven rack to middle position and heat oven to 325 degrees. Position steak on cutting board so long edge is parallel to counter edge. Using meat pounder, gently pound steak between 2 pieces of plastic wrap to even ½-inch thickness. Trim any ragged edges to create rough rectangle about 11 by 9 inches. Pat steak dry with paper towels.

2. Combine oil and garlic in bowl and microwave until fragrant, about 1 minute. Let cool slightly, then remove garlic from oil with fork. Separately reserve garlic and garlic oil. Combine raisins, Parmesan, ¼ cup basil, parsley, ½ teaspoon oregano, ¼ teaspoon pepper flakes, and half of garlic in bowl.

3. Brush exposed side of steak with 1 tablespoon garlic oil and season with pepper and salt. Spread raisin mixture evenly over steak, pressing to adhere, leaving 1-inch border along top edge. Starting from bottom edge and rolling away from you, roll steak into tight log, finally resting it seam side down. Tie kitchen twine around braciole at 1-inch intervals.

4. Heat 1 tablespoon garlic oil in 12-inch nonstick skillet over medium-high heat until just smoking. Add braciole, seam side down, and cook until lightly browned all over, about 5 minutes. Transfer to 13 by 9-inch baking dish.

5. Reduce heat to medium and add onion, remaining garlic oil, remaining ½ teaspoon oregano, and remaining ¼ teaspoon pepper flakes to now-empty skillet. Cook until onion just begins to soften, about 3 minutes. Stir in tomato paste and remaining garlic and cook until fragrant and tomato paste is lightly browned, about 1 minute. Stir in tomatoes and bring to simmer. Pour sauce over braciole and cover dish tightly with aluminum foil. Bake until fork slips easily in and out of braciole, 1½ to 1¾ hours. Transfer dish to wire rack, spoon sauce over braciole, re-cover, and let rest in sauce for 30 minutes.

6. Transfer braciole to carving board, seam side down. Discard twine and slice braciole ¾ inch thick. Stir remaining ¼ cup basil into sauce and season with salt and pepper to taste. Ladle 2 cups sauce onto serving platter. Transfer braciole slices to platter. Serve, passing remaining sauce and extra Parmesan separately.

TO MAKE AHEAD
Follow recipe through step 5, letting braciole cool completely in sauce. Refrigerate braciole and sauce separately. To serve, adjust oven rack to middle position and heat oven to 350 degrees. Bring sauce to simmer in large saucepan over medium heat. Stir remaining ¼ cup basil into sauce; season with salt and pepper to taste. Transfer braciole to carving board, seam side down; discard twine and slice braciole ¾ inch thick. Pour 2 cups sauce into 13 by 9-inch baking dish and arrange braciole slices on top of sauce. Cover dish tightly with aluminum foil and bake until meat is heated through, about 15 minutes. Serve, passing remaining sauce separately.

HEARTY BEEF LASAGNA

Serves 10 to 12

Why This Recipe Works There are many variations on lasagna, but we think the ultimate version features meat sauce (similar to Bolognese) and a rich béchamel sauce rather than ricotta cheese. Lasagna is always a project, and making a béchamel sauce makes it even more laborious. We found a perfect middle ground: a no-cook cream sauce using heavy cream and cottage cheese as the base. Grated Pecorino Romano cheese, which is bolder than Parmesan, and a bit of cornstarch thickened the sauce. Since the sauce cooks in the oven as the lasagna bakes, we were able to skip the simmer on the stovetop. As for the tomato-meat sauce, we amped up the meatiness by using 1½ pounds of beef and just one can of tomatoes—a much higher meat-to-tomato ratio than usual. But because of its increased presence, the beef's tendency to turn dry and pebbly was amplified. To ensure a more pleasant consistency, we stole a trick from our favorite meatball recipes and added a panade—a mixture of bread and milk—to the beef. Since the meat sauce in the assembled lasagna continues to cook for nearly an hour in the oven, we found it possible to slash the stovetop cooking time to just 15 minutes. We developed this recipe using dried curly-edged lasagna noodles; do not use no-boil noodles. There are about 20 individual noodles in a 1-pound box of lasagna noodles, enough for this recipe.

Lasagna

- 17 curly-edged lasagna noodles
- 1 tablespoon table salt
- 12 ounces mozzarella cheese, shredded (3 cups)
- ¼ cup grated Pecorino Romano cheese

Meat Sauce

- 2 slices hearty white sandwich bread, torn into small pieces
- ¼ cup milk
- 1½ pounds 90 percent lean ground beef
- ¾ teaspoon table salt
- ½ teaspoon pepper
- 1 tablespoon extra-virgin olive oil
- 1 onion, chopped fine

- 6 garlic cloves, minced
- 1 teaspoon dried oregano
- ¼ teaspoon red pepper flakes
- 1 (28-ounce) can crushed tomatoes

Cream Sauce

- 8 ounces (1 cup) cottage cheese
- 4 ounces Pecorino Romano cheese, grated (2 cups)
- 1 cup heavy cream
- 2 garlic cloves, minced
- 1 teaspoon cornstarch
- ¼ teaspoon table salt
- ¼ teaspoon pepper

1. For the lasagna Adjust oven rack to middle position and heat oven to 375 degrees. Spray rimmed baking sheet and 13 by 9-inch baking dish with oil spray. Bring 4 quarts water to boil in large Dutch oven. Add noodles and salt and cook, stirring often, until al dente. Drain noodles and transfer to prepared sheet. Using tongs, gently turn noodles to coat lightly with oil spray. Cut 2 noodles in half crosswise.

2. For the meat sauce Mash bread and milk in bowl until smooth. Add beef, salt, and pepper and knead with your hands until well combined; set aside. Heat oil in now-empty Dutch oven over medium heat until shimmering. Add onion and cook until softened, about 5 minutes. Stir in garlic, oregano, and pepper flakes and cook until fragrant, about 1 minute.

3. Add beef mixture, breaking meat into small pieces with wooden spoon, and cook until no longer pink, about 4 minutes. Stir in tomatoes and bring to simmer, scraping up any browned bits. Reduce heat to medium-low and simmer until flavors have melded, about 5 minutes.

4. For the cream sauce Whisk all ingredients in bowl until combined.

5. Lay 3 noodles lengthwise in prepared dish with ends touching 1 short side of dish, leaving gap at far end. Lay 1 half noodle crosswise to fill gap (if needed).

6. Spread 1½ cups meat sauce over noodles, followed by ½ cup cream sauce and finally ½ cup mozzarella. Repeat layering of noodles, meat sauce, cream sauce, and mozzarella 3 more times, switching position of half noodle to opposite end of dish each time.

7. Lay remaining 3 noodles over top (there is no half noodle for top layer). Spread remaining cream sauce over noodles, followed by remaining 1 cup mozzarella. Sprinkle Pecorino over top.

8. Spray sheet of aluminum foil with oil spray and cover lasagna. Set lasagna on rimmed baking sheet. Bake for 30 minutes. Discard foil and continue to bake until top layer of lasagna is spotty brown, 25 to 30 minutes. Let lasagna cool for 30 minutes. Slice and serve.

TO MAKE AHEAD
At end of step 7, cover dish with greased aluminum foil and refrigerate for up to 24 hours. When ready to eat, bake lasagna as directed in step 8, increasing covered baking time to 55 minutes.

HEARTY ITALIAN MEAT SAUCE (SUNDAY GRAVY)

Serves 8 to 10

Why This Recipe Works The Italian American classic known as Sunday gravy is not just a dish; it's a feast. Bowls of lightly sauced pasta and a slow-cooked tomato sauce (gravy) are served alongside a large platter of meats that have been braised for hours in the gravy. The meats can include ribs, meatballs, pork shoulder, hot and sweet sausages, and the dish's typical crowning glory: braciole (see page 174), the stuffed, rolled beef that's a meal on its own. Why such extravagance? Italians who immigrated to the United States in the late 19th and early 20th centuries found meat far more abundant and affordable here than in their home country. Sunday gravy became a weekly celebration of this good fortune. Even today, Italian grandmothers famously spend the better part of a day preparing Sunday gravy, and many recipes call for six cuts of meat. We wanted a full-flavored meal but with no more than an hour of hands-on cooking. To start, we limited ourselves to pork sausage and baby back ribs, and replaced the time-consuming braciole with standout meatballs. Cooking our sauce in the oven meant we could leave it unattended for most of the cooking time. Meatloaf mix is a prepackaged mix of ground beef, pork, and veal; if it's unavailable, use ½ pound each of ground pork and 85 percent lean ground beef. You can substitute 6 tablespoons plain yogurt mixed with 2 tablespoons milk for the buttermilk. You will need at least a 6-quart Dutch oven for this recipe.

Sauce

- 2 tablespoons extra-virgin olive oil
- 2¼ pounds baby back ribs, cut into 2-rib sections
- ¾ teaspoon table salt
- ¼ teaspoon pepper
- 1 pound hot Italian sausage
- 2 onions, chopped fine
- 1¼ teaspoons dried oregano
- 3 tablespoons tomato paste
- 4 garlic cloves, minced
- 2 (28-ounce) cans crushed tomatoes
- ⅔ cup beef broth

Meatballs and Pasta

- 2 slices hearty white sandwich bread, crusts removed and bread torn into small pieces
- ½ cup buttermilk
- 1 pound meatloaf mix
- 2 ounces thinly sliced prosciutto, chopped fine
- 1 ounce Pecorino Romano cheese, grated (½ cup)
- ¼ cup minced fresh parsley
- 2 garlic cloves, minced
- 1 large egg yolk
- ½ teaspoon table salt, plus salt for cooking pasta
- ¼ teaspoon red pepper flakes
- ½ cup extra-virgin olive oil
- 1½ pounds spaghetti or linguine
- ¼ cup chopped fresh basil
  Grated Parmesan cheese

1. For the sauce Adjust oven rack to lower-middle position and heat oven to 325 degrees. Heat oil in large Dutch oven over medium-high heat until just smoking. Pat ribs dry with paper towels and season with salt and pepper. Working in two batches, brown ribs well on both sides, 5 to 7 minutes; transfer to plate. Add sausage to pot and brown well on all sides, 5 to 7 minutes; transfer to plate.

2. Add onions and oregano to fat left in pot and cook over medium heat, stirring often, until softened and lightly browned, 5 to 7 minutes. Stir in tomato paste and cook until very dark, about 3 minutes. Stir in garlic and cook until fragrant, about 30 seconds. Stir in crushed tomatoes and broth, scraping up any browned bits. Nestle browned ribs and sausage into pot. Bring to simmer, cover, and transfer to oven. Bake until ribs are tender, about 2½ hours.

3. For the meatballs and pasta Mash bread and buttermilk to paste in large bowl; let stand for 10 minutes. Mix in meatloaf mix, prosciutto, Pecorino, parsley, garlic, egg yolk, ½ teaspoon salt, and pepper flakes with hands. Lightly shape mixture into 1½-inch round meatballs (about ¼ cup each; about 12 meatballs total); transfer to plate, cover, and refrigerate until needed.

4. During final ½ hour of sauce simmering time, heat oil in 12-inch nonstick skillet over medium-high heat until shimmering. Brown meatballs well on all sides, 5 to 7 minutes; transfer to paper towel–lined plate.

5. Remove sauce from oven and using wide, shallow spoon, skim excess fat from surface. Gently add meatballs to sauce. Cover, return pot to oven, and continue to cook until meatballs are just cooked through, about 15 minutes.

6. Meanwhile, bring 6 quarts water to boil in large pot. Add pasta and 2 tablespoons salt and cook, stirring often, until al dente. Reserve ½ cup cooking water, then drain pasta and return it to pot.

7. Using tongs, transfer meatballs, ribs, and sausage to serving platter; cut each sausage in half. Stir basil into sauce and season with salt and pepper to taste. Add 1 cup sauce and reserved cooking water to pasta and toss to combine. Serve with remaining sauce, platter of meat, and Parmesan.

TO MAKE AHEAD
After step 5, sauce and meats can be cooled and then refrigerated in Dutch oven for up to 2 days. To reheat, drizzle ½ cup water over sauce (do not stir it in) and heat on lower-middle rack of 325-degree oven for 1 hour.

PORK RAGU

Makes about 8 cups

Why This Recipe Works A meaty, long-cooked ragu can be made with pork instead of beef. It just requires the right cut, and we found that baby back ribs fit the bill, providing tender meat and lots of flavor and body from the bones. Browning the ribs first creates flavorful fond, and a base of onion, carrots, and fennel lends traditional Italian flavor. Braising the meat in the oven in broth, tomatoes, and wine renders it fork-tender, and cooking a whole head of garlic along with the meat requires less work than chopping a dozen cloves. We return the shredded meat to the savory cooking liquid along with the sweet, mellow garlic before tossing it all with pasta and topping it with Parmesan cheese. This recipe makes enough sauce to coat 2 pounds of pasta. Leftover sauce may be refrigerated for up to 3 days or frozen for up to 1 month.

- 2 (2¼- to 2½-pound) racks baby back ribs, trimmed and each rack cut into fourths
- 2 teaspoons ground fennel
- 4½ teaspoons kosher salt, plus salt for cooking pasta
- 1 teaspoon pepper
- 3 tablespoons extra-virgin olive oil
- 1 large onion, chopped fine
- 1 large fennel bulb, stalks discarded, bulb halved, cored, and chopped fine
- 2 large carrots, peeled and chopped fine
- ¼ cup minced fresh sage, divided
- 1½ teaspoons minced fresh rosemary
- 1 cup plus 2 tablespoons dry red wine, divided
- 1 (28-ounce) can whole peeled tomatoes, drained and crushed
- 3 cups chicken broth
- 1 garlic head, outer papery skins removed and top fourth of head cut off and discarded
- 1 pound pappardelle or tagliatelle
  Grated Parmesan cheese

1. Adjust oven rack to middle position and heat oven to 300 degrees. Sprinkle ribs with ground fennel and season with 4 teaspoons salt and pepper, pressing spices to adhere. Heat oil in Dutch oven over medium-high heat until just smoking. Add half of ribs, meat side down, and cook, without moving them, until meat is well browned, 6 to 8 minutes; transfer to plate. Repeat with remaining ribs; set aside.

2. Reduce heat to medium and add onion, fennel, carrots, 2 tablespoons sage, rosemary, and remaining ½ teaspoon salt to now-empty pot. Cook, stirring occasionally and scraping up any browned bits, until vegetables are well browned and beginning to stick to pot bottom, 12 to 15 minutes.

3. Add 1 cup wine and cook until evaporated, about 5 minutes. Stir in tomatoes and broth and bring to simmer. Submerge garlic and ribs, meat side down, in liquid; add any accumulated juices from plate. Cover and transfer to oven. Cook until ribs are fork-tender, about 2 hours.

4. Remove pot from oven and transfer ribs and garlic to rimmed baking sheet. Using large spoon, skim any fat from surface of sauce. Once cool enough to handle, shred meat from bones; discard bones and gristle. Return meat to pot. Squeeze garlic from its skin into pot. Stir in remaining 2 tablespoons sage and remaining 2 tablespoons wine. Season with salt and pepper to taste.

5. Meanwhile, bring 4 quarts water to boil in large pot. Add pasta and 2 tablespoons salt and cook, stirring often, until al dente. Reserve ½ cup cooking water, then drain pasta and return it to pot. Add half of sauce and toss to combine, adjusting consistency with reserved cooking water as needed. Serve, passing Parmesan separately.

Fine Dining at the VFW

As we drove into Cranston, Rhode Island, the lines in the center of the road changed from yellow to green, white, and red—an homage to the Italian flag. We suspected that following a road literally paved with Italian American pride would lead to excellent food. What we didn't know was that we'd find culinary treasure in a VFW (Veterans of Foreign Wars) dining hall.

Mike Lepizzera ran Mike's Kitchen out of the Tabor-Franchi VFW Post for more than three decades. (Mike recently passed away at the age of 86. The restaurant is now run by his niece and her husband.) The restaurant is open for lunch and dinner, except during VFW meetings. There are 125 seats scattered around Formica tables, and the place is so popular that a line of eager diners wraps around the building at peak hours.

A large chalkboard posted on the wood-paneled wall between military memorabilia and fading photos of soldiers serves as the menu.

We settled into seats and watched as a waitress wove through the crowded restaurant, doling out dozens of hellos, hugs, and kisses to regular customers on the way to our table. When she arrived, we inquired about the fluffy polenta and red sauce. Was it a side dish? No, she assured me. It's big enough for a meal.

A few minutes later, a 4-inch by 4-inch brick of golden polenta, swimming and smothered in a velvety red sauce, arrived at our table. It was light, airy, intensely flavorful, and substantial—anything but a side. The sauce was smooth, salty, and a tad sweet, until you tasted it with the cheesy polenta.

FLUFFY BAKED POLENTA WITH RED SAUCE

Serves 6

Why This Recipe Works Based on the perfectly squared-off profile of the polenta we enjoyed at Mike's Kitchen, it was clear that the slice had been cut out of a larger tray of polenta. We figured it must have had time to set up, probably in the cool environment of a refrigerator, transforming from a creamy porridge to something more solid. Back in the test kitchen, we tried applying this technique to several basic polenta recipes. Cooking the cornmeal in water instead of dairy gave us clean, sweet corn flavor and an airy texture. Garlic oil boosted the dish's savory quality, and adding half-and-half and nutty Pecorino contributed some welcome richness. While the polenta chilled, we processed canned whole tomatoes until smooth and then created a sweet-and-savory red sauce. We sliced the polenta and baked the blocks long enough to brown and heat through before serving. We developed this recipe using Quaker Yellow Corn Meal for its desirable texture and short cooking time. The timing may be different for other types of cornmeal, so be sure to cook the polenta until it is thickened and tender. Whole milk can be substituted for the half-and-half. Plan ahead: The polenta needs to be chilled for at least 3 hours before being cut, baked, and served.

Polenta

- 4 tablespoons unsalted butter
- 2 tablespoons extra-virgin olive oil
- 2 garlic cloves, smashed and peeled
- 7 cups water
- 1½ teaspoons table salt
- ½ teaspoon pepper
- 1½ cups cornmeal
- 3 ounces Pecorino Romano cheese, grated (1½ cups)
- ¼ cup half-and-half

Red Sauce

- 1 (14.5-ounce) can whole peeled tomatoes
- ¼ cup extra-virgin olive oil, divided
- 1 onion, peeled and halved through root end

- 1 (15-ounce) can tomato sauce
- 1 ounce Pecorino Romano cheese, grated (½ cup)
- 1½ tablespoons sugar
- ¾ teaspoon table salt
- ½ teaspoon garlic powder

1. For the polenta Lightly grease 8-inch square baking pan. Heat butter and oil in Dutch oven over medium heat until butter is melted. Add garlic and cook until lightly golden, about 4 minutes. Discard garlic.

2. Add water, salt, and pepper to butter mixture. Increase heat to medium-high and bring to boil. Add cornmeal in slow, steady stream, whisking constantly. Reduce heat to medium-low and continue to cook, whisking frequently and scraping sides and bottom of pot, until mixture is thick and cornmeal is tender, about 20 minutes.

3. Off heat, whisk in Pecorino and half-and-half. Transfer to prepared pan and let cool completely on wire rack. Once cooled, cover with plastic wrap and refrigerate until completely chilled, at least 3 hours.

4. For the red sauce Process tomatoes and their juice in blender until smooth, about 30 seconds. Heat 1 tablespoon oil in large saucepan over medium heat until shimmering. Add onion, cut sides down, and cook without moving until lightly browned, about 4 minutes. Add pureed tomatoes, tomato sauce, Pecorino, sugar, salt, garlic powder, and remaining 3 tablespoons oil. Bring mixture to boil, reduce heat to medium-low, and simmer until sauce is slightly thickened, about 15 minutes. Remove from heat, discard onion, cover, and keep warm.

5. Adjust oven rack to middle position and heat oven to 375 degrees. Line rimmed baking sheet with parchment paper, then grease parchment. Cut chilled polenta into 6 equal pieces (about 4 by 2⅔ inches each). Place on prepared sheet and bake until heated through and beginning to brown on bottom, about 30 minutes. Serve each portion covered with about ½ cup red sauce.

BAKED MANICOTTI

Serves 6 to 8

Why This Recipe Works Manicotti may look homey, but blanching and stuffing pasta tubes is a tedious chore, and the ricotta filling can be uninspired and watery. We wanted a simpler, better recipe that had all of the comforting, cheesy flavor but none of the fuss—and no pastry bag, please! We did away with the slippery pasta tubes and instead spread the filling onto no-boil lasagna noodles that we had briefly soaked in hot water to make them pliable enough to roll up easily. After baking the manicotti, we broiled the dish for a few minutes to give it a nicely bronzed crown. Note that some packages of no-boil lasagna noodles contain only 12 noodles; this recipe requires 16 noodles. If your baking dish isn't broiler-safe, brown the manicotti at 500 degrees for about 10 minutes.

Sauce

- 2 tablespoons extra-virgin olive oil
- 3 garlic cloves, minced
- 1/2 teaspoon red pepper flakes (optional)
- 2 (28-ounce) cans crushed tomatoes
- 2 tablespoons chopped fresh basil

Manicotti

- 1 1/2 pounds (3 cups) whole-milk or part-skim ricotta cheese
- 8 ounces whole-milk mozzarella cheese, shredded (2 cups)
- 4 ounces Parmesan cheese, grated (2 cups), divided
- 2 large eggs, lightly beaten
- 2 tablespoons minced fresh parsley
- 2 tablespoons chopped fresh basil
- 3/4 teaspoon table salt
- 1/2 teaspoon pepper
- 16 no-boil lasagna noodles

1. For the sauce Cook oil, garlic, and pepper flakes, if using, in large saucepan over medium heat until fragrant but not brown, about 2 minutes. Stir in tomatoes, bring to simmer, and cook until thickened slightly, about 15 minutes. Off heat, stir in basil and season with salt and pepper to taste.

2. For the manicotti Combine ricotta, mozzarella, 1 cup Parmesan, eggs, parsley, basil, salt, and pepper in bowl.

3. Pour 1 inch of boiling water into 13 by 9-inch broiler-safe baking dish. Slip noodles into water, 1 at a time. Let noodles soak, separating them with tip of knife to prevent sticking, until pliable, about 5 minutes. Remove noodles from water and place in single layer on clean dish towels. Discard water and dry baking dish.

4. Adjust oven rack to middle position and heat oven to 400 degrees. Spread 1 1/2 cups sauce over bottom of now-empty dish. Working with several noodles at a time, spread 1/4 cup ricotta mixture evenly over bottom three-quarters of each noodle. Roll noodles up around filling, then arrange seam side down in dish. Spread remaining sauce over manicotti.

5. Sprinkle manicotti with remaining 1 cup Parmesan, cover dish tightly with greased aluminum foil, and place on foil-lined rimmed baking sheet. Bake until bubbling, about 40 minutes. Remove baking dish from oven. Adjust oven rack 6 inches from broiler element and heat broiler. Uncover dish and broil until Parmesan is spotty brown, 4 to 6 minutes. Let casserole cool for 10 minutes before serving.

TO MAKE AHEAD
Assembled manicotti can be covered with sheet of parchment paper, wrapped tightly in aluminum foil, and refrigerated for up to 3 days or frozen for up to 1 month. If frozen, thaw manicotti in refrigerator for 1 to 2 days. To bake, remove parchment, replace foil, and increase baking time to 1 to 1 1/4 hours.

VARIATION
Baked Manicotti with Sausage
Cook 1 pound hot or sweet Italian sausage, casings removed, in 2 tablespoons olive oil in large saucepan over medium-high heat, breaking sausage into 1/2-inch pieces with wooden spoon, until no longer pink, about 6 minutes. Omit olive oil in sauce and cook remaining sauce ingredients in saucepan with sausage.

BAKED ZITI

Serves 8 to 10

Why This Recipe Works Many cooks don't mind lavishing time and tender loving care on lasagna—the outcome speaks for itself. Baked ziti, however, is another matter. It's supposed to be simple: just pasta and a robust tomato sauce baked under a cover of bubbling, gooey cheese. But over time the dish has devolved from simple to merely lazy. Most versions seem as though they went directly from the pantry into the oven, calling for little more than cooked pasta, jarred sauce, a container of ricotta, and some pre-shredded cheese. The results—overcooked ziti in a dull, grainy sauce topped with a rubbery mass of mozzarella—more than earn the dish its reputation as mediocre church-supper fare. To get a baked ziti recipe with perfectly al dente pasta, a rich and flavorful sauce, and melted cheese in every bite, we parted from convention in several ways. First, we substituted cottage cheese for ricotta because the larger cheese curds baked up pillowy instead of grainy, the way ricotta did. For al dente pasta in our ziti recipe, we cooked the pasta only halfway, then added extra sauce to the dish so the pasta could absorb more liquid without drying out the finished dish. Finally, we cut the mozzarella into small cubes rather than shredding it, so it melted into distinct but delectable little pockets of cheese rather than congealing into an unappetizing mass. We prefer baked ziti made with heavy cream, but whole milk can be substituted by increasing the amount of cornstarch to 2 teaspoons and increasing the cooking time in step 3 by 1 to 2 minutes. You can use part-skim mozzarella, if desired.

1 pound ziti, penne, or other short, tubular pasta

Table salt for cooking pasta

1 pound (2 cups) whole-milk or 1 percent cottage cheese

3 ounces Parmesan cheese, grated (1½ cups), divided

2 large eggs

2 tablespoons extra-virgin olive oil

5 garlic cloves, minced

1 (28-ounce) can tomato sauce

1 (14.5-ounce) can diced tomatoes

1 teaspoon dried oregano

½ cup plus 2 tablespoons chopped fresh basil, divided

1 teaspoon sugar

1 cup heavy cream

¾ teaspoon cornstarch

8 ounces whole-milk mozzarella cheese, cut into ¼-inch pieces (1½ cups), divided

1. Adjust oven rack to middle position and heat oven to 350 degrees. Bring 4 quarts water to boil in large pot. Add pasta and 1 tablespoon salt and cook, stirring often, until pasta begins to soften but is not yet cooked through, 5 to 7 minutes. Drain and leave in colander.

2. Meanwhile, whisk cottage cheese, 1 cup Parmesan, and eggs together in medium bowl; set aside. Heat oil and garlic in 12-inch skillet over medium heat. Cook, stirring often, until garlic turns golden but not brown, about 3 minutes. Stir in tomato sauce, diced tomatoes and their juice, and oregano; bring to simmer and cook until thickened, about 10 minutes. Off heat, stir in ½ cup basil and sugar and season with salt and pepper to taste.

3. Stir cream and cornstarch together in small bowl; transfer to now-empty pasta pot and set over medium heat. Bring to simmer and cook until thickened, 3 to 4 minutes. Off heat, stir in cottage cheese mixture, 1 cup tomato sauce, and ¾ cup mozzarella. Add pasta to pot and toss to combine.

4. Transfer pasta mixture to 13 by 9-inch baking dish and spread remaining tomato sauce evenly over top. Sprinkle with remaining ¾ cup mozzarella and remaining ½ cup Parmesan. Cover dish tightly with greased aluminum foil. Bake for 30 minutes, then remove foil and continue to bake until cheese is bubbling and beginning to brown, about 30 minutes. Let casserole cool for 20 minutes, then sprinkle with remaining 2 tablespoons basil and serve.

CHICKEN, BROCCOLI, AND ZITI CASSEROLE

Serves 8

Why This Recipe Works Pseudo-Italian chain restaurants known for cheap wine and doughy breadsticks are also notorious for serving dreadful plates of chicken and broccoli with ziti. Drowned in a fatty cream sauce whose only flavor is that of old chopped garlic, ziti casserole can be the perfect example of all the bad things that happen to "Italian" recipes in the wrong hands. That said, chicken, broccoli, and ziti is such a crowd-pleaser (pasta, protein, and vegetable all in one dish) that we decided to give it another look and turn the combination into a hearty casserole to feed a crowd. We wanted our recipe to have it all: moist chicken, crisp-tender broccoli, and firm ziti served in a cheesy sauce that stayed creamy even after baking. We made an enhanced béchamel sauce by sautéing onion, lots of garlic, and red pepper flakes before stirring in flour, milk, and savory chicken broth. The strips of boneless, skinless chicken breast needed to be precooked to prevent the other ingredients from overcooking by the time the chicken was done. We found that poaching the chicken in the sauce was the best method—it flavored the meat and kept it moist. Our first disastrous attempt at simmering the broccoli right in the sauce infused the whole dish with an off-flavor and dirty color. Microwaving the broccoli was easy and reliable. To prepare the pasta for the oven, we undercooked it and then rinsed it with cold water to stop any carryover cooking. A final topping of fresh bread crumbs, minced garlic, and Asiago cheese is as flavorful as the casserole itself. If you can't find Asiago, Parmesan is an acceptable alternative.

4 slices hearty white sandwich bread, torn into pieces

8 garlic cloves, minced, divided

5 ounces grated Asiago cheese (2½ cups), divided

5 tablespoons unsalted butter, 2 tablespoons melted, divided

1 pound ziti
   Table salt for cooking pasta

1 onion, chopped fine

¼ teaspoon red pepper flakes

¼ cup all-purpose flour

½ cup white wine

3 cups whole milk

2 cups chicken broth

4 boneless, skinless chicken breasts (about 1½ pounds), cut crosswise into ¼-inch slices

12 ounces broccoli florets, cut into 1-inch pieces

1. Pulse bread, one-fourth of garlic, ½ cup Asiago, and melted butter in food processor until coarsely ground. Set aside.

2. Adjust oven rack to middle position and heat oven to 400 degrees. Bring 4 quarts water to boil in large pot. Add ziti and 1 tablespoon salt to boiling water and cook until nearly al dente. Drain in colander and rinse under cold water until cool.

3. Melt remaining 3 tablespoons butter in now-empty pot over medium heat. Cook onion until softened, about 5 minutes. Add remaining garlic and pepper flakes and cook until fragrant, about 30 seconds. Stir in flour and cook until golden, about 1 minute. Slowly whisk in wine, scraping up any browned bits and smoothing out any lumps, and cook until liquid is almost evaporated, about 1 minute. Slowly whisk in milk and broth and bring to boil. Add chicken and simmer until no longer pink, about 5 minutes. Off heat, stir in remaining 2 cups cheese until melted.

4. Microwave broccoli, covered, in large bowl until bright green and nearly tender, 2 to 4 minutes. Stir cooked broccoli and drained ziti into pot and season with salt and pepper. Transfer to 13 by 9-inch baking dish. Sprinkle with bread crumb mixture and bake until sauce is bubbling around edges and topping is golden brown, 20 to 25 minutes. Cool 5 minutes. Serve.

TO MAKE AHEAD
Casserole can be assembled, minus bread crumbs, and refrigerated 24 hours in advance. Bring to room temperature before adding bread crumbs and baking.

STUFFED SHELLS

Serves 6 to 8

Why This Recipe Works Bad stuffed shell recipes can be frustrating. Most call for precooking the shells and then using a spoon or pastry bag to try to fill them without ripping them to shreds. Some demand that you simmer a sauce for hours before it goes over the shells. Some cheater recipes don't even bother with stuffing the shells, instructing you to just stir everything together and bake, leaving you with a mess of torn pasta and grainy cheese. For a quicker version of stuffed shells with better results, we got right down to stuffing them—no parboiling. We found that the quickest and easiest way to fill the raw pasta shells was to choose jumbo shells with wide openings and pipe in the filling using a pastry bag. For a supercheesy filling, we mixed creamy ricotta, shredded fontina, and grated Pecorino Romano cheeses with savory minced garlic, fragrant fresh basil, and dried oregano. Stirring cornstarch into the filling kept the ricotta from becoming grainy once it was baked. We also added two eggs to make the filling pipable and keep it from oozing out of the shells during baking. Smothering the filled shells in a thin tomato sauce meant the raw pasta cooked through properly during baking, absorbing liquid while still leaving behind a full-bodied—not chunky or dehydrated—sauce. We first baked the shells covered to trap in as much moisture as possible and cook the pasta, and then uncovered the pan to brown the cheesy top and reduce the sauce. Shred the fontina on the large holes of a box grater. Be sure to use open, unbroken shells. We developed this recipe using Barilla Jumbo Shells and were able to find at least 25 open shells in each 1-pound box.

Sauce

- 2 tablespoons extra-virgin olive oil
- 1 onion, chopped
- ½ teaspoon table salt
- ½ teaspoon pepper
- 6 garlic cloves, minced
- ¼ teaspoon red pepper flakes
- 1 (28-ounce) can tomato puree
- 2 cups water
- 1 teaspoon sugar

Filling

- 10 ounces (1¼ cups) whole-milk ricotta cheese
- 4 ounces fontina cheese, shredded (1 cup)
- 2 ounces Pecorino Romano cheese, grated (1 cup)
- 2 large eggs
- 3 tablespoons chopped fresh basil
- 1½ tablespoons cornstarch
- 2 garlic cloves, minced
- 1 teaspoon dried oregano
- ½ teaspoon table salt

Shells

- 25 jumbo pasta shells (from 1-pound package)
- 8 ounces fontina cheese, shredded (2 cups)
- 1 tablespoon chopped fresh basil

1. For the sauce Heat oil in large saucepan over medium heat until shimmering. Add onion, salt, and pepper and cook, stirring occasionally, until softened and lightly browned, about 10 minutes.

2. Stir in garlic and pepper flakes and cook until fragrant, about 30 seconds. Stir in tomato puree, water, and sugar and bring to simmer. Reduce heat to medium-low and cook until flavors meld, about 5 minutes. (Cooled sauce can be refrigerated for up to 3 days.)

3. For the filling Stir all ingredients in bowl until thoroughly combined. Transfer filling to pastry bag, or to large zipper-lock bag (if using zipper-lock bag, cut 1 inch off 1 corner of bag).

4. For the shells Adjust oven rack to middle position and heat oven to 400 degrees. Place shells open side up on counter. Pipe filling into shells until each is about three-quarters full. Divide remaining filling evenly among shells.

5. Spread 1 cup sauce over bottom of 13 by 9-inch baking dish. Transfer shells, open side up, to prepared dish. Pour remaining sauce evenly over shells to completely cover.

6. Cover dish tightly with greased aluminum foil and set on rimmed baking sheet. Bake until shells are tender and sauce is boiling rapidly, about 45 minutes. Remove dish from oven and discard foil; sprinkle fontina over top. Bake, uncovered, until fontina is lightly browned, about 15 minutes. Let shells cool for 25 minutes. Sprinkle with basil. Serve.

TO MAKE AHEAD

At end of step 2, let sauce cool completely. At end of step 5, cover dish tightly with aluminum foil and refrigerate for up to 24 hours. When ready to eat, bake shells as directed in step 6.

If You Wanna Find Me, You'll Find Me

La Campagna is easy to miss if you're not looking for it. Owner Carmella Fragassi tells us the original sign was three inches too big for the town's building code, and rather than redo it she decided to do without. "If you wanna find me, you'll find me," she says.

After 21 years as a narcotics agent, Carmella "retired" by opening a restaurant. Her first place was a big operation, and after it burned down she decided the next venture would be smaller.

In the intervening three-year period, Carmella traveled to Puglia, Italy, to visit family and reflect. It was during this trip that she decided to change the way she wrote menus. With her new restaurant she would follow the practical Italian model of an ever-changing menu based on seasonality, availability, and what needed to be used up.

In 1996, she reopened La Campagna in a suburban strip mall 25 minutes outside of downtown Cleveland. She wasn't looking for this location and when it came to her it was supposed to be a temporary situation. It's just big enough for 10 tables and small enough that you can see into the kitchen from the front door.

Carmella's earliest kitchen memories fall back to both her grandmothers in Puglia, where she's traveled since she was 14 years old. "If you went to their houses they never kicked you out of the kitchen. They would teach you how to cook." And now in her own restaurant she tells me, "the biggest compliment I can receive is when someone tells me they haven't had something like that since their grandma cooked it."

EGGPLANT PECORINO

Serves 6

Why This Recipe Works Read the words "eggplant Parmesan" on almost any menu and you know what you're in for: A mountain of mozzarella, a loaf's worth of bread crumbs, a swimming pool of red sauce, and buried deep beneath, a fat slab of mushy eggplant. But at La Campagna, they showcase the eggplant. It is sliced super thin, which nixes the possibility of a big bite of mush. In re-creating this dish, we decided early on to skip the bread crumbs and instead focus on frying the eggplant in a thin flour-and-egg coating, which creates a light, fluffy shell around each eggplant slice rather than a thick bready coating. Pecorino Romano's nutty, tangy flavor paired beautifully with the soft, mild eggplant. A final flourish of creamy, tangy shredded fontina cheese, melted and browned under the broiler, made the dish extra special. Do not use eggplants any larger than 1 pound each or the slices won't fit in the baking dish. If your baking dish isn't broiler-safe, brown the casserole at 500 degrees for about 10 minutes.

Sauce

- 2 tablespoons unsalted butter
- ¼ cup finely chopped onion
- 3 garlic cloves, minced
- 2 anchovy fillets, minced
- ¾ teaspoon table salt
- ¼ teaspoon red pepper flakes
- ¼ teaspoon dried oregano
- 1 (28-ounce) can crushed tomatoes
- 1 (15-ounce) can diced tomatoes
- ½ teaspoon sugar
- ¼ cup chopped fresh basil
- 1 tablespoon extra-virgin olive oil

Eggplant

- 3 (10- to 16-ounce) eggplants
- ½ cup all-purpose flour
- 4 large eggs
- 1 cup extra-virgin olive oil
- 4 ounces Pecorino Romano cheese, grated (2 cups)
- 4 ounces fontina cheese, shredded (1 cup)

1. For the sauce Melt butter in medium saucepan over medium-low heat. Add onion, garlic, anchovies, salt, pepper flakes, and oregano and cook until onions are softened, about 3 minutes. Stir in crushed tomatoes, diced tomatoes and their juice, and sugar and bring to simmer. Reduce heat to medium-low and simmer until slightly thickened, about 10 minutes. Off heat, stir in basil and oil. Season with salt and pepper to taste. Set aside. (Sauce can be prepared and refrigerated up to 48 hours in advance.)

2. For the eggplant Cut stem end off eggplants and discard. Cut off ¼-inch-thick slice from 1 long side of each eggplant and discard. Using mandoline or slicing knife and starting on cut side, slice eggplants lengthwise into ¼-inch-thick slices until you have 20 slices total (you may not need all 3 eggplants).

3. Place flour in shallow dish. Beat eggs together in second shallow dish. Line baking sheet with triple layer of paper towels. Heat oil in 12-inch skillet over medium heat to 350 degrees (tilt skillet to pool oil to one side to take temperature). Working with 3 to 4 slices of eggplant per batch (depending on size of eggplant), dredge eggplant in flour, shaking off excess; dunk in egg, allowing excess to drip off. Place in hot oil and fry until lightly browned on both sides, about 1½ minutes per side. Transfer to prepared sheet and repeat with remaining eggplant. (As eggplant cools, you can stack the slices to make room.)

4. Adjust oven rack 6 inches from broiler element and heat oven to 375 degrees. Spread 1 cup sauce in bottom of broiler-safe 13 by 9-inch baking dish. Starting with largest slices of eggplant, place 4 slices side-by-side in bottom of dish. Spread ½ cup sauce over eggplant, then sprinkle ½ cup Pecorino over top. Repeat layering 3 more times, building individual stacks of eggplant. Cover top layer of eggplant with remaining sauce, then sprinkle with fontina.

5. Bake until bubbling around edges and center of casserole is hot, about 30 minutes. Switch oven to broil and broil until cheese is lightly browned on top, 1 to 3 minutes. Let cool for 20 minutes. Serve.

LINGUINE AI FRUTTI DI MARE

Serves 6

Why This Recipe Works This pasta traditionally incorporates whatever is available in the daily catch into a dish resplendent with flavors of the sea—from briny mollusks to succulent shellfish. It's a celebration of freshness and everything that makes Italian food so delicious. We wanted a pasta dish with uncomplicated, clean elements that highlighted and complemented the delicate flavor of the seafood. We chose tomatoes, red pepper flakes, and saffron—a classic combination—and fortified the sauce with clam juice and white wine in which we'd simmered the shrimp shells to extract their flavor. For a smooth sauce that coated the pasta, canned whole tomatoes, pulsed in a food processor, worked best; tasters appreciated the texture of this sauce as opposed to one made with canned crushed tomatoes. We also added tomato paste and anchovies for savory depth. Adding the different types of seafood in stages ensured that each was cooked perfectly. A sprinkle of toasted lemon-chili bread crumbs served as a perfect aromatic accompaniment.

- 3 tablespoons extra-virgin olive oil, divided, plus extra for serving
- 8 ounces large shrimp (26 to 30 per pound), peeled and deveined, shells reserved
- 1 cup dry white wine
- 1 (28-ounce) can whole peeled tomatoes, drained
- 2 shallots, sliced thin
- 6 garlic cloves, sliced thin
- 2 tablespoons tomato paste
- 1 anchovy fillet, rinsed and minced
- 1/8 teaspoon red pepper flakes
- 1/8 teaspoon saffron threads, crumbled
- 1 (8-ounce) bottle clam juice
- 8 ounces mussels, scrubbed and debearded
- 8 ounces large sea scallops, tendons removed
- 8 ounces squid, bodies sliced crosswise into 1/4-inch-thick rings, tentacles halved
- 1 pound linguine
  Table salt for cooking pasta
- 1/3 cup minced fresh parsley
- 1 recipe Lemon-Chili Bread Crumbs (recipe follows)

1. Heat 1 tablespoon oil in Dutch oven over medium heat until shimmering. Add shrimp shells and cook, stirring frequently, until beginning to turn spotty brown and pot starts to brown, 2 to 4 minutes. Add wine and simmer, stirring occasionally, for 5 minutes. Strain mixture through fine-mesh strainer into bowl, pressing on solids to extract as much liquid as possible; discard solids.

2. Pulse tomatoes in food processor until finely ground, about 10 pulses. Heat remaining 2 tablespoons oil in now-empty pot over medium heat until shimmering. Add shallots and cook until softened and lightly browned, 2 to 3 minutes. Stir in garlic, tomato paste, anchovy, pepper flakes, and saffron and cook until fragrant, about 1 minute. Stir in wine mixture, scraping up any browned bits, and cook until nearly evaporated, about 30 seconds. Stir in tomatoes and clam juice, bring to simmer, and cook, stirring occasionally, until thickened and flavors meld, about 20 minutes.

3. Add mussels, bring to boil, cover, and cook, shaking pot occasionally, until mussels open, 3 to 6 minutes. As mussels open, transfer with slotted spoon to bowl. Discard any mussels that refuse to open.

4. Reduce sauce to simmer, gently stir in scallops, and cook for 2 minutes. Gently stir in shrimp and cook until just opaque throughout, about 2 minutes. Off heat, stir in squid, cover, and let sit until squid is just opaque and tender, 1 to 2 minutes.

5. Meanwhile, bring 4 quarts water to boil in large pot. Add pasta and 1 tablespoon salt and cook, stirring often, until al dente. Reserve 1/2 cup cooking water, then drain pasta and add to pot with sauce. Add mussels and parsley and toss to combine: Season with salt and pepper to taste and adjust consistency with reserved cooking water as needed. Serve, sprinkling individual portions with bread crumbs and drizzling with extra oil.

LEMON-CHILI BREAD CRUMBS

Makes 1 cup

2 slices hearty white sandwich bread

2 tablespoons extra-virgin olive oil

¼ teaspoon red pepper flakes

1 tablespoon grated lemon zest

Pulse bread in food processor until finely ground, 10 to 15 pulses. Heat oil in 12-inch nonstick skillet over medium heat until shimmering. Add bread crumbs and cook, stirring constantly, until crumbs begin to brown, 3 to 5 minutes. Add pepper flakes and cook, stirring constantly, until crumbs are golden brown, 1 to 2 minutes. Transfer to bowl, stir in zest, and season with salt and pepper to taste.

SEAFOOD RISOTTO

Serves 6 to 8

Why This Recipe Works The risottos of northern Italy are among its culinary glories, and seafood risotto is a favorite in better restaurants in Italian neighborhoods along the East Coast. This classic Venetian dish promises a luxurious mix of flavors and textures against a lush backdrop of creamy short-grain rice. It's the perfect dish for celebrations and is often prepared in Italian American homes for Christmas Eve. Venetians are known for enjoying their risottos *all'onda,* meaning they are wavier, more fluid, and looser than in other Italian regions, and we decided to follow suit. With a wide array of seafood to choose from, the preparation can easily become overloaded, so we decided to set some limits. We chose universally appealing shrimp and made a quick seafood broth by simmering the shrimp shells in a base of bottled clam juice, chicken broth, and water, to which we added bay leaves and canned tomatoes. Once the risotto was fully cooked, we stirred in the shrimp along with mussels and squid and allowed them to steam gently in the warm rice, resulting in flawlessly tender seafood. You may have broth left over once the rice is finished cooking; different rice products cook differently, and we prefer to err on the side of slightly too much broth rather than too little. If you do use all the broth and the rice has not finished cooking, add hot water.

12 ounces large shrimp (26 to 30 per pound), peeled and deveined, shells reserved

2 cups chicken broth

3½ cups water

4 (8-ounce) bottles clam juice

1 (14.5-ounce) can diced tomatoes, drained

2 bay leaves

5 tablespoons unsalted butter, cut into 5 pieces, divided

1 onion, chopped fine

2 cups Arborio rice

5 garlic cloves, minced

1 teaspoon minced fresh thyme or ¼ teaspoon dried

1 cup dry white wine

12 mussels, scrubbed and debearded

8 ounces squid, bodies sliced crosswise into ¼-inch-thick rings, tentacles halved

2 tablespoons chopped fresh parsley

1 tablespoon lemon juice

1. Bring shrimp shells, broth, water, clam juice, tomatoes, and bay leaves to boil in large saucepan. Reduce to simmer and cook for 20 minutes. Strain mixture through fine-mesh strainer into large bowl, pressing on solids to extract as much liquid as possible; discard solids. Return broth to now-empty saucepan, cover, and keep warm over low heat.

2. Melt 2 tablespoons butter in Dutch oven over medium heat. Add onion and cook until softened, about 5 minutes. Add rice, garlic, and thyme and cook, stirring frequently, until grain edges begin to turn translucent, about 5 minutes.

3. Add wine and cook, stirring frequently, until fully absorbed, about 2 minutes. Stir in 3½ cups warm broth, bring to simmer, and cook, stirring occasionally, until almost fully absorbed, 10 to 12 minutes.

4. Continue to cook rice, stirring frequently and adding warm broth, 1 cup at a time, every few minutes as liquid is absorbed, until rice is creamy and loose and cooked through but still slightly firm in center, 14 to 18 minutes.

5. Stir in shrimp, mussels, squid, and 1 cup broth and cook, stirring frequently, until shrimp and squid are opaque throughout, about 3 minutes. Remove pot from heat, cover, and let sit until all mussels have opened, about 5 minutes; discard any mussels that have not opened. Adjust consistency with remaining warm broth as needed. (Risotto should be somewhat loose; you may have broth left over.) Stir in remaining 3 tablespoons butter, parsley, and lemon juice and season with salt and pepper to taste. Serve immediately.

SIDES AND BREADS

GARLICKY BROCCOLINI

Serves 4

Why This Recipe Works Garlicky broccoli is a classic Italian American side dish. We like to make it with broccolini—a cross between broccoli and Chinese broccoli with crisp yet tender stalks and delicate tips. It's easier to prepare and cook than broccoli, especially if you want a one-pan stovetop method. While broccolini mingles well with just about any flavoring sympathetic to broccoli, we like it best with the seasonings Italians apply to all manner of greens: extra-virgin olive oil, garlic, crushed red pepper flakes, and Parmesan cheese. We tried sautéing the broccolini before adding a little water to let it steam through (a method we often use with broccoli), but the delicate broccolini tips scorched during the sauté. Instead, we brought salted water to a boil in a skillet, added the broccolini, and covered the pan to trap the steam. A few minutes later, we removed the lid to reveal tender, emerald-green broccolini stalks. Another minute over the heat evaporated any remaining water. A simple combination of minced garlic and red pepper flakes sautéed in oil, plus a sprinkling of Parmesan cheese before serving, was all the broccolini needed. Halving the bottom 2 inches of the thicker broccolini stalks lengthwise ensured the stalks cooked evenly. Broccolini is also sold as baby broccoli or aspiration. You will need a 12-inch nonstick skillet with a tight-fitting lid for this recipe.

2 tablespoons extra-virgin olive oil

2 garlic cloves, minced

⅛ teaspoon red pepper flakes

⅓ cup water

½ teaspoon table salt

1 pound broccolini, trimmed, bottom 2 inches of stems thicker than ½ inch halved lengthwise

2 tablespoons grated Parmesan cheese

1. Combine oil, garlic, and pepper flakes in bowl. Bring water and salt to boil in 12-inch nonstick skillet. Add broccolini, cover, reduce heat to medium-low, and cook until bright green and tender, about 5 minutes.

2. Uncover and cook until liquid evaporates, about 30 seconds. Clear center of skillet, add garlic mixture, and cook, mashing mixture into skillet, until fragrant, about 30 seconds. Stir garlic mixture into broccolini. Transfer to platter, sprinkle with Parmesan, and serve.

VARIATIONS

Broccolini with Shallots
Combine 2 tablespoons extra-virgin olive oil, 2 teaspoons minced shallot, 1 teaspoon grated lemon zest, 1 teaspoon minced fresh thyme, and ¼ teaspoon pepper in bowl. Replace garlic mixture with shallot mixture.

Broccolini with Capers and Lemon
Combine 2 tablespoons extra-virgin olive oil, 1 tablespoon rinsed and minced capers, 1 teaspoon grated lemon zest, and ¼ teaspoon pepper in bowl. Replace garlic mixture with caper mixture.

GRILLED BROCCOLI WITH LEMON AND PARMESAN

Serves 4

Why This Recipe Works Americans have translated many Italian preparations for the grill and this recipe might just be an improvement on the classic Italian cooking methods for broccoli. Steaming or sautéing broccoli is fine, but if you want vivid green florets with flavorful charred accents, you can't beat the grill. To avoid toughness and promote even cooking, we peeled the stems and cut the broccoli heads into spears small enough to cook quickly but large enough to grill easily. To cook the broccoli through without charring, we wrapped it in aluminum foil packs and let it steam first on the grill (flipping the packs halfway through to ensure even cooking). We then removed the spears and placed them directly on the grill to char. Grilled lemon halves added brightness and grill flavor, while shredded Parmesan provided a salty bite. To keep the packs from tearing, use heavy-duty aluminum foil. Use the large holes of a box grater to shred the Parmesan.

- ¼ cup extra-virgin olive oil, plus extra for drizzling
- 1 tablespoon water
- ¾ teaspoon table salt
- ½ teaspoon pepper
- 2 pounds broccoli
- 1 lemon, halved
- ¼ cup shredded Parmesan cheese

1. Cut two 26 by 12-inch sheets of heavy-duty aluminum foil. Whisk oil, water, salt, and pepper together in large bowl.

2. Trim stalk ends so each entire head of broccoli measures 6 to 7 inches long. Using vegetable peeler, peel away tough outer layer of broccoli stalks (about ⅛ inch). Cut stalks in half lengthwise into spears (stems should be ½ to ¾ inch thick and florets 3 to 4 inches wide). Add broccoli spears to oil mixture and toss well to coat.

3. Divide broccoli between sheets of foil, cut side down and alternating direction of florets and stems. Bring short sides of foil together and crimp tightly. Crimp long ends to seal packs tightly.

4A. For a charcoal grill Open bottom vent completely. Light large chimney starter filled with charcoal briquettes (6 quarts). When top coals are partially covered with ash, pour evenly over half of grill. Set cooking grate in place, cover, and open lid vent completely. Heat grill until hot, about 5 minutes.

4B. For a gas grill Turn all burners to high, cover, and heat grill until hot, about 15 minutes. Turn all burners to medium-high. (Adjust burners as needed to maintain grill temperature around 400 degrees.)

5. Clean and oil cooking grate. Arrange packs evenly on grill (over coals if using charcoal), cover, and cook for 8 minutes, flipping packs halfway through cooking.

6. Transfer packs to rimmed baking sheet and, using scissors, carefully cut open, allowing steam to escape away from you. (Broccoli should be bright green and fork inserted into stems should meet some resistance.)

7. Discard foil and place broccoli and lemon halves cut side down on grill (over coals if using charcoal). Grill (covered if using gas), turning broccoli about every 2 minutes, until stems are fork-tender and well charred on all sides, 6 to 8 minutes total. (Transfer broccoli to now-empty sheet as it finishes cooking.) Grill lemon halves until well charred on cut side, 6 to 8 minutes.

8. Transfer broccoli to cutting board and cut into 2-inch pieces; transfer to platter. Season with salt and pepper to taste. Squeeze lemon over broccoli to taste, sprinkle with Parmesan, and drizzle with extra oil. Serve.

SWEET AND SOUR BROCCOLI RABE

Serves 4 to 6

Why This Recipe Works Broccoli rabe, a cruciferous vegetable often associated with Italian cooking, is known for its bitter, peppery bite. In other words, it definitely stands out on a plate. The traditional cooking method of sautéing it with olive oil and aromatics brings its big, bold flavors to the forefront, but many Americans prefer vegetables with less bitterness. We found that blanching—quickly cooking in salted boiling water—the broccoli rabe before sautéing simultaneously softened its crunch and tamed its mustardy bite. To guarantee that it cooked properly, we trimmed the bottom 2 inches of the stems (they remained tough even when we tried peeling them before cooking) and then chopped the remaining rabe into 1-inch pieces before cooking. Once blanched and drained in a colander, our broccoli rabe was ready to be sautéed with any number of seasonings, but we were particularly interested in using assertive flavors that could stand up to this vegetable's subtle bitterness. In southern Italy, broccoli rabe is often flavored with a vibrant sauce called *agrodolce* (which roughly translates as "sweet and sour"). Italians make the sauce by simmering vinegar with sugar and sometimes aromatics until the mixture is syrupy. This seemed like the perfect pairing, so we set out to replicate it. In the empty pot that we had used to blanch the broccoli rabe, we sautéed onion and garlic in a little oil. Next, we added some red wine vinegar. (We tested the traditional balsamic vinegar, but found that it became unpleasantly heavy when reduced to a syrup.) Most agrodolce recipes call for granulated sugar, but tasters preferred brown sugar, which added warmth along with sweetness. At this point, the mixture was certainly lively, but tasters petitioned for more complexity. Raisins and orange juice, common additions in some agrodolce recipes, successfully rounded out our sauce. Once the mixture had reduced to a syrup, we tossed in the blanched broccoli rabe and turned an aggressive vegetable into a gentle giant. Sweet golden raisins balance the somewhat bitter broccoli rabe. If using black raisins, increase the brown sugar by 1 teaspoon.

1 pound broccoli rabe, bottom 2 inches trimmed, cut into 1-inch pieces

Table salt for blanching broccoli rabe

2 tablespoons extra-virgin olive oil

1 onion, chopped fine

2 garlic cloves, minced

¼ cup golden raisins

3 tablespoons red wine vinegar

1 tablespoon orange juice

1 tablespoon packed brown sugar

1. Bring 4 quarts water to boil in a large pot. Add broccoli rabe and 1 tablespoon salt and cook until just tender, about 2 minutes. Drain thoroughly.

2. Heat oil in empty pot over medium heat until shimmering. Cook onion until softened, about 5 minutes. Stir in garlic and cook until fragrant, about 30 seconds. Add raisins, vinegar, orange juice, and sugar and cook until syrupy, 3 to 5 minutes. Add drained broccoli rabe to pot and cook, stirring occasionally, until well coated and just beginning to brown, about 2 minutes. Season with salt and pepper. Serve.

UTICA GREENS

Serves 6

Why This Recipe Works While researching our recipe for Chicken Riggies in Utica, New York, we ate out at dozens of local restaurants, sampling every version of this regional favorite we could find. Every time we ordered riggies in Utica, the server would ask cheerfully, "Do you want the greens with that?" Once we figured out what the greens were—escarole braised on the stovetop with capicola, garlic, and cherry peppers until tender and then tossed with grated Pecorino Romano cheese and crispy bread crumbs—our answer was always an enthusiastic yes. By the end of our trip, we were hooked: We'd have to find a way to make these tender, meaty greens at home and introduce them to a wider national audience. Escarole is a gently bitter green that's popular in Italian cooking. The leaves are tender and meaty and, because the flavor is only mildly bitter, many people who claim not to like greens actually enjoy escarole. Its leaves have a tendency to hide a lot of dirt and grit, so make sure to give them a good rinse and a spin in the salad spinner before chopping and adding to the pot. The winning flavor of this dish comes from capicola (also called coppa), an Italian dry-cured cold cut made from pork shoulder and neck meat; we found that both hot and sweet varieties put this dish on the right track. Browning the meat first established a savory base of flavor. After braising the escarole with the browned meat, onions, hot cherry peppers, and garlic, we stirred in toasted homemade bread crumbs to absorb excess moisture. Grated Pecorino Romano along with another helping of bread crumbs contributed great crunchy texture to complement the greens' bold, hearty flavors. You can use either hot or sweet capicola here. Whichever you choose, buy a ½-inch-thick slice (or use prosciutto) at the deli counter; avoid the prepackaged thin slices, as hearty cubes of meat are traditional for this dish. Do not use store-bought bread crumbs here. This dish is traditionally served with Chicken Riggies (page 122).

1 slice hearty white sandwich bread, torn into 1-inch pieces

3 tablespoons extra-virgin olive oil, divided

4 ounces ½-inch-thick capicola, cut into ½-inch pieces

1 onion, chopped

¼ cup jarred sliced hot cherry peppers, chopped fine

4 garlic cloves, minced

2 large heads (2½ pounds) escarole, trimmed and chopped

½ cup chicken broth

¾ teaspoon table salt

½ teaspoon pepper

1 ounce Pecorino Romano cheese, grated (½ cup)

1. Pulse bread and 1 tablespoon oil in food processor to coarse crumbs, about 5 pulses. Toast bread crumbs in Dutch oven over medium heat, stirring occasionally, until golden brown, about 5 minutes. Transfer crumbs to bowl; set aside. Wipe out pot with paper towels. Add remaining 2 tablespoons oil and capicola to now-empty pot and cook, stirring occasionally, until capicola begins to brown, 3 to 5 minutes. Stir in onion and cook until onion is softened and capicola is browned and crispy, about 5 minutes. Add cherry peppers and garlic and cook until fragrant, about 30 seconds.

2. Stir in half of escarole, broth, salt, and pepper. Cover and cook until greens are beginning to wilt, about 1 minute. Add remaining escarole, cover, and cook over medium-low heat, stirring occasionally, until stems are tender, about 10 minutes. Off heat, stir in Pecorino and ⅓ cup reserved bread crumbs. Top with remaining bread crumbs before serving.

SAUTÉED KALE

Serves 6 to 8

Why This Recipe Works Simple sautéed greens prepared Italian style—with garlic and red pepper flakes—pair well with hearty pastas and meats. For a quick dish of sautéed kale, a notoriously fibrous and tough green, we had to account for the leaves and woody stems cooking at different rates. Cutting the leaves into rough 2-inch pieces and the stems into smaller ½-inch pieces ensured that they cooked in the same amount of time. Cooking the kale in oil in a skillet took a long time since we had to wait for each handful to wilt before adding the next. Our solution? We softened all the kale at once by blanching it in boiling water in a Dutch oven first. Once the kale was drained and pressed of excess water, we heated sliced garlic and a dash of red pepper flakes in extra-virgin olive oil in the now-empty Dutch oven and then added the kale. After 5 minutes of stirring, the kale was completely tender and infused with garlicky flavor. A final drizzle of olive oil gave it a glossy sheen and extra richness. For a more assertively flavored variation, we incorporated chopped pepperoni and hot cherry peppers. You can substitute Lacinato kale (also known as dinosaur or Tuscan kale) for the curly kale in this recipe. It's important to boil the kale in the full 4 quarts of water; with less water it can become too salty.

1½ pounds curly kale

   Table salt for blanching kale

6 tablespoons extra-virgin olive oil, divided

4 garlic cloves, sliced thin

¼ teaspoon red pepper flakes

1. Bring 4 quarts water to boil in Dutch oven over medium-high heat.

2. Meanwhile, stem kale by grasping leaves between your thumb and index finger at base of stem and pulling from bottom to top of stem to strip off leaves. Cut leaves into 2-inch pieces. Trim and discard bases of stems thicker than ½ inch. Cut remaining stems into ½-inch pieces. Transfer kale to large bowl and wash thoroughly.

3. Add 2 tablespoons salt to boiling water. Add kale to pot, 1 handful at a time, submerging with tongs as needed. Cook, stirring occasionally, until leaves are tender and stems are just al dente, about 5 minutes. Drain in colander and let sit for 5 minutes, occasionally pressing on kale with rubber spatula to release excess moisture. (Drained kale can be refrigerated for up to 3 days.)

4. Heat ¼ cup oil in now-empty pot over medium heat until shimmering. Add garlic and pepper flakes and cook until garlic is lightly browned, 30 to 60 seconds. Add kale and cook, stirring frequently, until stems are tender, about 5 minutes. Season with salt and pepper to taste. Transfer to serving platter and drizzle with remaining 2 tablespoons oil. Serve.

VARIATION
Sautéed Kale with Crispy Pepperoni and Cherry Peppers
Add ½ cup pepperoni, cut into ¼-inch pieces, to shimmering oil in step 4 and cook until rust-colored, 3 to 5 minutes. Using slotted spoon, transfer pepperoni to plate, then add garlic and pepper flakes to remaining oil in pot and continue with recipe. Before serving, sprinkle kale with pepperoni and 2 tablespoons chopped jarred hot cherry peppers.

PITTSBURGH BEANS AND GREENS

Serves 4

Why This Recipe Works Hearty greens, such as escarole or kale, cooked down until tender in a flavorful broth and then tossed with tender white beans is a staple menu item in restaurants in Pittsburgh's Strip District (home to many Italian Americans), where it's dubbed "beans and greens." We wanted a version for cooks around the country to make at home. Although we found recipes that added sausage, potatoes, tomatoes, and more, we decided that simplicity is key in this recipe. We began by sautéing some onion, garlic, and rosemary and then added one head of escarole, which we had cut into 2-inch pieces. Once the greens were wilted, we added some drained canned cannellini beans, cooked them for a few minutes, and finished the dish by sprinkling some nutty Parmesan cheese and extra olive oil over the mixture before serving. Don't be alarmed by what may seem like the large amount of greens we call for. Once added to the pot, they wilt down significantly within minutes.

- 2 tablespoons extra-virgin olive oil, plus extra for drizzling
- 1 onion, chopped fine
- ½ teaspoon table salt
- ½ teaspoon pepper
- 3 garlic cloves, minced
- 1 teaspoon chopped fresh rosemary
- ½ teaspoon red pepper flakes
- ½ cup chicken broth
- 1 head escarole (1 pound), trimmed and cut into 2-inch pieces
- 1 (15-ounce) can cannellini beans, rinsed
- 1 ounce Parmesan cheese, grated (½ cup), divided

1. Heat oil in Dutch oven over medium-high heat until shimmering. Add onion, salt, and pepper and cook until softened and beginning to brown, 5 to 7 minutes. Add garlic, rosemary, and pepper flakes and cook until fragrant, about 30 seconds.

2. Reduce heat to medium-low. Stir in broth, scraping up any browned bits. Stir in escarole; cover and cook, stirring occasionally, until wilted, 6 to 8 minutes.

3. Add beans and cook, uncovered and stirring occasionally, until escarole is tender, about 5 minutes. Off heat, stir in ¼ cup Parmesan. Season with salt and pepper to taste. Transfer greens to serving dish. Sprinkle with remaining ¼ cup Parmesan and drizzle with extra oil. Serve.

THE ITALIAN AMERICAN KITCHEN
Escarole

Escarole, a kind of chicory, is a leafy green that looks like green leaf lettuce. Its slightly bitter flavor makes it a great choice for peppery salads, a good accent for romaine, or delicious with just a simple vinaigrette. Escarole is less assertive than its cousins, Belgian endive and frisée, and is a good choice when you want something slightly, rather than full-on, bitter. Unlike lettuce, escarole stands up well to cooking. Its resilient leaves turn supple but don't fall apart, and the base and spine of each leaf add a little texture. Look for heads bristling with sturdy, unblemished leaves. Use a salad spinner to wash escarole since the fine, feathery leaves tend to≈hold a lot of soil.

BRAISED GREEN BEANS

Serves 4 to 6

Why This Recipe Works Quickly steamed or sautéed, lightly crisp green beans are commonplace. But there's a lesser-known approach—a slow braise—that turns beans into something altogether different. The time-honored take on the method calls for sautéing garlic and onions in olive oil, adding tomatoes and green beans along with water, and then simmering until the sauce is thickened and the beans are infused with tomato and garlic. The slow cooking renders them so meltingly tender that they're almost creamy. There are just two problems: First, it takes at least 2 hours of cooking to turn the beans ultratender. (Some recipes call for shorter cooking times, but they don't produce the truly silky texture that makes this dish so special.) Second, we often find that by the time the skins have fully softened, the interiors have nearly disintegrated. We wanted the beans to turn velvety-soft but remain intact. We also wanted a reasonable cooking time—no more than an hour. It turns out the tomatoes' acidity prevents the pectin in the beans from breaking down. Until the pectin breaks down, the beans will remain stubbornly firm. Waiting to add the tomatoes and adding some baking soda to the pot at the outset (to create an alkaline environment and speed the break-down of the pectin) were the keys to perfecting this dish. Cooking the beans in the oven, rather than the stovetop, minimized agitation in the pot and kept the beans from becoming ragged around the edges.

5 tablespoons extra-virgin olive oil, divided

1 onion, chopped fine

4 garlic cloves, minced

Pinch cayenne pepper

1½ cups water

½ teaspoon baking soda

1½ pounds green beans, trimmed and cut into 2- to 3-inch lengths

1 (14.5-ounce) can diced tomatoes, drained with juice reserved, chopped coarse

1 tablespoon tomato paste

1 teaspoon table salt

¼ teaspoon pepper

¼ cup chopped fresh parsley

Red wine vinegar

1. Adjust oven rack to lower-middle position and heat oven to 275 degrees. Heat 3 tablespoons oil in Dutch oven over medium heat until shimmering. Add onion and cook, stirring occasionally, until softened, 3 to 5 minutes. Add garlic and cayenne and cook until fragrant, about 30 seconds. Add water, baking soda, and green beans and bring to simmer. Reduce heat to medium-low and cook, stirring occasionally, for 10 minutes. Stir in tomatoes and their juice, tomato paste, salt, and pepper.

2. Cover pot, transfer to oven, and cook until sauce is slightly thickened and green beans can be easily cut with side of fork, 40 to 50 minutes. Stir in parsley and season with vinegar to taste. Drizzle with remaining 2 tablespoons oil and serve warm or at room temperature.

VARIATION

Braised Green Beans with Potatoes and Basil
Substitute 2 teaspoons dried oregano for cayenne, 3 tablespoons chopped fresh basil for parsley, and 2 teaspoons lemon juice for red wine vinegar. In step 1, add 1 pound peeled Yukon Gold potatoes, cut into 2- to 3-inch lengths, to pot with green beans and increase salt to 2 teaspoons.

THE ITALIAN AMERICAN KITCHEN
Tomato Paste

Tomato paste is an inexpensive flavor powerhouse. We deploy its concentrated sweetness and umami to bring depth and complexity to sauces, soups, and other slow-cooked dishes. Historically, tomato paste has been sold in cans in the United States, but in recent years tubed pastes have popped up. Studying the market, we found an intriguing pattern: Most tubes are made in Italy; all the cans are made in the United States. Does it matter? It's no surprise that you can't detect much difference in finished dishes given how little paste is used in a recipe. But tubes are so much more convenient to use and store. Our favorite, **Cento Double Concentrated Tomato Paste,** has an "intense, roasty tomato flavor" and "good acidity."

GRILLED ARTICHOKES WITH LEMON BUTTER

Serves 4 to 6

Why This Recipe Works The center of the artichoke universe is Monterey County, California. Locals love artichokes' delicate flavor, especially when grilled and seasoned with Italian flavors. Artichokes are part of the thistle family and are technically the bud of a flower; the spiky tips of the leaves evolved to protect the bud from predators—except for those with a sharp knife. After experimenting, we found it best to use a vegetable peeler to remove the fibrous outer skin of the stem before snapping off the bottom rows of the remaining tough leaves. Placing each artichoke on its side and lopping off the top quarter got rid of most of the spikes. We pruned the rest of the leaves with scissors. With the artichokes prepared, it was time to cook them. Parboiling them in a broth with lemon juice, red pepper flakes, and salt ensured that they were completely tender and thoroughly seasoned. Brushing them in extra-virgin olive oil before grilling helped develop a flavorful char. Because the artichokes were mostly cooked through, all we needed from the fire was a solid char, which we achieved with just 2 to 4 minutes per side over hot coals. A simple blend of lemon zest and juice, garlic, and butter came together easily in the microwave and was perfect for dipping or drizzling. To eat, use your teeth to scrape the flesh from the inner part of the exterior leaves. The tender inner leaves, heart, and stem are entirely edible.

- 4 artichokes (8 to 10 ounces each)
- ½ teaspoon table salt, plus salt for cooking artichokes
- ½ teaspoon red pepper flakes
- 2 lemons
- 6 tablespoons unsalted butter
- 1 garlic clove, minced to paste
- ¼ teaspoon pepper
- 2 tablespoons extra-virgin olive oil

1. Cut off and discard bottom ¼ inch of each artichoke stem. Remove any leaves attached to stems. Using vegetable peeler, peel away outer layer of stems. Pull bottom row of tough outer leaves downward toward stems and break off at base. Cut off and discard top quarter of each artichoke. Using scissors, cut off sharp tips of remaining leaves all around artichokes.

2. Combine 3 quarts water, 3 tablespoons salt, and pepper flakes in Dutch oven. Cut 1 lemon in half; squeeze juice into pot, then add spent halves. Bring to boil over high heat. Add artichokes, cover, and reduce heat to medium-low. Simmer until tip of paring knife inserted into base of artichoke slips easily in and out, 25 to 28 minutes, stirring occasionally.

3. Meanwhile, grate 2 teaspoons zest from remaining lemon; combine with butter, garlic, remaining ½ teaspoon salt, and pepper in bowl. Microwave at 50 percent power until butter is melted and bubbling and garlic is fragrant, about 2 minutes, stirring occasionally. Squeeze 1½ tablespoons juice from zested lemon and stir into butter mixture. Season with salt and pepper to taste.

4. Set wire rack in rimmed baking sheet. Place artichokes stem side up on prepared rack and let drain for 10 minutes. Cut artichokes in half lengthwise. Using spoon, scoop out fuzzy choke, leaving small cavity in center of each half.

5A. For a charcoal grill Open bottom vent completely. Light large chimney starter filled with charcoal briquettes (6 quarts). When top coals are partially covered with ash, pour evenly over grill. Set cooking grate in place, cover, and open lid vent completely. Heat grill until hot, about 5 minutes.

5B. For a gas grill Turn all burners to high, cover, and heat grill until hot, about 15 minutes. Leave all burners on high.

6. Clean and oil cooking grate. Brush artichokes with oil. Place artichokes on grill and cook (covered if using gas) until lightly charred, 2 to 4 minutes per side. Transfer artichokes to platter and tent with aluminum foil. Briefly rewarm lemon butter in microwave, if necessary, and serve with artichokes.

STUFFED TOMATOES

Serves 6

Why This Recipe Works Stuffed tomatoes always sound delicious, but too often you get tasteless tomatoes and a lackluster stuffing that falls out in a clump. To concentrate flavor and get rid of excess moisture, we scooped the pulp out of our tomatoes, seasoned hollowed-out tomato shells with salt and sugar, and let them drain. Separately, we pressed and strained the pulp to extract its flavorful juices for later. Bread crumbs are the classic choice for the stuffing, but even with the tomatoes salted, the crumbs turned soggy and bloated in test after test. Couscous (a tiny pasta) proved to be the best base for the filling. It could absorb some of the reserved tomato juice without becoming bloated. A topping of panko bread crumbs—pretoasted for proper browning—mixed with cheese added crunch and richness and satisfied our desire for some crumbs, with no risk of sogginess. A drizzle of the cooking liquid supplemented with red wine vinegar provided a piquant final touch. Look for large tomatoes, about 3 inches in diameter.

- 6 large vine-ripened tomatoes (8 to 10 ounces each)
- 1 tablespoon sugar
- 1 tablespoon plus ½ teaspoon kosher salt, divided
- 4½ tablespoons extra-virgin olive oil, divided
- ¼ cup panko bread crumbs
- 3 ounces Gruyère cheese, shredded (¾ cup), divided
- 1 onion, halved and sliced thin
- 2 garlic cloves, minced
- ⅛ teaspoon red pepper flakes
- 8 ounces (8 cups) baby spinach, chopped coarse
- 1 cup couscous
- ½ teaspoon grated lemon zest
- 1 tablespoon red wine vinegar

1. Adjust oven rack to middle position and heat oven to 375 degrees. Cut top ½ inch off stem end of tomatoes and set aside. Using melon baller, scoop out tomato pulp and transfer to fine-mesh strainer set over bowl. Press on pulp with wooden spoon to extract juice; set aside juice and discard pulp. (You should have about ⅔ cup tomato juice; if not, add water as needed to equal ⅔ cup.)

2. Combine sugar and 1 tablespoon salt in bowl. Sprinkle each tomato cavity with 1 teaspoon sugar mixture, then turn tomatoes upside down on plate to drain for 30 minutes.

3. Combine 1½ teaspoons oil and panko in 10-inch skillet and toast over medium-high heat, stirring frequently, until golden brown, about 3 minutes. Transfer to bowl and let cool for 10 minutes. Stir in ¼ cup Gruyère.

4. Heat 2 tablespoons oil in now-empty skillet over medium heat until shimmering. Add onion and remaining ½ teaspoon salt and cook until softened, 5 to 7 minutes. Stir in garlic and pepper flakes and cook until fragrant, about 30 seconds. Add spinach, 1 handful at a time, and cook until wilted, about 3 minutes. Stir in couscous, lemon zest, and reserved tomato juice. Cover, remove from heat, and let stand until couscous has absorbed liquid, about 7 minutes. Transfer couscous mixture to bowl and stir in remaining ½ cup Gruyère. Season with salt and pepper to taste.

5. Coat bottom of 13 by 9-inch baking dish with remaining 2 tablespoons oil. Blot tomato cavities dry with paper towels and season with salt and pepper. Pack each tomato with couscous mixture, about ½ cup per tomato, mounding excess. Top stuffed tomatoes with 1 heaping tablespoon panko mixture. Place tomatoes in prepared dish. Season reserved tops with salt and pepper and place in empty spaces in dish.

6. Bake, uncovered, until tomatoes have softened but still hold their shape, about 20 minutes. Using slotted spoon, transfer to serving platter. Whisk vinegar into oil remaining in dish, then drizzle over tomatoes. Place tops on tomatoes and serve.

CRISPY PARMESAN POTATOES

Serves 6 to 8

Why This Recipe Works This dish is a purely American invention but it is good enough to belong on the table at the finest restaurants in Italy. These crispy, cheesy potato slices are a habit-forming snack or elegant side dish to the Sunday roast. Trust us: Once you try them you will be making them again. Using thinly sliced, creamy Yukon Gold potatoes ensures that the potatoes won't dry out during roasting, and tossing the slices with seasoned cornstarch promotes crisping. Parmesan, rosemary, and a little more cornstarch make for a savory coating that clings evenly to the slices. Baked in a very hot oven until golden brown and served with a cool chive sour cream, these may just be the best potatoes you will ever make. Try to find potatoes that are 2½ to 3 inches long. Spray the baking sheet with an aerosol (not pump) vegetable oil spray. Use a good-quality Parmesan cheese here.

Chive Sour Cream

- 1 cup sour cream
- ¼ cup minced fresh chives
- ½ teaspoon minced fresh rosemary
- ½ teaspoon table salt
- ½ teaspoon pepper
- ½ teaspoon garlic powder
- ¼ teaspoon onion powder

Potatoes

- 2 pounds medium Yukon gold potatoes, unpeeled
- 4 teaspoons cornstarch, divided
- 1 teaspoon table salt
- 1½ teaspoons pepper, divided
- 1 tablespoon extra-virgin olive oil
- 6 ounces Parmesan cheese, cut into 1-inch pieces
- 2 teaspoons minced fresh rosemary

1. For the chive sour cream Combine all ingredients in bowl. Cover and refrigerate for at least 30 minutes to allow flavors to meld.

2. For the potatoes Adjust oven rack to lower-middle position and heat oven to 500 degrees. Spray rimmed baking sheet liberally with vegetable oil spray. Cut thin slice from 2 opposing long sides of each potato; discard slices. Cut potatoes crosswise into ½-inch-thick slices and transfer to large bowl.

3. Combine 2 teaspoons cornstarch, salt, and 1 teaspoon pepper in small bowl. Sprinkle cornstarch mixture over potatoes and toss until potatoes are thoroughly coated and cornstarch is no longer visible. Add oil and toss to coat.

4. Arrange potatoes in single layer on prepared sheet and bake until golden brown on top, about 20 minutes.

5. Meanwhile, process Parmesan, rosemary, remaining 2 teaspoons cornstarch, and remaining ½ teaspoon pepper in food processor until cheese is finely ground, about 1 minute.

6. Remove potatoes from oven. Sprinkle Parmesan mixture evenly over and between potatoes (cheese should cover surface of baking sheet), pressing on potatoes with back of spoon to adhere. Using two forks, flip slices over into same spot on sheet.

7. Bake until cheese between potatoes turns light golden brown, 5 to 7 minutes. Transfer sheet to wire rack and let potatoes cool for 15 minutes. Using large metal spatula, transfer potatoes, cheese side up, and accompanying cheese to platter. Serve with chive sour cream.

REALLY GOOD GARLIC BREAD

Serves 8

Why This Recipe Works Have you ever been to an Italian American restaurant that *doesn't* serve garlic bread? Probably not. But how often has this American invention (related, at least tangentially, to bruschetta) been memorable? Garlic bread is simple to make but it is often a disappointment to eat, with either too much or too little garlic flavor and bread that's steamed and unevenly browned. While bruschetta (page 22) is made with slices of crusty artisan bread brushed with olive oil and toasted, American garlic bread starts with butter and a soft loaf of supermarket Italian bread. Now, we weren't about to change the bread or choice of fat, but could we produce a recipe that was crisp and browned? For an evenly toasted version with garlic flavor that was prominent but not harsh, we briefly microwaved fresh garlic (grated to a paste with a rasp-style grater) and butter. We then combined the melted garlic butter with solid butter and just a bit of cayenne, salt, and garlic powder, which provided sweet, roasty notes. This gave us a spreadable paste that could be smeared evenly onto the bread. We first baked the bread cut side up on a baking sheet and then flipped it and compressed it with a second baking sheet. The panini-like setup pressed the cut side onto the hot sheet so that it evenly crisped and browned while also compressing the bread for a better balance of crust to crumb. A 12 by 5-inch loaf of supermarket Italian bread, which has a soft, thin crust and fine crumb, works best here. Do not use a rustic or crusty artisan-style loaf. A rasp-style grater makes quick work of turning the garlic into a paste. The amount of time needed to brown the bread after flipping it in step 3 depends on the color of your baking sheet. If using a dark sheet, the browning time will be on the shorter end of the range.

1 teaspoon garlic powder

1 teaspoon water

8 tablespoons unsalted butter, divided

½ teaspoon table salt

⅛ teaspoon cayenne pepper

4–5 garlic cloves, minced to paste (1 tablespoon)

1 (1-pound) loaf soft Italian bread, halved horizontally

1. Adjust oven rack to lower-middle position and heat oven to 450 degrees. Combine garlic powder and water in medium bowl. Add 4 tablespoons butter, salt, and cayenne to bowl; set aside.

2. Place remaining 4 tablespoons butter in small bowl and microwave, covered, until melted, about 30 seconds. Stir in garlic and continue to microwave, covered, until mixture is bubbling around edges, about 1 minute, stirring halfway through microwaving. Transfer melted butter mixture to bowl with garlic powder–butter mixture and whisk until homogeneous loose paste forms. (If mixture melts, set aside and let solidify before using.)

3. Spread cut sides of bread evenly with butter mixture. Transfer bread, cut sides up, to rimmed baking sheet. Bake until butter mixture has melted and seeped into bread, 3 to 4 minutes. Remove sheet from oven. Flip bread cut sides down, place second rimmed baking sheet on top, and gently press. Return sheet to oven, leaving second sheet on top of bread, and continue to bake until cut sides are golden brown and crisp, 4 to 12 minutes longer, rotating sheet halfway through baking. Transfer bread to cutting board. Using serrated knife, cut each half into 8 slices. Serve immediately.

PARMESAN BREADSTICKS

Makes 18 breadsticks

Why This Recipe Works The best part about going to an "Italian" chain restaurant might be the Parmesan breadsticks. Our goal was to re-create these flavorful, golden breadsticks—and serve them warm and fresh at home. First, we wanted to ensure that the flavor of our breadsticks' namesake really came through. In addition to sprinkling Parmesan on top, we mixed some into the dough for a rich cheese taste that wasn't just an afterthought. Adding a small amount of onion powder to our dough enhanced the nutty taste of the cheese and further boosted the savory appeal. Nailing down the perfect texture proved more complex. We wanted chewy yet soft-crumbed breadsticks, so we used all-purpose flour rather than higher-protein bread flour. But we found that our sticks were still too tough and dry inside. Our first thought, adding more water to the dough, left us with a sticky mess that was too difficult to shape. Doubling the amount of extra-virgin olive oil in the dough from 2 tablespoons to ¼ cup was the perfect solution. The oil acted as a tenderizer and coated the gluten strands, preventing them from sticking to one another and forming a strong gluten network. This created an easy-to-shape dough that baked up with a soft crumb. We set our oven to 500 degrees to ensure that our breadsticks took on a nice golden hue in the short time required to cook them through. Brushing our breadsticks with an egg-and-oil wash enhanced browning and flavor, while making the exterior chewy, not crunchy. Breadsticks can be stored in a zipper-lock bag at room temperature for up to 3 days. Wrapped in aluminum foil before being placed in the bag, the breadsticks can be frozen for up to 1 month. To reheat, wrap the breadsticks (thawed if frozen) in foil, place them on a baking sheet, and bake in a 350-degree oven for 10 minutes.

- 4 cups (20 ounces) all-purpose flour
- 1 tablespoon instant or rapid-rise yeast
- 1 tablespoon table salt
- 2 teaspoons onion powder
- 1½ cups water, room temperature
- ¼ cup extra-virgin olive oil
- 3 ounces Parmesan cheese, grated (1½ cups), divided
- 1 large egg, lightly beaten with 2 tablespoons extra-virgin olive oil and pinch salt

1. Whisk flour, yeast, salt, and onion powder together in bowl of stand mixer. Combine water and oil in 4-cup liquid measuring cup.

2. Using dough hook on low speed, slowly add water mixture to flour mixture and mix until cohesive dough starts to form and no dry flour remains, about 2 minutes, scraping down bowl as needed. Increase speed to medium-low and knead until dough is smooth and elastic and clears sides of bowl but sticks to bottom, about 8 minutes. Reduce speed to low, slowly add 1 cup Parmesan, ¼ cup at a time, and mix until mostly incorporated, about 2 minutes.

3. Transfer dough to lightly floured counter and knead by hand until Parmesan is evenly distributed and dough forms smooth, round ball, about 30 seconds. Place dough seam side down in lightly greased large bowl or container, cover tightly with plastic wrap, and let rise until doubled in size, 1 to 1½ hours. (Unrisen dough can be refrigerated for at least 8 hours or up to 16 hours; let sit at room temperature for 1 hour before shaping.)

4. Press down on dough to deflate. Transfer dough to clean counter and divide in half. Stretch each half into 9-inch log, cut log into 9 equal pieces (about 2 ounces each), and cover loosely with greased plastic.

5. Working with 1 piece of dough at a time (keep remaining pieces covered), form into rough ball by stretching dough around your thumbs and pinching edges together so that top is smooth. Place ball seam side down on clean counter and, using your cupped hand, drag in small circles until dough feels taut and round. Cover balls loosely with greased plastic and let rest for 30 minutes.

6. Line 2 rimmed baking sheets with greased parchment paper. Stretch and roll each dough ball into 8-inch-long cylinder. Moving your hands in opposite directions, use back and forth motion to roll ends of cylinder under your palms to form rounded points.

7. Arrange breadsticks on prepared sheets, spaced about 1½ inches apart. Cover loosely with greased plastic and let rise until nearly doubled in size and dough springs back minimally when poked gently with your knuckle, about 30 minutes.

8. Adjust oven racks to upper-middle and lower-middle positions and heat oven to 500 degrees. Gently brush breadsticks with egg mixture and sprinkle with remaining ½ cup Parmesan. Bake until golden brown, 12 to 14 minutes, switching and rotating sheets halfway through baking. Transfer breadsticks to wire rack and let cool for 15 minutes. Serve warm.

VARIATIONS
Asiago and Black Pepper Breadsticks
Add 1 tablespoon coarsely ground pepper to flour mixture in step 1. Substitute 1 cup shredded Asiago cheese for Parmesan; add ½ cup cheese to dough in step 2 and sprinkle breadsticks with remaining ½ cup cheese before baking in step 8.

Pecorino and Mixed Herb Breadsticks
Substitute 1½ cups grated Pecorino Romano for Parmesan. Combine 1 cup Pecorino, 2 tablespoons finely chopped fresh basil, 2 tablespoons minced fresh parsley, and 2 tablespoons minced fresh oregano in bowl before adding to dough in step 2. Sprinkle breadsticks with remaining ½ cup cheese before baking in step 8.

GARLIC KNOTS

Makes 12 knots

Why This Recipe Works Made from leftover pizza dough, buttery, supremely garlicky garlic knots are a pizzeria classic. Could we bring them home without the help of a pizza delivery driver? The pizza dough recipes we tried made knots that were too dry or too hard. We wanted something fluffier than pizza crust but chewier than dinner rolls. Substituting all-purpose flour for bread flour softened the knots, and kneading for about 8 minutes provided the right elasticity. To give our knots potent flavor, we first tried dousing them in garlic powder, which tasted artificial, and then in raw garlic, which was too harsh. So we gently cooked minced garlic—nine cloves of it—in butter, then stirred some of the butter and the reserved toasty garlic solids into the dough. We then brushed the knots with the garlic butter during baking and again just after taking them out of the oven to fully satisfy our garlic cravings. Knots can be stored in a zipper-lock bag at room temperature for up to 3 days. Wrapped in aluminum foil before being placed in the bag, the knots can be frozen for up to 1 month. To reheat, wrap the knots (thawed if frozen) in foil, place them on a baking sheet, and bake in a 350-degree oven for 10 minutes. See step photos on page 228.

9	garlic cloves, minced (2 tablespoons)
6	tablespoons unsalted butter, divided
¾	cup plus 1 teaspoon water, divided
2	cups (10 ounces) all-purpose flour
1½	teaspoons instant or rapid-rise yeast
1	teaspoon table salt
	Coarse sea salt

1. Cook garlic, 1 tablespoon butter, and 1 teaspoon water in 8-inch skillet over low heat, stirring occasionally, until garlic is straw-colored, 8 to 10 minutes. Stir in remaining butter until melted. Strain into bowl; reserve garlic solids.

2. Whisk flour, yeast, and table salt together in bowl of stand mixer. Whisk remaining ¾ cup water, 1 tablespoon garlic butter, and garlic solids together in 4-cup liquid measuring cup. Using dough hook on low speed, slowly add water mixture to flour mixture and mix until cohesive dough starts to form and no dry flour remains, about 2 minutes, scraping down bowl as needed. Increase speed to medium-low and knead until dough is smooth and elastic and clears sides of bowl but sticks to bottom, about 8 minutes.

3. Transfer dough to lightly floured counter and knead by hand to form smooth, round ball, about 30 seconds. Place dough seam side down in lightly greased large bowl or container, cover tightly with plastic wrap, and let rise until doubled in size, 1 to 1½ hours.

4. Line rimmed baking sheet with parchment paper. Press down on dough to deflate. Transfer dough to clean counter. Press and stretch dough into 12 by 6-inch rectangle, with long side parallel to counter edge. Using pizza cutter or chef's knife, cut dough vertically into 12 (6 by 1-inch) strips; cover loosely with greased plastic.

5. Working with 1 piece of dough at a time (keep remaining pieces covered), stretch and roll into 14-inch rope. Shape rope into U with 2-inch-wide bottom curve. Tie ends into single overhand knot, with 1½-inch open loop at bottom. Wrap 1 tail over loop and press through opening from top. Wrap other tail under loop and through opening from bottom. Pinch ends together to seal.

6. Arrange knots pinched side down on prepared sheet, spaced about 1 inch apart. Cover loosely with greased plastic and let rise until nearly doubled in size and dough springs back minimally when poked gently with your knuckle, 1 to 1½ hours. (Unrisen garlic knots can be refrigerated for at least 8 hours or up to 16 hours; let garlic knots sit at room temperature for 1 hour before baking.)

7. Adjust oven rack to middle position and heat oven to 500 degrees. Bake knots until set, about 5 minutes. Brush with 2 tablespoons garlic butter, rotate sheet, and bake until knots are golden brown, about 5 minutes.

8. Transfer knots to wire rack. Brush with remaining garlic butter, sprinkle with sea salt, and let cool for 15 minutes. Serve warm.

SCALI BREAD

Makes 1 loaf

Why This Recipe Works Boasting a soft crust and a relatively fluffy crumb, scali is the bread you want to have next to your big bowl of spaghetti and meatballs. A signature of Boston's Italian American community, scali is sold in most local grocery stores and cafés in the North End and is almost always braided and coated with a generous amount of sesame seeds. It has a more complex flavor than many fluffy Italian loaves thanks to the incorporation of a sponge, which ferments for 6 to 24 hours before being mixed with the remaining dough. We thought it was time to introduce this lovely loaf to the rest of the country. Unlike with most loaves, in which we want a sturdy, open crumb, we passed over bread flour in favor of all-purpose flour here; the lower-protein flour gave our bread its trademark soft, pillowy texture. When the sponge was ready, we kneaded it with the remaining dough ingredients in the mixer until smooth and elastic before letting the dough rise undisturbed. Incorporating 1 tablespoon of olive oil into the dough also helped create a soft crumb, along with providing a pleasing touch of richness. After dividing the dough into thirds and braiding the pieces into a loaf, we brushed the top with beaten egg and sprinkled on the traditional (but optional) dose of sesame seeds. See step photos on page 229.

Sponge
- ²/₃ cup (3¹/₃ ounces) all-purpose flour
- ½ cup water, room temperature
- ⅛ teaspoon instant or rapid-rise yeast

Dough
- 2²/₃ cups (13¹/₃ ounces) all-purpose flour
- 2 teaspoons table salt
- 1¼ teaspoons instant or rapid-rise yeast
- ¾ cup plus 2 tablespoons water, room temperature
- 3 tablespoons sugar
- 1 tablespoon extra-virgin olive oil
- 1 large egg, lightly beaten with 1 tablespoon water and pinch salt
- 1 tablespoon sesame seeds (optional)

1. For the sponge Stir all ingredients in 4-cup liquid measuring cup with wooden spoon until well combined. Cover tightly with plastic wrap and let sit at room temperature until sponge has risen and begins to collapse, about 6 hours (sponge can sit at room temperature for up to 24 hours).

2. For the dough Whisk flour, salt, and yeast together in bowl of stand mixer. Stir water, sugar, and oil into sponge with wooden spoon until well combined. Using dough hook on low speed, slowly add sponge mixture to flour mixture and mix until cohesive dough starts to form and no dry flour remains, about 2 minutes, scraping down bowl as needed. Increase speed to medium-low and knead until dough is smooth and elastic and clears sides of bowl, about 8 minutes.

3. Transfer dough to lightly floured counter and knead by hand to form smooth, round ball, about 30 seconds. Place dough seam side down in lightly greased large bowl or container, cover tightly with plastic, and let rise until doubled in size, 1½ to 2 hours.

4. Stack 2 rimmed baking sheets, line with aluminum foil, and spray with vegetable oil spray. Press down on dough to deflate. Transfer dough to lightly floured counter, divide into thirds (about 9½ ounces each), and cover loosely with greased plastic. Working with 1 piece of dough at a time (keep remaining pieces covered), stretch and roll into 10-inch rope. Arrange ropes side by side, perpendicular to counter edge, and pinch far ends together. Braid ropes into 10-inch loaf and pinch remaining ends together.

5. Transfer loaf to prepared sheet and reshape as needed, tucking edges under to form taut 10-inch loaf. Cover loosely with greased plastic and let rise until loaf increases in size by about half and dough springs back minimally when poked gently with your knuckle, 1 to 1½ hours.

6. Adjust oven rack to middle position and heat oven to 350 degrees. Gently brush loaf with egg mixture and sprinkle with sesame seeds, if using. Bake until golden brown and loaf registers 205 to 210 degrees, 35 to 40 minutes, rotating sheet halfway through baking. Transfer loaf to wire rack and let cool completely, about 3 hours, before serving.

Shaping Garlic Knots (page 225)

1. Press and stretch dough into 12 by 6-inch rectangle, with long side parallel to counter edge.

2. Using pizza cutter or chef's knife, cut dough vertically into 12 (6 by 1-inch) strips; cover loosely with greased plastic wrap.

3. Working with 1 piece of dough at a time, stretch and roll into 14-inch rope.

4. Shape rope into U with 2-inch-wide bottom curve.

5. Tie ends into single overhand knot, with 1½-inch open loop at bottom.

6. Wrap 1 tail over loop and press through opening from top. Wrap other tail under loop and through opening from bottom. Pinch ends together to seal.

7. Arrange knots pinched side down on prepared sheet, spaced 1 inch apart. Cover loosely with greased plastic and let rise until nearly doubled in size, 1 to 1½ hours.

8. Bake knots until set, about 5 minutes. Brush with 2 tablespoons garlic butter, rotate sheet, and bake until knots are golden brown, about 5 minutes.

9. Transfer knots to wire rack. Brush with remaining garlic butter, sprinkle with sea salt, and let cool for 15 minutes. Serve warm.

Making Scali Bread (page 226)

1. Stir sponge ingredients in liquid measuring cup with wooden spoon until well combined. Cover tightly with plastic wrap and let sit at room temperature until sponge has risen and collapses, about 6 hours.

2. Using stand mixer fitted with dough hook, slowly add sponge mixture to flour mixture on low speed and mix until cohesive dough starts to form and no dry flour remains, about 2 minutes, scraping down bowl as needed.

3. Increase speed to medium-low and knead until dough is smooth and elastic and clears sides of bowl, about 8 minutes.

4. Transfer dough to lightly floured counter and knead by hand to form smooth, round ball, about 30 seconds. Place dough seam side down in greased large bowl, cover tightly with plastic, and let rise until doubled in size, 1½ to 2 hours.

5. Press down on dough to deflate. Transfer dough to lightly floured counter, divide into thirds (about 9½ ounces each), and cover loosely with greased plastic. Working with 1 piece of dough at a time (keep remaining pieces covered), stretch and roll into 10-inch rope.

6. Arrange ropes side by side, perpendicular to counter edge, and pinch far ends together. Braid ropes into 10-inch loaf and pinch remaining ends together.

7. Transfer loaf to prepared sheet and reshape as needed, tucking edges under to form taut 10-inch loaf. Cover loosely with greased plastic and let rise until loaf increases in size by half, 1 to 1½ hours.

8. Gently brush loaf with egg mixture and sprinkle with sesame seeds, if using. Bake until golden brown, 35 to 40 minutes, rotating sheet halfway through baking.

A Scrappy Brooklyn Loaf Comes of Age

A giant fiberglass pig in chef's clothing stands proudly at the door of G. Esposito & Sons Jersey Pork Store in Brooklyn, New York, simultaneously welcoming customers and warning away miscreants. When we step inside, the relative quiet is pierced by a wailing band saw manned by a stocky, gray-haired butcher breaking down a pork loin into thin, even chops. Beneath a canopy of salami, we wait for the sawing to stop so we can inquire about the house specialty, prosciutto bread. The butcher responds curtly, talking as much with his hands as with his words, "So you wanna talk about prosciutt' bread?"

George Esposito and his brother, John, took over the store after their dad, Frank, passed away in 2004. Frank's father established the store in 1933, adding the word "Jersey" to the name to indicate

the origin of the hogs they butchered, which came from New Jersey and were, at the time, considered particularly high quality. Prosciutto bread, studded with prosciutto, salami, and other cured cuts of pork, has long been a staple here; early on it was a good way to use up odds and ends of cured meats, but the bread soon graduated from a landing place for scraps to a marquee item. The crew at Esposito's makes 5 to 25 loaves most days and up to 100 loaves around the holidays.

PROSCIUTTO BREAD

Makes 2 loaves

Why This Recipe Works Among the myriad offerings of cured and fresh meat at G. Esposito & Sons Jersey Pork Store in Brooklyn, New York, one of its house-made specialties, prosciutto bread, is legendary among the locals. Studded with prosciutto, salami, and other cured cuts of pork, it is a dream come true for aficionados of great bread and Italian meats. Back at the test kitchen, we set to work creating a version of this delicious but humble bread, the star of one of the few Italian American butcher shops remaining in the once bustling Court Street region of Brooklyn. To make this bread extra-meaty, it all came down to the cut of prosciutto. Thinly sliced deli meat became wadded up and was swallowed by the dough, but thicker slabs cut into ½-inch pieces proved to be just right. Using a combination of three meats—prosciutto, capicola, and pepperoni—gave each bite a satisfying, savory mix of flavors. We added beer to boost the yeasty, fermented flavor of the bread without having to let it rise all day, and opted for bread flour, with its high protein content, to form a strong gluten structure. We love the combination of prosciutto, pepperoni, and capicola (also called coppa) in this bread, but you can use 9 ounces of any combination of your favorite cured meats; just be sure to have each sliced ¼ inch thick at the deli counter. Do not use thinly sliced deli meats as they will adversely affect the bread's texture. Use a mild lager, such as Budweiser; strongly flavored beers will make the bread taste bitter.

- 3 cups (16½ ounces) bread flour
- 1½ teaspoons instant or rapid-rise yeast
- 1 teaspoon table salt
- 1 cup mild lager, room temperature
- 6 tablespoons water, room temperature
- 3 tablespoons extra-virgin olive oil
- 3 ounces (¼-inch-thick) sliced prosciutto, cut into ½-inch pieces
- 3 ounces (¼-inch-thick) sliced pepperoni, cut into ½-inch pieces
- 3 ounces (¼-inch-thick) sliced capicola, cut into ½-inch pieces
- 1½ teaspoons coarsely ground pepper
- Cornmeal

1. Whisk flour, yeast, and salt together in bowl of stand mixer. Whisk beer, water, and oil together in 2-cup liquid measuring cup.

2. Fit mixer with dough hook. Mix flour mixture on low speed while slowly adding beer mixture until cohesive dough starts to form and no dry flour remains, about 2 minutes, scraping down bowl as needed. Increase speed to medium and knead until dough is smooth and elastic and clears sides of bowl, about 8 minutes.

3. Reduce speed to low and add prosciutto, pepperoni, capicola, and pepper. Continue to knead until combined, about 2 minutes longer (some meats may not be fully incorporated into dough at this point; this is OK). Transfer dough and any errant pieces of meats to lightly floured counter and knead by hand to evenly incorporate meats into dough, about 1 minute.

4. Form dough into smooth, round ball and place seam side down in lightly greased large bowl. Cover tightly with plastic wrap and let dough rise at room temperature until doubled in size, about 1½ hours.

5. Line baking sheet with parchment paper and lightly dust with cornmeal. Turn out dough onto counter and gently press down to deflate any large air pockets. Cut dough into 2 even pieces. Press each piece of dough into 8 by 5-inch rectangle with long side parallel to counter's edge.

6. Working with 1 piece of dough at a time, fold top edge of rectangle down to midline, pressing to seal. Fold bottom edge of rectangle up to midline and pinch to seal. Flip dough seam side down and gently roll into 12-inch loaf with tapered ends. Transfer loaf to 1 side of prepared sheet. Repeat shaping with second piece of dough and place loaf about 3 inches from first loaf on sheet. Cover with greased plastic and let rise at room temperature until puffy and dough springs back slowly when pressed lightly with your finger, about 45 minutes.

continued

7. Adjust oven rack to middle position and heat oven to 450 degrees. Using sharp paring knife in swift, fluid motion, make ½-inch-deep lengthwise slash along top of each loaf, starting and stopping about 1½ inches from ends. Bake until loaves register 205 to 210 degrees, 22 to 25 minutes. Transfer loaves to wire rack and let cool completely, about 3 hours. Serve.

TO MAKE AHEAD

Make dough through placing ball in lightly greased bowl in step 4. Cover tightly with plastic wrap and refrigerate for at least 16 hours or up to 24 hours. Let dough come to room temperature, about 3 hours, before proceeding with step 5.

VARIATION

Prosciutto Bread with Provolone

Add 5 ounces provolone cheese, sliced ¼ inch thick and cut into ½-inch pieces, with meat in step 3.

Making Prosciutto Bread

1. Using dough hook on low speed, slowly add beer mixture to flour mixture until no dry flour remains, about 2 minutes, scraping down bowl as needed. Increase speed to medium and knead until dough is smooth and elastic and clears sides of bowl, about 8 minutes.

2. Reduce speed to low and add prosciutto, pepperoni, capicola, and pepper. Continue to knead until combined, about 2 minutes longer.

3. Transfer dough and any errant pieces of meats to lightly floured counter and knead by hand to evenly incorporate meats into dough, about 1 minute.

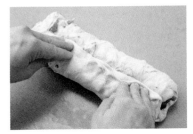

4. After dough has risen, cut dough into 2 even pieces. Press each piece into 8 by 5-inch rectangle with long side parallel to counter's edge. Working with 1 piece of dough at a time, fold top edge of rectangle down to midline, pressing to seal. Fold bottom edge of rectangle up to midline and pinch to seal.

5. Flip dough seam side down and gently roll into 12-inch loaf with tapered ends. Transfer loaf to 1 side of prepared sheet. Repeat shaping with second piece of dough and place loaf about 3 inches from first loaf on sheet.

6. After loaves have risen, use sharp paring knife in swift, fluid motion to make 1/2-inch-deep lengthwise slash along top of each loaf, starting and stopping about 1 1/2 inches from ends.

DESSERTS

TIRAMISU

Serves 10 to 12

Why This Recipe Works You could argue about which dessert, in the canon of Italian classics, reigns supreme, but there is no arguing that tiramisu created a sensation in the 1980s that has endured to this day. Is there an Italian restaurant in New York City that doesn't have a version of it on their menu? We doubt it. It is definitely beloved. A good tiramisu is a seamless union of flavors and textures—it's difficult to tell where cookie ends and cream begins, where bitter espresso gives over to the bite of alcohol, and whether unctuous or uplifting is the better adjective to describe it. For our version, instead of making a custard filling, we simply whip egg yolks, sugar, salt, rum, and mascarpone together and lighten it with whipped cream. We briefly moisten the ladyfingers in a mixture of coffee, espresso powder, and more rum. Simple to prepare but grand enough to serve the most discerning *famiglia,* this tiramisu is an ideal holiday dessert and worth every creamy, coffee-flavored, rum-spiked calorie. We prefer a tiramisu with a pronounced rum flavor; for a less potent dessert, reduce the amount of rum in the coffee mixture. Brandy or whiskey can be substituted for the rum. Don't let the mascarpone warm to room temperature before whipping. Dried ladyfingers (see page 260) are also called *savoiardi;* you will need between 42 and 60, depending on their size and the brand.

2½ cups strong brewed coffee, room temperature

9 tablespoons dark rum, divided

1½ tablespoons instant espresso powder

6 large egg yolks

⅔ cup (4⅔ ounces) sugar

¼ teaspoon table salt

1½ pounds mascarpone cheese (3 cups)

¾ cup heavy cream, chilled

14 ounces dried ladyfingers (savoiardi)

3½ tablespoons Dutch-processed cocoa, divided

¼ cup grated semisweet or bittersweet chocolate (optional)

1. Stir coffee, 5 tablespoons rum, and espresso in wide bowl or baking dish until espresso dissolves; set aside.

2. Using stand mixer fitted with whisk, whip egg yolks on low speed until just combined. Add sugar and salt and whip on medium-high speed until pale yellow, 1½ to 2 minutes, scraping down bowl once or twice. Add remaining ¼ cup rum and whip on medium speed until just combined, 20 to 30 seconds; scrape down bowl. Add mascarpone and whip on medium speed until no lumps remain, 30 to 45 seconds, scraping down bowl once or twice. Transfer mixture to large bowl and set aside.

3. In now-empty mixer bowl, whip cream on medium-low speed until foamy, about 1 minute. Increase speed to high and whip until stiff peaks form, 1 to 3 minutes. Using rubber spatula, fold one-third of whipped cream into mascarpone mixture to lighten, then gently fold in remaining whipped cream until no white streaks remain. Set mascarpone mixture aside.

4. Working with one at a time, drop half of ladyfingers into coffee mixture, roll to coat, remove, and transfer to 13 by 9-inch glass or ceramic baking dish. (Do not submerge ladyfingers in coffee mixture; entire process should take no longer than 2 to 3 seconds for each cookie.) Arrange soaked cookies in single layer in baking dish, breaking or trimming ladyfingers as needed to fit neatly into dish.

5. Spread half of mascarpone mixture over ladyfingers with spatula, spreading mixture to sides and into corners of dish, then smooth surface. Place 2 tablespoons cocoa in fine-mesh strainer and dust cocoa over mascarpone.

6. Repeat dipping and arrangement of ladyfingers; spread remaining mascarpone mixture over lady-fingers and dust with remaining 1½ tablespoons cocoa. Wipe edges of dish clean with paper towel. Cover with plastic wrap and refrigerate for at least 6 hours or up to 24 hours. Garnish with grated chocolate, if using; cut into pieces and serve chilled. (Tiramisu can be refrigerated for up to 1 day.)

CLASSIC PANNA COTTA

Serves 8

Why This Recipe Works The literal translation of panna cotta, "cooked cream," does nothing to suggest its ethereal qualities. In fact, panna cotta isn't cooked at all. Instead, sugar and gelatin are melted in cream and milk and the mixture is then turned into ramekins and chilled. It is typically unmolded onto a plate and accompanied by a sauce or fruit. Panna cotta is about nothing if not texture. The cream must be robust enough to unmold but delicate enough to shiver on the plate. Our mission was to find the correct proportions of ingredients and the most effective way to thicken the dessert with the gelatin. Because cream gave the panna cotta a rich mouthfeel and a creamier, more rounded flavor, we concurred with those recipes that favored a heavier proportion of cream to milk. The amount of sugar was enough to sweeten our concoction without making it too sweet. For a flavor accent, we found that a vanilla bean contributed a richer flavor than vanilla extract. The bean gives the panna cotta the deepest flavor, but 2 teaspoons vanilla extract can be used instead. Serve the panna cotta cold, with lightly sweetened berries or Berry Coulis (we like it made with raspberries here). Though traditionally served unmolded, panna cotta may be chilled and served in wine glasses with sauce.

1 cup whole milk

2¾ teaspoons unflavored gelatin

3 cups heavy cream

1 vanilla bean

6 tablespoons (2⅔ ounces) sugar

Pinch table salt

1. Pour milk into medium saucepan, sprinkle gelatin over top, and let sit until gelatin softens, about 10 minutes. Meanwhile, place cream in 4-cup liquid measuring cup. Cut vanilla bean in half lengthwise. Using tip of paring knife, scrape out seeds. Add vanilla bean and seeds to cream. Set eight 4-ounce ramekins on rimmed baking sheet. Fill large bowl halfway with ice and water.

2. Heat milk mixture over high heat, stirring constantly, until gelatin is dissolved and mixture registers 135 degrees, about 1½ minutes. Off heat, stir in sugar and salt until dissolved, about 1 minute.

3. Stirring constantly, slowly pour cream into milk mixture. Transfer mixture to clean bowl and set over ice bath. Stir mixture often until slightly thickened and mixture registers 50 degrees, about 10 minutes. Strain mixture through fine-mesh strainer into large liquid measuring cup, then distribute evenly among ramekins.

4. Cover ramekins and baking sheet with plastic wrap and refrigerate until custards are set (panna cottas should wobble when shaken gently), about 4 hours or up to 24 hours.

5. To unmold, run paring knife around perimeter of each ramekin. Hold serving plate over top of each ramekin and invert; set plate on counter and gently shake ramekin to release custard. Serve.

BERRY COULIS
Makes about 1½ cups

12 ounces (2½ cups) fresh or thawed frozen raspberries and/or blueberries

5–7 tablespoons sugar, divided

¼ cup water

⅛ teaspoon table salt

2 teaspoons lemon juice

1. Bring berries, 5 tablespoons sugar, water, and salt to bare simmer in medium saucepan over medium heat, stirring occasionally; cook until sugar is dissolved and berries are heated through, about 1 minute.

2. Process mixture in blender until smooth, about 20 seconds. Strain through fine-mesh strainer set over small bowl, pressing on solids to extract as much puree as possible. Stir in lemon juice and additional sugar, if desired. Transfer coulis to airtight container and refrigerate for at least 1 hour or up to 4 days. Stir to recombine before serving, adding 1 to 2 teaspoons water to adjust consistency if needed.

INDIVIDUAL FRESH BERRY GRATINS WITH ZABAGLIONE

Serves 4

Why This Recipe Works Zabaglione is a traditional Italian custard flavored with wine and often accompanied by fresh berries. To make this simple combination into a full-flavored dessert worthy of serving to guests, we turned it into a gratin. We macerated the berries with a little bit of sugar to encourage them to release their flavorful juices. For the custard, we whisked together egg yolks, sugar, and wine over a pot of barely simmering water; keeping the heat low and using a glass bowl rather than a metal one guarded against overcooking. Tasters preferred the flavor of light, crisp white wine to the more traditional Marsala, but the decreased sugar made our custard runny. To make up for the loss of structure without making the custard achingly sweet, we folded in some whipped cream. Dividing the berries and custard among individual ramekins made for a pretty presentation and easier serving. Running the gratins briefly under the broiler produced warm, succulent berries and a golden-brown crust on the zabaglione. You will need four shallow 6-ounce broiler-safe gratin dishes, but a broiler-safe pie plate or gratin dish can be used instead. When making the zabaglione, be sure to cook the egg mixture in a glass bowl over water that is barely simmering; glass conducts heat more evenly and gently than metal. Although we prefer to make this recipe with a mixture of blackberries, blueberries, raspberries, and strawberries, you can use 3 cups of just one type of berry. Do not use frozen berries for this recipe. To prevent scorching, pay close attention to the gratins when broiling. Use a medium-bodied dry white wine such as Sauvignon Blanc or Chardonnay in this recipe.

Berry Mixture

- 11 ounces (2¼ cups) blackberries, blueberries, and/or raspberries
- 4 ounces strawberries, hulled and halved lengthwise if small or quartered if large (¾ cup)
- 2 teaspoons granulated sugar
   Pinch table salt

Zabaglione
- 3 large egg yolks
- 3 tablespoons granulated sugar, divided
- 3 tablespoons dry white wine
- 2 teaspoons packed light brown sugar
- 3 tablespoons heavy cream, chilled

1. For the berry mixture Line rimmed baking sheet with aluminum foil. Toss berries, strawberries, sugar, and salt together in bowl. Divide berry mixture evenly among 4 shallow 6-ounce gratin dishes set in prepared sheet; set aside.

2. For the zabaglione Whisk egg yolks, 2 tablespoons plus 1 teaspoon granulated sugar, and wine together in medium bowl until sugar has dissolved, about 1 minute. Set bowl over saucepan of barely simmering water and cook, whisking constantly, until mixture is frothy. Continue to cook, whisking constantly, until mixture is slightly thickened, creamy, and glossy, 5 to 10 minutes (mixture will form loose mounds when dripped from whisk). Remove bowl from saucepan and whisk constantly for 30 seconds to cool slightly. Transfer bowl to refrigerator and chill until egg mixture is completely cool, about 10 minutes.

3. Meanwhile, adjust oven rack 6 inches from broiler element and heat broiler. Combine brown sugar and remaining 2 teaspoons granulated sugar in bowl.

4. Whisk heavy cream in large bowl until it holds soft peaks, 30 to 90 seconds. Using rubber spatula, gently fold whipped cream into cooled egg mixture. Spoon zabaglione over berries and sprinkle sugar mixture evenly on top. Let sit at room temperature for 10 minutes, until sugar dissolves.

5. Broil gratins until sugar is bubbly and caramelized, 1 to 4 minutes. Serve immediately.

A Walk Through History, Ending with Cannoli

If you find yourself lost in the jumble of narrow streets in Boston's North End, keep walking. You're sure to stumble on the directional sign planted on a prominent corner indicating the way home. To… Napoli? Calabria? Milano? There's no chance the arrows are accurate—they point in every direction—but the message they convey is true: Here, Italy is an idea, an identity, a state of mind. As it has been for a century and a half.

The first significant wave of Italian immigrants arrived in Boston's North End in the 1860s, during a period when America was struggling to recalibrate after the Civil War. Over the next decades, Irish and German-speaking Jewish communities moved out of the city's North End as Italians moved in. Soon, the main streets of the

neighborhood—Prince, Salem, Hanover—were filled with Italian bakeries, butchers, greengrocers, and restaurants, all just steps away from Revolutionary and Colonial landmarks like Faneuil Hall and the Old North Church. A central location with plenty of foot traffic has made it one of the city's most vibrant neighborhoods over the years, filled with little restaurants where hungry residents can grab a dish of pasta with clams or a spicy calzone for a fair price.

Today, locals celebrate street festivals like the annual Saint Agrippina's Feast, and tourists line up for the cannolis at Mike's Pastry, perhaps to fuel up for a walking tour of the Freedom Trail or an afternoon lazing around Christopher Columbus Waterfront Park.

PISTACHIO CANNOLI

Makes 10 cannoli

Why This Recipe Works Cannoli might just be the most well-known sweet sold in bakeries in Italian neighborhoods across the United States. The name translates as "little tubes," a reference to the fried pastry tubes that are filled with creamy, sweetened ricotta. Too bad that most versions sold in Italian bakeries are terrible. That's because this sweet is best filled to order. If filled in advance, the shells gets soggy and you lose the contrast between the lush filling and crisp pastry. For this recipe, we filled store-bought cannoli shells with a traditional filling of ricotta cheese enriched with creamy, rich mascarpone, sugar, and chopped pistachios—a nod to the Sicilian origins of the treat. Instead of draining the ricotta overnight, we placed the ricotta in cheese-cloth and then weighted it with heavy cans to remove maximum moisture in minimal time, resulting in a desirably dense filling in only an hour. To pipe the filling into the shells, a zipper-lock bag makes a convenient stand-in for a pastry bag. We garnished one end of each cannoli with shaved chocolate as a flavorful and elegant alternative to mini chocolate chips. You can find cannoli shells at most markets in either the international foods aisle, the gourmet cheese section, or the bakery. Make sure to use a high-quality whole-milk ricotta (see page 141). Use a vegetable peeler or the large holes of a box grater to shave or grate chocolate for a garnish.

- 12   ounces (1½ cups) ricotta cheese
- 12   ounces (1½ cups) mascarpone cheese
- ¾   cup (3 ounces) confectioners' sugar
- ½   cup shelled pistachios, chopped
- 1½   teaspoons vanilla extract
     Pinch table salt
- 10   cannoli shells
- ¼   cup shaved or grated bittersweet chocolate

1. Line colander with triple layer of cheesecloth and place in sink. Place ricotta in prepared colander, pull edges of cheesecloth together to form pouch, and twist to squeeze out as much liquid as possible. Place taut, twisted cheese pouch in pie plate and set heavy plate on top. Weight plate with 2 large heavy cans and refrigerate for 1 hour.

2. Discard drained ricotta liquid and transfer dry ricotta to medium bowl. Stir in mascarpone, sugar, pistachios, vanilla, and salt. Cover and refrigerate until needed, or up to 1 day.

3. Transfer chilled cheese mixture into pastry bag or large zipper-lock bag. (If using zipper-lock bag, cut ¾ inch off one bottom corner.) Pipe filling evenly into cannoli shells from both ends, working outward from center. Sprinkle 1 end of each cannoli with grated chocolate and serve.

THE ITALIAN AMERICAN KITCHEN
Mascarpone

Tiramisu is just the tip of the iceberg when it comes to mascarpone. This soft, creamy cow's milk cheese from Italy is both slightly sweet and slightly tangy. It's versatile enough to be used in both sweet applications (tiramisu, tarts, dolloped on berries, drizzled with honey) and savory dishes (stirred into pasta or risotto, served alongside baked or roasted potatoes). Mascarpone is an acid-set cheese, which means that the cream and/or milk is coagulated using acids such as citric instead of rennet. It's then cooked until it reaches a thick and spreadable consistency similar to that of crème fraîche or sour cream. It used to be available only in Italian markets or specialty shops, but now can be found in most supermarkets. Although we liked all of the brands we tasted in the test kitchen, the sole Italian import emerged as our favorite. **Polenghi Mascarpone** boasts an especially "luscious" texture and yielded ultrasmooth desserts that sliced neatly but weren't too thick or heavy.

ZEPPOLES

Makes 15 to 18 zeppoles

Why This Recipe Works Go to an Italian American festival, such as the annual Feast of San Gennaro in New York's Little Italy, and you'll likely pass multiple booths selling fresh zeppoles. These deep-fried Italian confections are golden brown and crispy on the outside and soft and airy inside, with a light sprinkle of powdered sugar on top. They usually aren't eccentric or fancy in their flavorings, nor are they meant to be; their charm is their simplicity. To make zeppoles, a cross between doughnuts and fried dough, we discovered that two leaveners were better than one. Although typically used independently, in the case of these Italian fritters, a combination of baking powder and yeast created the perfect fluffy confection. The baking powder ensured a light rather than doughy interior, and the yeast provided the requisite flavor and more lift. Frying the wet, sticky dough at 350 degrees yielded a crispy exterior that didn't overcook by the time the interior had finished cooking. These light, tender zeppoles are best served warm with a dusting of powdery confectioners' sugar. The dough is very wet and sticky. If you own a 4-cup liquid measuring cup, you can combine the dough in it to make it easier to tell when it has doubled in volume in step 1.

1⅓ cups (6⅔ ounces) all-purpose flour

1 tablespoon granulated sugar

2 teaspoons instant or rapid-rise yeast

1 teaspoon baking powder

½ teaspoon table salt

1 cup warm water (110 degrees)

½ teaspoon vanilla extract

2 quarts peanut or vegetable oil

Confectioners' sugar

1. Combine flour, granulated sugar, yeast, baking powder, and salt in large bowl. Whisk water and vanilla into flour mixture until fully combined. Cover tightly with plastic wrap and let rise at room temperature until doubled in size, 15 to 25 minutes.

2. Set wire rack in rimmed baking sheet and line rack with triple layer of paper towels. Adjust oven rack to middle position and heat oven to 200 degrees. Add oil to large Dutch oven until it measures about 1½ inches deep and heat over medium-high heat to 350 degrees.

3. Using greased tablespoon measure, add 6 heaping tablespoonfuls of batter to oil. (Use dinner spoon to help scrape batter from tablespoon if necessary.) Fry until golden brown and toothpick inserted in center of zeppole comes out clean, 2 to 3 minutes, flipping once halfway through frying. Adjust burner, if necessary, to maintain oil temperature between 325 and 350 degrees.

4. Using wire skimmer or slotted spoon, transfer zeppoles to prepared wire rack; roll briefly so paper towels absorb grease. Transfer sheet to oven to keep warm. Return oil to 350 degrees and repeat twice more with remaining batter. Dust zeppoles with confectioners' sugar and serve.

CHOCOLATE CHIP PANETTONE

Makes 1 loaf

Why This Recipe Works Panettone is a sweetened and enriched bread (think brioche) studded with dried and candied fruit or sometimes nuts. It's not a fruitcake! Originating in Milan, this tall, luxurious bread is made during the Christmas season in bakeries throughout Italy and sold in pretty boxes in countless Italian markets in the United States. Some bakers in this country have Americanized this recipe by replacing most of the candied fruit with crowd-pleasing chocolate chips. We decided to follow suit and develop a variation that hews closer to the Italian original. To avoid having to special-order the customary paper panettone baking molds, we discovered that using an 8-inch cake pan produced the signature dome shape. While panettone traditionally takes multiple days to make due to its long rising time, we sped up the process by using warm milk and corn syrup; yeast acts faster in warm environments and can metabolize invert sugars (such as corn syrup) faster than white sugar. Using corn syrup also helped the panettone stay moist longer. Use an instant-read thermometer to make sure the milk is the correct temperature. If using a traditional 6 by 4-inch paper panettone mold, which you can find online or at kitchen supply stores, extend the baking time in step 6 by 10 minutes.

- ¾ cup warm milk (110 degrees)
- 2 large eggs plus 2 large yolks, divided
- 3 tablespoons light corn syrup
- 1 teaspoon vanilla extract
- ½ teaspoon almond extract
- 2¾ cups (13¾ ounces) all-purpose flour
- 2¼ teaspoons instant or rapid-rise yeast
- 1 teaspoon table salt
- 8 tablespoons unsalted butter, cut into 8 pieces and softened
- 1 cup (6 ounces) mini chocolate chips
- 3 ounces finely chopped candied orange peel

1. Whisk milk, 1 egg and yolks, corn syrup, vanilla, and almond extract in 2-cup liquid measuring cup until combined. Using stand mixer fitted with dough hook, mix flour, yeast, and salt on medium-low speed until combined, about 5 seconds. With mixer running, slowly add milk mixture and knead until cohesive dough forms and no dry flour remains, 3 to 5 minutes, scraping down bowl and dough hook as needed.

2. With mixer running, add butter 1 piece at a time until incorporated. Increase speed to medium-high and knead until dough pulls away from sides of bowl but still sticks to bottom, about 10 minutes. Reduce speed to low, add chocolate chips and orange peel, and knead until fully incorporated, about 2 minutes.

3. Turn out dough onto lightly floured counter and knead until smooth, about 1 minute. Form dough into tight ball and transfer to greased large bowl. Cover with plastic wrap and let rise until doubled in size, about 2 hours.

4. Grease 8-inch cake pan. Pat dough into 12-inch disk on lightly floured counter. Working around circumference of dough, fold edges of dough toward center to form rough square. Flip dough over and, applying gentle pressure, move your hands in small circular motions to form dough into smooth, taut ball. Transfer ball, seam side down, to prepared pan. Cover loosely with greased plastic and let rise until center is about 2 inches above lip of pan, 2 to 2½ hours.

5. Adjust oven rack to middle position and heat oven to 350 degrees. Lightly beat remaining egg and brush over dough. Bake until golden brown, 15 to 20 minutes.

6. Rotate pan, tent with aluminum foil, and continue to bake until center of loaf registers 190 degrees, 30 to 40 minutes longer. Transfer pan to wire rack and let cool for 15 minutes. Remove loaf from pan and let cool completely on wire rack, about 3 hours. Serve.

VARIATION

Orange and Raisin Panettone
Omit chocolate chips. Combine ¾ cup golden raisins and 2 tablespoons orange juice in small bowl, cover, and microwave until steaming, about 1 minute. Let sit until raisins are softened, about 15 minutes. Add 2 teaspoons grated orange zest to milk mixture in step 1. Add raisins (plus any juice remaining in bowl) with candied orange peel in step 2.

ITALIAN ALMOND CAKE

Serves 8 to 10

Why This Recipe Works Simple, rich almond cake makes a sophisticated and delicately sweet dessert, but traditional Italian versions tend to be heavy and dense. For a slightly cakier version with plenty of nutty flavor, we swapped out the usual almond paste for toasted blanched sliced almonds (we disliked the slight bitterness imparted by skin-on almonds) and added a bit of almond extract for extra depth. A generous amount of lemon zest provided subtle brightness. For an even lighter crumb, we increased the flour slightly and added baking powder—an untraditional ingredient—to ensure proper rise. Making the batter in a food processor broke down some of the protein structure in the eggs, ensuring that the cake had a level, not domed, top, which was especially important for this unfrosted dessert. We swapped some butter for oil and lowered the oven temperature to produce an evenly baked, moist cake. For a crunchy finishing touch, we topped the cake with sliced almonds and a sprinkle of lemon-infused sugar. If you can't find blanched sliced almonds, grind slivered almonds for the batter and use unblanched sliced almonds for the topping. The Orange Crème Fraîche is optional but well worth the extra 10 minutes of effort.

Orange Crème Fraîche

- 2 oranges
- 1 cup crème fraîche
- 2 tablespoons sugar
- 1/8 teaspoon table salt

Almond Cake

- 1 1/2 cups plus 1/3 cup blanched sliced almonds, toasted, divided
- 3/4 cup (3 3/4 ounces) all-purpose flour
- 3/4 teaspoon table salt
- 1/4 teaspoon baking powder
- 1/8 teaspoon baking soda
- 4 large eggs
- 1 1/4 cups (8 3/4 ounces) plus 2 tablespoons sugar, divided

- 1 tablespoon plus 1/2 teaspoon grated lemon zest (2 lemons), divided
- 3/4 teaspoon almond extract
- 5 tablespoons unsalted butter, melted
- 1/3 cup vegetable oil

1. For the orange crème fraîche Finely grate 1 teaspoon zest from 1 orange. Cut away peel and pith from oranges. Slice between membranes to release segments and cut segments into 1/4-inch pieces. Combine orange pieces and zest, crème fraîche, sugar, and salt in bowl and mix well. Refrigerate for at least 1 hour, or until serving.

2. For the almond cake Adjust oven rack to middle position and heat oven to 300 degrees. Grease 9-inch round cake pan and line with parchment paper. Pulse 1 1/2 cups almonds, flour, salt, baking powder, and baking soda in food processor until almonds are finely ground, 5 to 10 pulses. Transfer almond mixture to bowl.

3. Process eggs, 1 1/4 cups sugar, 1 tablespoon lemon zest, and almond extract in now-empty processor until very pale yellow, about 2 minutes. With processor running, add melted butter and oil in steady stream until incorporated. Add almond mixture and pulse to combine, 4 to 5 pulses. Transfer batter to prepared pan.

4. Using your fingers, combine remaining 2 tablespoons sugar and remaining 1/2 teaspoon lemon zest in small bowl until fragrant, 5 to 10 seconds. Sprinkle top of cake evenly with remaining 1/3 cup almonds followed by sugar-zest mixture.

5. Bake until center of cake is set and bounces back when gently pressed and toothpick inserted in center comes out clean, 55 minutes to 1 hour 5 minutes, rotating pan after 40 minutes. Let cake cool in pan on wire rack for 15 minutes. Run thin knife around edge of pan. Invert cake onto greased wire rack, discarding parchment, and reinvert cake onto second wire rack. Let cake cool completely on rack, about 2 hours. Serve with orange crème fraîche. (Cake can be stored at room temperature for up to 3 days.)

PIGNOLI

Makes about 18 cookies

Why This Recipe Works With an appealingly light texture from egg whites (no yolks) and a nutty flavor profile, pine nut macaroons from southern Italy are standard after-dinner fare with espresso or maybe some grappa. *Pignoli* require only a few ingredients and are simple to make, plus they are naturally gluten-free. For the base, most recipes we found rely on almond paste, but we achieved a deeper, richer almond flavor and more controlled sweetness by simply processing slivered almonds with granulated sugar. Some recipes include lemon or orange zest, but we found that these additions were more a distraction than an asset. Our base was a little sticky, but it was still easy enough to roll the dough into balls, then coat in pine nuts for the traditional finish. There was no need to toast the pine nuts ahead of time since they toasted as the cookies baked. If desired, the cookies can be dusted with confectioners' sugar just after they come out of the oven.

$1\frac{2}{3}$ cups slivered almonds

$1\frac{1}{3}$ cups ($9\frac{1}{3}$ ounces) sugar

2 large egg whites

1 cup pine nuts

1. Adjust oven racks to upper-middle and lower-middle positions and heat oven to 375 degrees. Line 2 baking sheets with parchment paper.

2. Process almonds and sugar in food processor until finely ground, about 30 seconds. Scrape down sides of bowl and add egg whites. Continue to process until smooth (dough will be wet), about 30 seconds; transfer mixture to bowl. Place pine nuts in shallow dish.

3. Working with 1 scant tablespoon dough at a time, roll into balls, roll in pine nuts to coat, and space 2 inches apart on prepared sheets.

4. Bake cookies until light golden brown, 13 to 15 minutes, switching and rotating sheets halfway through baking. Let cookies cool on sheets for 5 minutes, then transfer to wire rack. Let cookies cool to room temperature before serving. (Cookies can be stored in airtight container at room temperature for up to 4 days.)

THE ITALIAN AMERICAN KITCHEN

Pine Nuts

Also called *pignoli* (Italian) or *piñons* (Spanish), these diminutive nut-like seeds are harvested from pine cones. There are two main types of pine nuts: the delicately flavored, torpedo-shaped Mediterranean pine nuts and the more assertive, corn kernel–shaped Chinese pine nuts (shown below). The less-expensive Chinese variety is more widely available, but both can be used interchangeably. Pine nuts have a mild taste and a slightly waxy texture and need to be stored with care to prevent rancidity. They are best transferred to an airtight container as soon as their original packaging is opened. They will keep in the refrigerator for up to 3 months or in the freezer for up to 9 months.

ITALIAN ANISE COOKIES

Makes about 32 cookies

Why This Recipe Works *Angeletti*, also known as anisette cookies, are a staple at any big Italian celebration. Cakey, with a little heft, they share similarities with scones and biscuits. To achieve their unique texture, we used vegetable shortening in addition to butter. The shortening gave the cookies a lighter texture and an appealing crisp edge, while the butter contributed plenty of flavor. A combination of 4 tablespoons shortening and 4 tablespoons butter struck the right balance, giving us cookies with both ethereal texture and rich flavor. A couple of teaspoons of baking powder provided just enough lift. Lemon zest ably complemented the refreshing hit of anise. To ensure the anise flavor fully permeated our cookies, we used extract in both the cookie dough and the glaze. These cookies are traditionally decorated with cheery multicolored nonpareils after their bright white, lemony glaze is applied, but feel free to use any sprinkles you like. Just be sure to glaze and decorate only a few cookies at a time so the sprinkles stick before the glaze dries.

- 2 cups (10 ounces) all-purpose flour
- ½ cup (3½ ounces) granulated sugar
- 2 teaspoons baking powder
- ½ teaspoon table salt
- 4 tablespoons unsalted butter, cut into ½-inch pieces and chilled
- 4 tablespoons vegetable shortening, cut into ½-inch pieces and chilled
- 2 large eggs
- 1¼ teaspoons anise extract, divided
- 1 teaspoon vanilla extract
- 1 teaspoon grated lemon zest plus 2 tablespoons juice
- 1½ cups (6 ounces) confectioners' sugar
  Multicolored nonpareils (optional)

1. Adjust oven racks to upper-middle and lower-middle positions and heat oven to 375 degrees. Line 2 baking sheets with parchment paper.

2. Process flour, granulated sugar, baking powder, and salt in food processor until combined, about 5 seconds. Scatter butter and shortening over top and pulse until mixture appears sandy, 10 to 12 pulses. Add eggs, 1 teaspoon anise extract, vanilla, and lemon zest and process until dough forms, 20 to 30 seconds.

3. Working with 1 tablespoon dough at a time, roll into balls and space them 2 inches apart on prepared sheets. Bake until tops have puffed and cracked and bottoms are light golden brown, 14 to 16 minutes, switching and rotating sheets halfway through baking. Let cookies cool on sheets for 5 minutes, then transfer to wire rack. Let cookies cool completely.

4. Whisk confectioners' sugar, lemon juice, and remaining ¼ teaspoon anise extract in bowl until smooth. Working with a few cookies at a time, spread each cookie with glaze and decorate with nonpareils, if using. Let glaze dry for at least 30 minutes before serving.

SPUMONI BARS

Makes 48 cookies

Why This Recipe Works One of the best things about cookies is that they're a blank slate, just waiting for your creative contribution. These cookies are inspired by the frozen Italian dessert spumoni. Striped just like the slabs of ice cream, they feature three traditional flavors—nuts, chocolate, and cherry. Instead of emptying and washing the mixer three times for three flavored doughs, we streamlined the process by making one dough, dividing it into thirds, and simply stirring the flavorings into each batch of dough. Then, to shape the cookies, we formed the doughs into ropes and pressed three ropes (one of each color) together, rolled out the tricolored dough, and sliced it into bars. We refrigerated the dough as needed to keep the process from getting messy. In the end we had an eye-catching and colorful cookie featuring three delicious flavors. And the best part? Unlike ice cream, we could savor them for as long as we liked without them melting. If the ropes don't stick together well, lightly brush their sides with water to help them adhere.

- 2 cups (10 ounces) all-purpose flour
- ¼ teaspoon baking powder
- ⅛ teaspoon salt
- 12 tablespoons unsalted butter, softened
- ⅔ cup (4⅔ ounces) sugar
- 3 large egg yolks
- 1 teaspoon vanilla extract
- 12 maraschino cherries, drained, stemmed, and chopped fine
- ¼ cup walnuts, toasted and chopped fine
- ¼ cup semisweet chocolate chips, melted and slightly cooled

1. Adjust oven racks to upper-middle and lower-middle positions and heat oven to 375 degrees. Line 2 baking sheets with parchment paper.

2. Whisk flour, baking powder, and salt together in bowl. Using stand mixer fitted with paddle, beat butter and sugar on medium-high speed until pale and fluffy, about 2 minutes. Add egg yolks and vanilla and beat until incorporated. Reduce speed to low, add flour mixture, and mix until just combined. Divide dough into 3 equal pieces and transfer each piece to separate bowl.

3. Add cherries to first bowl of dough and mix with wooden spoon until incorporated. Add walnuts to second bowl and mix until incorporated. Add melted chocolate to third bowl and mix until incorporated. Refrigerate until doughs are slightly firm, about 10 minutes.

4. Divide each dough in half. Roll each dough half into 12-inch rope on lightly floured counter. Place 1 rope of each color side-by-side and gently press together. Refrigerate dough ropes until slightly firm, about 10 minutes. Roll each set of ropes into 24 by 3-inch rectangle. Cut rectangles crosswise into 1-inch cookies and space them ¾ inch apart on prepared sheets.

5. Bake until just set but not browned, 12 to 14 minutes, switching and rotating sheets halfway through baking. Let cookies cool on sheets for 5 minutes, then transfer to wire rack. Let cookies cool completely before serving.

ITALIAN RAINBOW COOKIES

Makes 60 cookies

Why This Recipe Works Rainbow cookies, Napoleon cookies, tricolor cookies, seven layer cookies, or Venetian cookies: Whatever you call them, these multilayered treats are part cake, part cookie, part confection, and unabashedly sweet. With their green, white, and red stripes, these Italian American cookies are meant to look like miniature Italian flags. Each colorful layer is made from an almond paste–enhanced sponge cake for a sturdy, slightly dense confection that's easy to stack, slice, and eat in cookie form. For tricolored cake layers, we made just one batter and then separated it into thirds, adding red and green food coloring to two of the portions. We baked each batter separately and then once the layers cooled we spread them with raspberry jam and stacked them. For a crowning touch, we spread a generous amount of melted chocolate over the surface, taking the final layer of these cookies over the top. Running a fork through the melted chocolate in waves once it had set and thickened for a few minutes provided the final flourish. After the chocolate coating was completely set, we trimmed the sides and cut the cookies into beautifully layered bars packed with almond, raspberry, and chocolate flavor in every bite.

- 2 cups (8 ounces) cake flour
- ½ teaspoon baking powder
- 1½ cups (10½ ounces) sugar
- 8 ounces almond paste, cut into 1-inch pieces
- 7 large eggs
- 1 teaspoon vanilla extract
- ½ teaspoon table salt
- 8 tablespoons unsalted butter, melted and cooled slightly
- ⅛ teaspoon red food coloring
- ⅛ teaspoon green food coloring
- ⅔ cup seedless raspberry jam
- 1 cup (6 ounces) bittersweet chocolate chips

1. Adjust oven rack to middle position and heat oven to 350 degrees. Grease 13 by 9-inch baking pan. Make parchment paper sling by folding 1 long sheet of parchment 13 inches wide and laying across width of pan, with extra parchment hanging over edges of pan. Push parchment into corners and up sides of pan, smoothing parchment flush to pan. Grease parchment.

2. Combine flour and baking powder and sift into bowl; set aside. Process sugar and almond paste in food processor until combined, 20 to 30 seconds. Transfer sugar mixture to bowl of stand mixer; add eggs, vanilla, and salt. Fit mixer with whisk attachment and whip mixture on medium-high speed until pale and thickened, 5 to 7 minutes. Reduce speed to low and add melted butter. Slowly add flour mixture until just combined.

3. Transfer 2 cups batter to prepared pan and spread in even layer with offset spatula. Bake until top is set and edges are just starting to brown, 10 to 12 minutes. Let cool in pan for 5 minutes. Using parchment overhang, remove cake from pan and transfer to wire rack. Let cake and pan cool completely.

4. Divide remaining batter between 2 bowls. Stir red food coloring into first bowl and green food coloring into second bowl. Make new parchment sling for now-empty pan and repeat baking with each colored batter, letting pan cool after each batch.

5. Invert red layer onto cutting board and gently remove parchment. Spread ⅓ cup jam evenly over top. Invert plain layer onto red layer and gently remove parchment. Spread remaining ⅓ cup jam evenly over top. Invert green layer onto plain layer and gently remove parchment.

6. Microwave chocolate chips in bowl at 50 percent power, stirring occasionally, until melted, 2 to 4 minutes. Spread chocolate evenly over green layer. Let set for 2 minutes, then run fork in wavy pattern through chocolate. Let chocolate set, 1 to 2 hours. Using serrated knife, trim away edges. Cut lengthwise into 5 equal strips (about 1½ inches wide) and then crosswise into 12 equal strips (about 1 inch wide). Serve.

FLORENTINE LACE COOKIES

Makes 24 cookies

Why This Recipe Works Florentines are slim, lacy disks of ground almonds bound with buttery caramel and gilded with bittersweet chocolate. They are pretty much a given at any bakery in an Italian American neighborhood. By making just a few tweaks to the recipes that the pros use for these wafer-thin citrus-flavored almond cookies, we were able to achieve foolproof, fantastic Florentines for the home kitchen. Our main challenge was making the batter thin enough that it would spread before becoming rock hard. Processing the almonds until they were coarsely ground gave the cookies a flatter profile, and upping the cream encouraged spread. But the Florentines still lacked crispness and a delicate filigreed appearance. Two quick fixes solved these problems: A touch less flour helped them spread even thinner, and a few extra minutes in the oven allowed the cookies to crisp and turn deep golden brown from edge to edge. It's important to cook the cream mixture in the saucepan until it's thick and starting to brown at the edges; undercooking will result in a dough that is too runny to portion. Don't be concerned if some butter separates from the dough. For the most uniform cookies, make sure that your parchment paper lies flat. When melting the chocolate, pause the microwave and stir the chocolate often to ensure that it doesn't get much warmer than body temperature.

- 2 cups slivered almonds
- ¾ cup heavy cream
- 4 tablespoons unsalted butter, cut into 4 pieces
- ½ cup (3½ ounces) sugar
- ¼ cup orange marmalade
- 3 tablespoons all-purpose flour
- 1 teaspoon vanilla extract
- ¼ teaspoon grated orange zest
- ¼ teaspoon table salt
- 4 ounces bittersweet chocolate, chopped fine

1. Adjust oven racks to upper-middle and lower-middle positions and heat oven to 350 degrees. Line 2 baking sheets with parchment paper. Process almonds in food processor until they resemble coarse sand, about 30 seconds.

2. Bring cream, butter, and sugar to boil in medium saucepan over medium-high heat. Cook, stirring frequently, until mixture begins to thicken, 5 to 6 minutes. Continue to cook, stirring constantly, until mixture begins to brown at edges and is thick enough to leave trail that doesn't immediately fill in when spatula is scraped along pan bottom, 1 to 2 minutes (it's OK if some darker speckles appear in mixture). Remove pan from heat and stir in almonds, marmalade, flour, vanilla, orange zest, and salt until combined.

3. Drop six 1-tablespoon portions of dough onto each prepared sheet, spaced at least 3½ inches apart. When cool enough to handle, use your dampened fingers to press each portion into 2½-inch circle.

4. Bake cookies until deep brown from edge to edge, 15 to 17 minutes, switching and rotating sheets halfway through baking. Transfer cookies, still on parchment, to wire racks. Repeat with remaining dough. Let cookies cool completely.

5. Microwave 3 ounces chocolate in bowl at 50 percent power, stirring frequently, until about two-thirds melted, 1 to 2 minutes. Remove bowl from microwave, add remaining 1 ounce chocolate, and stir until melted, returning to microwave for no more than 5 seconds at a time to complete melting if necessary. Transfer chocolate to small zipper-lock bag and snip off corner, making hole no larger than 1/16 inch.

6. Pipe zigzag of chocolate over each cookie on wire racks, distributing chocolate evenly among all cookies. Refrigerate until chocolate is set, about 30 minutes, before serving. (Cookies can be stored at cool room temperature for up to 4 days.)

CHOCOLATE SALAMI

Makes 24 cookies

Why This Recipe Works Don't worry: No pork products were used in the making of this confection. This no-bake cookie may get its name from its resemblance to the Italian cured sausage, but any similarity is in appearance only: With a chocolate ganache base akin to a chocolate truffle, chocolate salami is typically chock-full of dried fruit, nuts, and crushed cookies. The mixture is then formed into a log that's cut into rounds, much like slice-and-bake cookies—minus the "bake." The result is something that's a little bit like a cookie, a little bit like a candy—and very delicious. To complete the salami look, we dredged the logs of dough in confectioners' sugar. For our recipe, we liked the combination of tart dried cherries, which we macerated in Grand Marnier for extra flavor, and rich pistachios. We used dried ladyfingers as the cookie component, although any dry, biscuit-like cookie will work. We found that chocolate chips worked better than bar chocolate here; they made a smooth mixture that was easy to mold. The result is an exquisite, unique cookie that's deceptively simple to make.

½ cup dried cherries, chopped coarse

2 tablespoons Grand Marnier

4 ounces dried ladyfingers (savoiardi), cut into ½-inch pieces, divided

1 cup (6 ounces) semisweet or bittersweet chocolate chips

⅓ cup heavy cream

Pinch table salt

⅔ cup pistachios, toasted

½ cup confectioners' sugar

1. Combine cherries and Grand Marnier in small bowl and microwave until hot, about 30 seconds; let sit until cherries have softened and mixture is cool, about 15 minutes. Set aside 1 cup ladyfingers. Process remaining ladyfingers in food processor to fine crumbs, 15 to 20 seconds. (You should have about ¾ cup crumbs.)

2. Microwave chocolate chips and cream in bowl at 50 percent power, stirring frequently, until melted and smooth, 30 to 60 seconds. Add salt and ladyfinger crumbs and stir to combine. Add pistachios, reserved ladyfingers, and cherry mixture and stir until thick dough forms.

3. Transfer dough to counter. Divide dough in half and place each half on large sheet of plastic wrap. Use plastic to roll each dough half into tight 6-inch log, twisting ends well to secure. Refrigerate logs until firm, at least 3 hours or up to 3 days.

4. When ready to serve, spread confectioners' sugar in shallow dish. Unwrap logs and roll in sugar until well coated, brushing off excess. Cut each log into ½-inch-thick slices and serve.

THE ITALIAN AMERICAN KITCHEN

Ladyfingers

Ladyfingers (also called *savoiardi*) are the base for several Italian sweets, including tiramisu (see recipe on page 236). At some markets you will find two options: soft, cake-like ladyfingers with a texture akin to sponge cake as well as dried ladyfingers with a crisp, cookie-like texture. Make sure to buy dried ladyfingers for this recipe as well as for tiramisu.

LEMON ICE

Serves 8 (Makes 1 quart)

Why This Recipe Works We wanted a refreshing lemon ice that struck a perfect sweet-tart balance and hit lots of high notes—without so much as a trace of bitterness. A cup of sugar gave our lemon ice the ideal amount of sweetness; less sugar left it with a pronounced bitterness, and more sugar made it taste like frozen lemonade. Spring water had a cleaner, less metallic flavor than tap water and a pinch of salt boosted flavors. Alcohol, because it has anti-freezing properties, is often added to icy frozen desserts such as lemon ice to help counter the mixture's solidity and stiffness when frozen. Usually vodka is the spirit of choice—it is colorless, odorless, and relatively tasteless and so can go unnoticed. When we added 2 tablespoons vodka, the finished ice was softer and creamier with a slightly slushy texture. Of course, the single most important determinant of the texture of lemon ice is the freezing method. An ice cream machine will produce a very fine-grained, creamy, and smooth sorbet-like texture. We also tried freezing the lemon mixture in ice cube trays and then processing the cubes in a food processor and transferring the mixture to a chilled bowl. This simple method produced a fluffy, coarse-grained texture. Since many home cooks are without an ice cream machine, we decided to use the ice cube tray method, but you can use an ice cream machine if you prefer. The addition of vodka yields the best texture, but it can be omitted.

2¼ cups water, preferably spring water

1 cup lemon juice (6 lemons)

1 cup (7 ounces) sugar

2 tablespoons vodka (optional)

⅛ teaspoon table salt

1. Whisk all ingredients together in bowl until sugar has dissolved. Pour mixture into 2 ice cube trays and freeze until solid, at least 3 hours or up to 5 days.

2. Place medium bowl in freezer. Pulse half of ice cubes in food processor until creamy and no large lumps remain, about 18 pulses. Transfer mixture to chilled bowl and return to freezer. Repeat pulsing remaining cubes; transfer to bowl. Serve immediately.

VARIATIONS
Orange Ice
Reduce lemon juice to 2 tablespoons and add ¾ cup orange juice (3 oranges). Reduce sugar to ¾ cup.

Lemon-Lime Ice
Substitute ½ cup lime juice (4 limes) for ½ cup lemon juice.

Minted Lemon Ice
Bring 1 cup water, sugar, and salt to simmer in small saucepan over medium-high heat, stirring occasionally. Off heat, stir in ½ cup fresh mint leaves, roughly torn; let steep for 5 minutes, then strain mixture through fine-mesh strainer into medium bowl. Stir in remaining 1¼ cups water, lemon juice, and vodka, if using; let cool to room temperature, about 15 minutes. Freeze as directed.

Lemon-Lavender Ice
Bring 1 cup water, sugar, and salt to simmer in small saucepan over medium-high heat, stirring occasionally. Off heat, stir in 2½ teaspoons dried lavender; let steep for 5 minutes, then strain mixture through fine-mesh strainer into medium bowl. Stir in remaining 1¼ cups water, lemon juice, and vodka, if using; let cool to room temperature, about 15 minutes. Freeze as directed.

NUTRITIONAL INFORMATION FOR OUR RECIPES

We calculate the nutritional values of our recipes per serving; if there is a range in the serving size, we used the highest number of servings to calculate the nutritional values. We entered all the ingredients, using weights for important ingredients such as most vegetables. We also used our preferred brands in these analyses. We did not include additional salt or pepper for food that's "seasoned to taste."

	Calories	Total Fat (G)	Sat Fat (G)	Chol (MG)	Sodium (MG)	Total Carb (G)	Dietary Fiber (G)	Total Sugars (G)	Protein (G)
Appetizers and Snacks									
Marinated Olives	170	18	2	0	510	3	1	0	0
Marinated Bocconcini	320	29	13	70	200	1	0	0	14
Marinated Artichoke Hearts and Stuffed Pickled Sweet Peppers	390	31	8	45	970	14	4	5	15
Caponata	167	9	1	0	360	20	5	13	3
Prosciutto-Wrapped Figs with Gorgonzola	130	4.5	2	25	690	18	2	15	8
Prosciutto-Wrapped Melon	80	2.5	1	20	620	7	1	6	7
Italian Straws	200	13	6	5	400	20	1	1	7
Ricotta Crostini with Cherry Tomatoes and Basil	71	5	1	4	67	6	0	1	2
Ricotta Crostini with Asparagus and Radishes	71	5	1	4	73	6	0	1	2
Ricotta Crostini with Olives and Sun-Dried Tomatoes	88	6	1	4	100	6	1	1	2
Ricotta Crostini with Peas and Mint	76	5	1	4	73	7	1	1	2
Ricotta Crostini with Roasted Red Peppers and Capers	72	5	1	4	84	6	0	1	2
Bruschetta	151	6	1	0	195	18	1	2	4
Bruschetta with Black Olive Pesto, Ricotta, and Basil Topping	320	17	5	20	600	28	1	1	12
Bruschetta with Grape Tomato, White Bean Puree, and Rosemary Topping	196	10	2	2	241	22	3	1	6
Bruschetta with Artichoke and Parmesan Topping	230	10	2.5	5	550	26	1	1	8
Stuffed Mushrooms	33	3	1	1	42	1	0	1	1
Stuffed Mushrooms with Olives and Goat Cheese	33	3	1	1	39	1	0	1	1
Fried Asparagus	404	43	4	28	190	5	1	1	2
Fried Calamari	190	8	0.5	130	180	18	0	0	12
Mozzarella Sticks	450	27	12	115	800	30	0	3	22
Sandwiches, Soups, and Salads									
New Orleans Muffuletta	440	19	3	0	1290	57	0	6	9
Roasted Eggplant and Mozzarella Panini	560	28	9	30	1240	61	4	8	19
Meatball Subs	713	36	12	201	1079	53	4	7	43
Grilled Sausage Subs with Bell Peppers and Onions	633	20	6	45	1486	75	5	10	37
Chicago-Style Italian Beef Sandwiches	700	25	7	100	2260	76	0	4	41

	Calories	Total Fat (G)	Sat Fat (G)	Chol (MG)	Sodium (MG)	Total Carb (G)	Dietary Fiber (G)	Total Sugars (G)	Protein (G)
Sandwiches, Soups, and Salads (continued)									
Philadelphia Pork Sandwiches	711	40	16	138	1051	37	3	2	50
Iron Range Porketta Sandwiches	588	30	10	134	869	34	3	2	44
Hearty Minestrone	220	7	2	9	254	27	7	5	12
Pittsburgh Wedding Soup	203	7	3	29	1009	22	2	3	14
White Bean Soup	350	14	3.5	15	780	40	21	4	17
Pasta e Fagioli	440	13	4	17	786	58	9	7	23
Monterey Bay Cioppino	451	15	2	115	1512	35	3	8	43
Ultimate Caesar Salad	510	45	8	53	507	21	4	2	8
Chopped Caprese Salad	220	16	6	30	605	10	4	5	11
Simple Tomato Salad	151	13	2	0	300	8	2	5	2
Simple Tomato Salad with Capers and Parsley	126	11	1	1	387	7	2	5	2
Simple Tomato Salad with Pecorino Romano and Oregano	151	12	3	7	401	8	2	5	4
Marinated Antipasto Salad	137	8	3	11	527	11	5	3	6
Italian Pasta Salad	403	20	7	45	898	37	2	1	16
Panzanella	501	29	4	0	465	51	4	10	10
White Bean Salad with Sautéed Squid and Pepperoncini	340	15	2.5	175	980	28	7	4	21
Pizza and More									
New York Thin-Crust Pizza	495	15	6	33	736	66	4	8	20
Chicago Deep-Dish Pizza	826	42	20	94	895	83	5	8	29
Chicago Thin-Crust Pizza	776	36	17	101	1127	71	3	7	41
New England Bar Pizza	504	23	10	51	626	54	4	7	20
St. Louis Pizza	291	10	4	13	429	42	2	6	9
Detroit Pizza	616	29	15	63	636	62	4	5	26
Philadelphia Tomato Pie	430	13	2	0	651	71	4	8	10
Sicilian-Style Pizza	649	31	9	39	706	68	4	4	23
Thin-Crust Whole-Wheat Pizza with Garlic Oil, Three Cheeses, and Basil	507	29	11	54	456	42	4	2	20
Grilled Pizza	699	39	11	43	638	63	3	4	23
Spinach Ricotta Calzones	460	21	10	110	960	42	2	6	24
Three-Meat Calzones	640	37	16	170	1920	40	0	5	35
Broccoli Rabe and Salami Stromboli	595	26	12	107	1426	60	4	2	30
Pasta Night									
Spaghetti with Fresh Tomato Sauce	540	13	1.5	0	450	91	3	8	16
Spaghetti with Amatriciana Sauce	130	10	3	12	407	7	2	5	4
Spaghetti with Arrabbiata Sauce	95	7	1	2	378	7	2	4	2
Spaghetti with Puttanesca Sauce	550	14	1.5	0	680	93	3	9	16
Pasta with Classic Marinara	390	8	1	0	430	65	2	7	11
Pasta alla Norma	700	22	5	20	1120	108	9	16	23
Penne alla Vodka	769	24	11	61	946	105	9	13	20
Tagliatelle with Weeknight Bolognese	664	25	9	76	756	65	3	5	34
Pasta with Sausage Ragu	596	17	6	45	1074	71	7	7	36
Drop Meatballs	459	28	9	85	863	25	5	11	29

	Calories	Total Fat (G)	Sat Fat (G)	Chol (MG)	Sodium (MG)	Total Carb (G)	Dietary Fiber (G)	Total Sugars (G)	Protein (G)
Pasta Night (continued)									
Aglio e Olio	390	14	2	0	220	56	0	1	10
Fettuccine Alfredo	439	16	9	38	266	57	2	2	17
Spaghetti Carbonara	790	33	12	196	699	87	3	3	32
Pasta Primavera	469	17	3	6	607	66	6	6	15
Chicken Riggies	868	33	14	202	1369	77	8	13	65
Spaghetti with Fresh Clams	698	16	2	43	887	92	4	3	36
Shrimp Piccata Pasta	707	22	9	174	857	89	4	4	32
Easy Weekday Meals									
Chicken Marsala	840	35	11	160	2240	44	2	23	52
Chicken Francese	544	26	13	286	862	20	1	2	50
Chicken Scaloppini with Mushrooms and Peppers	570	34	8	145	900	15	1	4	41
Scampi-Style Chicken	726	47	12	146	782	41	3	3	28
Chicken Parmesan	607	40	9	155	905	23	4	9	38
Baked Ricotta Chicken	607	34	10	183	912	16	2	6	57
Chicken Cacciatore	190	5	1	80	900	8	1	3	18
Chicken Vesuvio	541	31	7	155	140	25	3	1	29
Chicken Scarpariello	615	40	11	182	928	11	2	4	51
Rao's Lemon Chicken	841	58	18	272	1011	8	1	2	65
Grilled Chicken alla Diavola	640	45	10	165	1030	4	1	0	52
Steak Pizzaiola	474	33	9	95	618	15	1	1	29
Flank Steak Peperonata	433	27	7	103	851	13	4	4	34
Steak Modiga	1025	75	29	270	1195	19	2	3	64
Grilled Stuffed Flank Steak	208	13	5	49	694	2	0	0	17
Pork Milanese	325	12	4	159	457	24	2	1	29
Pork Chops with Vinegar Peppers	238	11	3	11	652	25	1	12	4
One-Pan Sweet Italian Sausage with Polenta	598	35	16	83	1122	41	5	10	30
Shrimp Scampi	371	20	8	244	969	13	0	7	23
Shrimp Fra Diavolo	363	19	2	216	1279	11	4	5	25
Sunday Suppers and Celebrations									
Chicago-Style Italian Roast Beef	541	35	13	172	835	6	1	1	47
Braciole	302	14	3	26	846	35	7	21	15
Hearty Beef Lasagna	543	35	16	109	642	30	3	6	27
Hearty Italian Meat Sauce (Sunday Gravy)	886	48	14	134	1088	70	6	11	43
Pork Ragu	1090	46	14	160	2110	79	3	14	60
Fluffy Baked Polenta with Red Sauce	470	29	11	44	1238	44	4	10	11
Baked Manicotti	576	28	15	128	733	48	5	7	31
Baked Manicotti with Sausage	772	46	21	171	1070	49	5	7	39
Baked Ziti	570	28	15	115	1210	54	2	10	28
Chicken, Broccoli, and Ziti Casserole	732	25	13	152	1125	65	3	8	59
Stuffed Shells	548	25	13	121	777	53	4	8	28
Eggplant Pecorino	736	58	16	177	1069	39	13	18	22
Linguine ai Frutti di Mare	580	15	2.5	145	800	71	4	6	32
Seafood Risotto	450	14	2	70	1120	56	2	3	21

	Calories	Total Fat (G)	Sat Fat (G)	Chol (MG)	Sodium (MG)	Total Carb (G)	Dietary Fiber (G)	Total Sugars (G)	Protein (G)
Sides and Breads									
Garlicky Broccolini	128	9	2	5	345	8	3	2	6
Broccolini with Shallots	110	9	1.5	5	390	4	3	1	5
Broccolini with Capers and Lemon	100	9	8	5	440	4	3	0	5
Grilled Broccoli with Lemon and Parmesan	230	16	3	5	619	17	7	4	9
Sweet and Sour Broccoli Rabe	150	8	1	0	45	18	4	13	4
Utica Greens	164	10	3	11	485	14	7	2	7
Sautéed Kale	134	11	1	0	226	8	3	2	4
Sautéed Kale with Crispy Pepperoni and Cherry Peppers	205	17	4	15	281	8	3	2	7
Pittsburgh Beans and Greens	240	9	2	6	460	29	6	2	12
Braised Green Beans	161	11	1	0	532	13	5	6	3
Braised Green Beans with Potatoes and Basil	180	7	1	0	820	27	6	7	4
Grilled Artichokes with Lemon Butter	162	16	8	31	157	5	2	1	1
Stuffed Tomatoes	316	15	4	16	567	35	4	7	11
Crispy Parmesan Potatoes	260	13	6	30	830	23	0	1	13
Really Good Garlic Bread	260	13	7	30	349	29	1	0	5
Parmesan Breadsticks	360	13	3	25	970	47	0	0	12
Asiago and Black Pepper Breadsticks	370	14	3.5	30	920	47	1	0	11
Pecorino and Mixed Herb Breadsticks	380	15	4.5	35	1060	47	0	0	13
Garlic Knots	132	6	4	15	107	17	1	0	3
Scali Bread	250	2.5	0	25	590	48	0	5	7
Prosciutto Bread	180	6	1.5	10	440	22	1	0	8
Prosciutto Bread with Provolone	210	8	3	20	520	22	1	0	10
Desserts									
Tiramisu	482	31	16	248	315	37	1	15	9
Classic Panna Cotta	368	34	21	125	85	13	0	13	3
Individual Fresh Berry Gratins with Zabaglione	190	8	4	150	40	26	4	21	3
Pistachio Cannoli	520	33	18	90	130	42	1	22	15
Zeppoles	80	4	0	0	110	10	0	3	1
Chocolate Chip Panettone	257	12	7	45	179	35	2	15	5
Orange and Raisin Panettone	258	9	5	53	198	39	1	15	5
Italian Almond Cake	610	40	14	135	340	55	4	43	10
Pignoli	170	10	1	0	5	18	2	15	4
Italian Anise Cookies	90	3	1.5	15	70	14	0	9	1
Spumoni Bars	66	4	2	19	9	8	0	4	1
Italian Rainbow Cookies	99	4	2	26	33	15	0	10	2
Florentine Lace Cookies	163	12	4	15	29	12	1	9	3
Chocolate Salami	120	6	2.5	10	15	16	0	11	2
Lemon Ice	110	0	0	0	40	27	0	26	0
Orange Ice	90	0	0	0	40	21	0	24	0
Lemon-Lime Ice	148	0	0	0	52	36	0	34	0
Minted Lemon Ice	110	0	0	0	40	27	0	26	0
Lemon-Lavender Ice	151	0	0	0	53	36	0	34	0

CONVERSIONS AND EQUIVALENTS

Some say cooking is a science and an art. We would say geography has a hand in it, too. Flours and sugars manufactured in the United Kingdom and elsewhere will feel and taste different from those manufactured in the United States. So we cannot promise that a loaf of bread you bake in Canada or England will taste the same as a loaf baked in the States, but we can offer guidelines for converting weights and measures. We also recommend that you rely on your instincts when making our recipes. Refer to the visual cues provided. If the dough hasn't come together as described, you may need to add more flour—even if the recipe doesn't tell you to. You be the judge.

The recipes in this book were developed using standard U.S. measures following U.S. government guidelines. The charts below offer equivalents for U.S. and metric measures. All conversions are approximate and have been rounded up or down to the nearest whole number.

EXAMPLE

| 1 teaspoon | = | 4.9292 milliliters, rounded up to 5 milliliters |
| 1 ounce | = | 28.3495 grams, rounded down to 28 grams |

Volume Conversions

U.S.	Metric
1 teaspoon	5 milliliters
2 teaspoons	10 milliliters
1 tablespoon	15 milliliters
2 tablespoons	30 milliliters
¼ cup	59 milliliters
⅓ cup	79 milliliters
½ cup	118 milliliters
¾ cup	177 milliliters
1 cup	237 milliliters
1¼ cups	296 milliliters
1½ cups	355 milliliters
2 cups (1 pint)	473 milliliters
2½ cups	591 milliliters
3 cups	710 milliliters
4 cups (1 quart)	0.946 liter
1.06 quarts	1 liter
4 quarts (1 gallon)	3.8 liters

Weight Conversions

Ounces	Grams
½	14
¾	21
1	28
1½	43
2	57
2½	71
3	85
3½	99
4	113
4½	128
5	142
6	170
7	198
8	227
9	255
10	283
12	340
16 (1 pound)	454

Conversions For Common Baking Ingredients

Because measuring by weight is far more accurate than measuring by volume, and thus more likely to produce reliable results, in our recipes we provide ounce measures in addition to cup measures for many ingredients. Refer to the chart below to convert these measures into grams.

Ingredient	Ounces	Grams
Flour		
1 cup all-purpose flour*	5	142
1 cup cake flour	4	113
1 cup whole-wheat flour	5½	156
Sugar		
1 cup granulated (white) sugar	7	198
1 cup packed brown sugar (light or dark)	7	198
1 cup confectioners' sugar	4	113
Cocoa Powder		
1 cup cocoa powder	3	85
Butter†		
4 tablespoons (½ stick or ¼ cup)	2	57
8 tablespoons (1 stick or ½ cup)	4	113
16 tablespoons (2 sticks or 1 cup)	8	227

* U.S. all-purpose flour, the most frequently used flour in this book, does not contain leaveners, as some European flours do. These leavened flours are called self-rising or self-raising. If you are using self-rising flour, take this into consideration before adding leaveners to a recipe.

† In the United States, butter is sold both salted and unsalted. We recommend unsalted butter. If you are using salted butter, take this into consideration before adding salt to a recipe.

Oven Temperature

Fahrenheit	Celsius	Gas Mark
225	105	¼
250	120	½
275	135	1
300	150	2
325	165	3
350	180	4
375	190	5
400	200	6
425	220	7
450	230	8
475	245	9

Converting Temperatures from an Instant-Read Thermometer

We include doneness temperatures in many of the recipes in this book. We recommend an instant-read thermometer for the job. Refer to the table above to convert Fahrenheit degrees to Celsius. Or, for temperatures not represented in the chart, use this simple formula:

Subtract 32 degrees from the Fahrenheit reading, then divide the result by 1.8 to find the Celsius reading.

EXAMPLE

"Flip chicken, brush with remaining glaze, and cook until breast registers 160 degrees, 1 to 3 minutes."

To convert:
$$160°F - 32 = 128°$$
$$128° \div 1.8 = 71.11°C, \text{ rounded down to } 71°C$$

Monterey Bay Cioppino (page 57)

INDEX

Note: Page references in *italics* indicate photographs.

R

Q

S